Renaissance Personhood

Renaissance Personhood

Materiality, Taxonomy, Process

Edited by Kevin Curran

EDINBURGH
University Press

Edinburgh University Press is one of the leading university presses in the UK. We publish academic books and journals in our selected subject areas across the humanities and social sciences, combining cutting-edge scholarship with high editorial and production values to produce academic works of lasting importance. For more information visit our website: edinburghuniversitypress.com

Edinburgh University Press Ltd
The Tun—Holyrood Road
12(2f) Jackson's Entry
Edinburgh EH8 8PJ

First published in hardback by Edinburgh University Press 2020

Typeset in 11/13 Adobe Sabon by
IDSUK (DataConnection) Ltd

A CIP record for this book is available from the British Library

ISBN 978 1 4744 4808 6 (hardback)
ISBN 978 1 4744 4809 3 (paperback)
ISBN 978 1 4744 4810 9 (webready PDF)
ISBN 978 1 4744 4811 6 (epub)

Contents

Acknowledgments

This volume began its life as two collaborative events: a roundtable I organized for the 2017 meeting of the Modern Language Association in Philadelphia called "Object Lessons in Personhood" and a seminar I directed at the 2018 meeting of the Shakespeare Association of America in Los Angeles called "Object Lessons in Renaissance Personhood." I want to thank all who participated in these events for their daring ideas. Our discussions changed how I thought about personhood in ways I could never have predicted. Moving this project from the interactive environments of the conference and seminar room to the more formal and atomized landscape of cooperative book creation was an absolute pleasure thanks to the truly stellar team of contributors who joined me. I am very fortunate to be in the company of such a rigorous, inventive, and intellectually generous group of scholars in these pages. Finally, Edinburgh University Press has been a delight to work with. Thank you to Michelle Houston, Ersev Ersoy, Rebecca Mackenzie, and Carla Hepburn for ushering *Renaissance Personhood* through review and production with professionalism and care.

Kevin Curran
Lausanne, Switzerland

Contributors

John Michael Archer is Professor of English at New York University. His first book, *Sovereignty and Intelligence: Spying and Court Culture in the English Renaissance* (Stanford University Press, 1993), discusses the portrayal of political surveillance in the works of Montaigne, Marlowe, Bacon, and other authors. *Old Worlds* (Stanford University Press, 2001), extends his interest in knowledge-gathering to the later seventeenth century by analyzing European travel writings along with literary works by Shakespeare, Milton, and Dryden. His third book, *Citizen Shakespeare: Freemen and Aliens in the Language of the Plays* (Palgrave, 2005), shows how the London citizen and the immigrant city-dweller figure in the action and verbal texture of Shakespeare's drama. *Technically Alive: Shakespeare's Sonnets* (Palgrave, 2012) traces the correspondence between Heidegger's thinking about technology and Shakespeare's poetics of natural productivity. Chapters take up agriculture, animals, memory, print culture, and ecological waste, as well as technology as a form of thought.

Amanda Bailey is Professor of English at the University of Maryland. She is the author of *Of Bondage: Debt, Property, and Personhood in Early Modern England* (University of Pennsylvania Press, 2013) and *Flaunting: Style and the Subversive Male Body in Renaissance England* (University of Toronto Press, 2007). She has edited *Masculinity and the Metropolis of Vice, 1550–1650*, with Roze Hentschell (Palgrave, 2010), and, more recently, *Affect Theory and Early Modern Texts: Politics, Ecologies, and Form* (Palgrave, 2017), with Mario DiGangi. She has published numerous essays and book chapters and is currently completing *Shakespeare on Consent*, under contract with Routledge. This book broadens and deepens the notion of consent underwriting the #MeToo movement by tracing its legacy to earlier understandings of erotic agency in relation to gender, embodiment, and collective politics. She is also working on a book-length study of racial economies of knowledge and the formation of the Humanities as an academic discipline.

Joseph Campana is a poet, arts writer, and scholar who serves as Alan Dugald McKillop Professor of English at Rice University where he is also an editor of *Studies in English Literature, 1500–1900*. He is the author of *The Pain of Reformation: Spenser, Vulnerability, and the Ethics of Masculinity* (Fordham University Press, 2012), co-editor with Scott Maisano of *Renaissance Posthumanism* (Fordham University Press, 2016), and the author of three collections of poetry, *The Book of Faces* (2005), *Natural Selections* (2012), which received the Iowa Poetry Prize, and *The Book of Life* (Tupelo Press, 2019). Current projects include a study of children and sovereignty in the works of Shakespeare, *The Child's Two Bodies*, a study of bees, trees, crocodile tears, and other forms of creaturely life called *Living Figures*, and a two-volume co-edited collection with Keith Botelho on insect life in the Renaissance, *Lesser Living Creatures*.

Kevin Curran is Professor of Early Modern Literature at the University of Lausanne in Switzerland and editor of the book series "Edinburgh Critical Studies in Shakespeare and Philosophy." He is the author of *Shakespeare's Legal Ecologies: Law and Distributed Selfhood* (Northwestern University Press, 2017) and *Marriage, Performance, and Politics at the Jacobean Court* (Ashgate, 2009). He is the editor of *Shakespeare and Judgment* (Edinburgh University Press, 2016) and co-editor, with James Kearney, of a special issue of the journal *Criticism* on "Shakespeare and Phenomenology" (2012). In 2017, Curran was named Distinguished International Visiting Fellow at the Center for the History of Emotions in Australia. He is also the founder and Director of the Lausanne Shakespeare Festival.

Holly Dugan is Associate Professor of English at the George Washington University. She is the author of *The Ephemeral History of Perfume: Scent and Sense in Early Modern England* (Johns Hopkins University Press, 2013), co-editor, with Lara Farina, of *Intimate Senses*, a special issue of *Postmedieval* (2012), and co-editor, with Karl Steel, of *Fabulous Animals*, a special issue of *EMC* (2016). She is currently working on *The Famous Ape*, a book project that explores the prehistory of primatology through the lens of Shakespeare's plays.

Stephanie Elsky is Assistant Professor of English at Rhodes College. She is the author of *Custom, Law, and the Constitution of English*

Renaissance Literature (Oxford University Press, forthcoming). Her work has appeared in journals including *English Literary Renaissance*, *Spenser Studies*, and *Law, Culture and the Humanities*. Her essay "Lady Anne Clifford's Common-Law Mind" was awarded the 2014 Louis Wilson Round Prize for Best Article from *Studies in Philology*. Her research has been supported by the Andrew W. Mellon Foundation; the American Council of Learned Societies; the Henry E. Huntington Library; and Volkswagen Foundation.

David B. Goldstein is a critic, poet, and food writer, and an Associate Professor at York University in Toronto. His first monograph, *Eating and Ethics in Shakespeare's England*, shared the 2014 biennial Shakespeare's Globe Book Award. He has also published two books of poetry and has co-edited two essay collections, *Culinary Shakespeare* (Duquesne University Press, 2016), with Amy Tigner, and *Shakespeare and Hospitality* (Routledge, 2016), with Julia Reinhard Lupton. His essays on early modern literature, Emmanuel Levinas, food studies, ecology, and contemporary poetry have appeared in *Studies in English Literature*, *Shakespeare Studies*, *Gastronomica*, and numerous other journals and collections. He is currently co-director of the Folger Shakespeare Library's Mellon-funded research project "Before 'Farm to Table': Early Modern Foodways and Cultures."

Colby Gordon earned a Ph.D. in Comparative Literature from UC Irvine and is currently an Assistant Professor of English at Bryn Mawr College. His work has been published in multiple journals, including articles on prosthetic bodies, transgender embodiment, and creation narratives in Shakespeare's sonnets; soft architecture and queer futurity in *Antony and Cleopatra*; political aesthetics and *The Tempest*'s soundscapes; Carl Schmitt, Sianne Ngai, and the aesthetics of political theology; and, with Julia Reinhard Lupton, a piece on Shakespeare and design theory. With Simone Chess and Will Fisher, he is currently editing a special issue of the *Journal of Early Modern Cultural Studies* on early modern trans studies. Professor Gordon is currently at work on a manuscript entitled "Glorious Bodies: Trans Theology and Renaissance Literature."

Wendy Beth Hyman is Associate Professor of English and Comparative Literature at Oberlin College. She is the author of *Impossible Desire and the Limits of Knowledge in Renaissance Poetry* (Oxford University Press, 2019), co-editor of *Teaching Social Justice Through Shakespeare: Why Renaissance Literature Matters Now* (Edinburgh

University Press, 2019), and editor of *The Automaton in English Renaissance Literature* (Ashgate, 2011). She has published essays on insect poetry and early modern microscopy, physics and metaphysics in Renaissance lyric, the role of metaphor in early modern science, jacquemart figures in Shakespeare's history plays, early modern mechanical birds, Spenser's *Faerie Queene*, Nashe's *Unfortunate Traveller*, and liberal arts colleges and book history. She has begun a second book project on myth and fiction in Shakespeare's late plays.

Gregory Kneidel is Associate Professor of English at the University of Connecticut. He is the author of *Rethinking the Turn to Religion in Early Modern English Literature* (Palgrave, 2008) and *John Donne and Early Modern Legal Culture* (Duquesne University Press, 2015), which won the John Donne Society Award for Distinguished Publication in Donne Studies in 2016. He is currently Associate General Editor of *The Variorum Edition of the Poetry of John Donne*.

Chapter 1

What Was Personhood?

Kevin Curran

If you're reading this, you're probably a person. Probably, but not definitely. I know you're not an embryo. I know you're not a crocodile. I know you're not a rock. But I can't be totally sure you're not a very young child, or someone with advanced dementia, or someone with a serious mental illness. I can't be entirely sure you're not a stateless person in a refugee camp or an advanced form of artificial intelligence, and though I'm quite sure you're not an extraterrestrial, I also can't rule it out completely.

Yes, you're probably, but not definitely, a person. Not just any person, mind you, but rather a certain type of person. Indeed, some persons are definitely *not* reading this. Westinghouse Electric Corporation is not reading this. Neither is the Government of India. And Mount Taranaki in New Zealand, I can assure you, is not reading this. No, if you're reading this, you're probably a "natural person," as opposed to a "juridical person." That is to say, you're a human being—a human being with personhood status. Probably.

Why so much uncertainty around personhood? Part of it is a simple problem of terminology. There is a difference between how we use the word "person" in an everyday context and how it gets used in a legal context. Colloquially, a "person" is a human. We talk about a four-person vehicle or a two-person tent; first-, second- or third-person point of view in a novel; or our Aunt Beatrice being the "the kind of person who . . . ." In all of these cases, "person" makes sense as a descriptor because it draws on some broadly shared ideas about the physical, cognitive, and behavioral features that make humans humans. In a legal context, however, personhood is a far more extrinsic status. A legal "person" denotes an entity, human or nonhuman, to which a bundle of rights and obligations have been attributed. Legal personhood, that is, might be thought of as a role to be stepped into or a mask to be worn. It is a kind of legal attire in which an entity is outfitted in order to function within society at a certain level of autonomy, protection, and/or culpability.

In this sense, the etymological links between *person* and words like *personage* ("character" or "role" in French) and *persona* ("mask" in Latin) are instructive.[1] Personhood is not something immanent or ontological, but rather something external, mobile, and social. The fact that personhood is nevertheless an abstraction, something impossible to touch or feel, can make this difficult to grasp. In his classic study of "the notion of person," the anthropologist Marcel Mauss describes how modern legal personhood, which he traces back to ancient Rome, developed gradually out of much more concretely prosthetic ways of thinking about identity.[2] The Zuñi tribe of the American southwest, for example, understands identity exclusively through social roles. Individuals are named according to their function within the collective, and these names/functions are concretized in masks that are used in certain rituals and festivals. As Mauss puts it, for the Zuñi, "the clan is conceived of as being made up of a certain number of persons, in reality characters (*personages*)."[3] Mauss also speaks of the Kwakiutl tribe of the Pacific Northwest, who believe that in addition to simply killing an important warrior or chief, one can "seize from him one of the trappings of ritual, robes or masks, so as to inherit his names, his goods, his obligations, his ancestors, his *person* in the fullest sense of the word."[4] We can see in these contexts how personhood is entirely prosthetic, how it's quite different from selfhood. Personhood has less to do with who you *are* in and of yourself and more to do with what you *do* in a community or other social context. It is active rather than passive, phenomenological rather than ontological.

Hobbes and Locke

One of the clearest articulations of personhood as a role or a mask comes from someone who had never heard of the Zuñi or the Kwakiutl tribes and was long dead by the time Marcel Mauss started writing about them: Thomas Hobbes. In his great work of political philosophy, *Leviathan* (1651), Hobbes developed a theory of personhood derived explicitly from the theater, and more specifically from acting. He describes the relationship like this:

> The word Person is latine: instead whereof the Greeks have *Prosopon*, which signifies the *Face*, as *Persona* in latine signifies the *disguise* or *outward appearance* of a man, counterfeited on the Stage; and sometimes more particularly that part of it, which disguiseth the face, as a Mask or Vizard: And from the Stage, hath been translated to any Representer

of speech and action, as well in Tribunalls, as Theaters. So that a *Person*, is the same that an *Actor* is, both on the Stage and in common Conversation; and to *Personate*, is to *Act*, or *Represent* himself, or an other; and he that acteth another, is said to beare his Person, or act in his name; . . . and is called in diverse occasions, diversely; as a *Representer*, or *Representative*, a *Lieutenant*, a *Vicar*, an *Attorney*, a *Deputy*, a *Procurator*, an *Actor*, and the like.[5]

For Hobbes, the most important thing about personhood is that it is not an essence, but instead a highly structured representational relationship. This relationship can obtain, for example, when a sovereign speaks for the commonwealth or when an adult speaks for a child: "A Multitude of men, are made *One* Person, when they are by one man, or one Person, Represented."[6] The relationship can also obtain among humans and nonhumans: "Inanimate things, as a Church, an Hospital, a Bridge, may be personated by a Rector, Master, or Overseer."[7] In all cases, though, the basic point remains the same: the legal status of person does not accrue from anything cognitively, spiritually, or physiologically intrinsic, but has to do instead with "words or actions" being "considered . . . as his own."[8] That is to say, in Hobbes's account of personhood, there is a space between utterance/action and ownership thereof. The person is at the front of that space, the mask or fiction that owns words and actions and therefore provides an interface of prerogative and accountability for society. On the other side, at the back of this space—a space prior to the question of ownership and social appearing—is the thing we might call selfhood, or even subjectivity. Personhood, therefore, even in the context of a single human being, is a relational and presentational concept, one entirely consistent with Hobbes's more general materialism and nominalism.[9]

It is perhaps because the story of modern personhood usually starts with John Locke rather than Hobbes that we have lost a full sense of how important materiality, collectivity, and relationality are to this key legal and political concept. In *An Essay Concerning Human Understanding* (1689), Locke lays out a theory of personhood that seems diametrically opposed to Hobbes's. Whereas for the latter, personhood denotes a transactional process, for the former, it denotes self-contained psychology. A person, in Locke's words, is an "intelligent" entity "that has reason and reflection," or what he calls "reflective consciousness."[10] Personhood, he continues,

is a forensic term, appropriating actions and their merit; and so belongs only to intelligent agents, capable of law, and happiness, and misery. This personality extends itself beyond present existence to what is past, only by consciousness—whereby it becomes concerned and accountable.[11]

For Locke, only those entities capable of being held accountable for their actions can be accorded the rights that go along with political accommodation. That is to say, only an entity "capable of law" can be a person, and this requires "consciousness." By consciousness, Locke does not mean the basic sensate awareness possessed to a greater or lesser extent by all animals, but rather a uniquely self-sentient and temporally expansive form of cognizance that he accords to rational humans alone. This version of "consciousness" makes personal identity integral to legal personhood. He describes the link as follows:

> For since consciousness always accompanies thinking, and 'tis that, that makes every one to be, what he calls self, and thereby distinguishes himself from all other thinking things, in this alone constitutes personal identity, i.e., the sameness of a rational Being. And as far as this consciousness can be extended backwards to any past Action or Thought, so far reaches the identity of that Person; it is the same self now as it was then; and 'tis by the same self with this present one that now reflects on it, that Action was done.[12]

Hermetic self-sameness, "the sameness of a rational being," is the locus of Lockean personhood. This is very different from Hobbes. Whereas Hobbes places personhood at the interface between actor and society, defining it, therefore, in terms of a relationship, Locke places personhood at the cognitive core of the actor, defining it, therefore, in terms of an individual essence.

These two ways of thinking about personhood, the Hobbesian model and the Lockean model, have different intellectual sources and lay different kinds of foundations for the story of modern personhood from the Enlightenment to the present day. For contemporary scholars, it is Locke who has emerged as the standard-bearer of seventeenth-century thought on personhood. Indeed, within legal scholarship on personhood, historical overviews of the concept almost systematically start with Locke's psychological theories.[13] Hobbes is left out, as are earlier sixteenth- and seventeenth-century sources. Of course, there is a certain sense to this. If you are, by default, thinking of personhood in terms of individual identity and tracing a genealogy that runs roughly from the Enlightenment to twentieth-century thinkers like Derek Parfit and John Perry, then there is no place for a materialist and nominalist thinker like Thomas Hobbes.[14] His theatrical, collaborative, and mechanistic account of personhood is misaligned with modern legal-philosophical debates that tend to be concerned with questions of individual moral agency vis-à-vis issues like dementia, euthanasia, abortion, and artificial intelligence. Locke's theories, on the other hand, fit comfortably with the notions of individuality and interiority that underpin so much post-Enlightenment legal and political thought.

It would be an oversimplification to suggest that the intellectual history of personhood can be divided neatly into Hobbesian and Lockean camps. But the difference in their respective reception histories nevertheless offers an object lesson in the way certain currents of thought in sixteenth- and seventeenth-century England have been distorted or silenced. Hobbes's model of personhood—relational, collaborative, material—grows much more coherently out of earlier Renaissance reflections on the topic than Locke's does. To be sure, Renaissance personhood is most often imagined in collective terms, as interfaces rather than essences. It is *ir*rational in the sense that it orients itself around bodily processes and transactions rather than intellectual characteristics and capacities. These distinctions are important, for once personhood is untethered from concepts like reason and moral agency, it becomes attributable to a much wider range of entities, both human and nonhuman. In addition, once personhood is recognized as relational rather than essential, the archive of personhood broadens considerably to include the variety of objects and environments through which it is made intelligible.

Personhood without Individualism

The idea at the heart of personhood was, and still is, that certain beings possess some fundamental degree of liberty and that communities work better when that liberty is protected. But personhood does not simply enshrine liberty. More precisely, it instrumentalizes it through basic legal transactions such as litigation, property transfer, and contract. It also balances it off with a set of responsibilities and obligations. This means that personhood is never just about the individual subject and their freedom. Instead, personhood denotes a relationship to one's lived environment, a form of liberty that only makes sense in a transactional context. Personhood describes an interface between self and world and provides scripts of consent, entitlement, and responsibility for managing that interface. Understanding personhood in the Renaissance means recovering a sense of its distributed structure and the wide circle of its franchise. It involves rethinking the idea of "rights" in specifically Renaissance terms, as something collective rather than individual, and as something that makes sense in a cross-species context. It also involves rethinking the importance of reason in theorizations of personhood, including reason's most concrete legal application in the form of contract making.

A good place to start this rethinking is with the established legal-historical narrative of enfranchisement in Renaissance England. We know that at least since Magna Carta (1215) there existed a baseline guarantee that no free man (*liber homo*) could be harmed save in accordance with the law of the land (*lex terrae*). Magna Carta, along with a subsequent series of related due-process statutes, is the closest we come to something like personhood *doctrine* in pre-modern England.[15] Of course, what constituted a "free man" before the sixteenth century was fairly narrow. A complex system of status and rank—peerage, knighthood, villeinage, and so on—worked to concentrate liberty among the lords. But over the course of the Tudor period we see a steady widening of the franchise such that legal personality was eventually able to function independent of principles of status and rank. One useful illustration of this is the demise of villeinage, a status of feudal servitude. According to a Gray's Inn moot of the 1520s, "villeinage is an odious thing in law and not to be favoured, for it is merely contrary to liberty and liberty is one of the things which the law most favours."[16] Increasingly, lawyers were willing to include villeins within the category of "free men" on the principle that although technically in a state of bondage, they were still protected from their lord by criminal law. By the end of the sixteenth century, the status had disappeared altogether. A second illustration of the gradual widening of the franchise emerges from the dissolution of the monasteries during the Reformation. Up to that point, the professed religious—monks, friars, and nuns—existed outside the ambit of personhood. When a monk took the habit and swore obedience to a religious order, he officially left the secular world, losing his surname and relinquishing all worldly possessions. He became dead in law (*civiliter mortus*). The dissolution of the monasteries brought with it a general resurrection of the professed religious to legal life. Triggered by a 1539 statute, they were "put at their liberties from the danger of servitude, and condition of their religion and profession" (31 Hen. VIII, c. 6).[17] They were free to purchase land and goods and to pass that property on to their heirs. They could both sue and be sued. They were persons.

The first thing we should notice in this narrative is that English common law was, at least at a theoretical level, oriented toward liberty.[18] This predisposition underpinned the gradual broadening of the franchise and reinforced a notion of legal personality that was distinct from status and rank. It is important to note, though, that in the Renaissance, liberty was not associated with individuality and personal freedom, as it would be later. On the contrary, liberty was understood first and foremost in collective terms, and this made ideas about interdependence and commonality central to Renaissance personhood. Anti-tyrannical writings, for example, carry this collectivist notion of liberty forward from the Greco-Roman tradition, frequently embedding it within a larger discourse of natural rights. Mary Nyquist notes how this linkage has been sidelined in modern intellectual historical work:

> Whether owing to . . . liberalism's individualist legacies, or to Cold War anxieties about positive freedom when associated with a collectivity, the extent to which early modern anti-tyrannism maintains the Greco-Roman emphasis on collective rather than individual agency and interests is frequently obscured.[19]

To be a free subject of the law, with rights and obligations, is not necessarily to be a rational self-reflective individual, as Locke describes it, but rather, in the largest sense, to be part of a transnational and transhistorical community, bound together by a common Greco-Roman lineage. Algernon Sidney, writing around the same time as Locke, describes "liberty" as

> The principle in which the Grecians, Italians, Spaniards, Gauls, Germans, and Britains, and all other generous Nations ever lived, before the name of Christ was known in the World; insomuch as the base effeminate Asiaticks and Africans, for being careless of their Liberty, or unable to govern themselves, were by Aristotle and other wise men called Slaves by Nature, and looked upon as little different from Beasts.[20]

Legal, religious, colonial, and even proto-evolutionary ideas converge around this collectivist notion of liberty in the Renaissance. Europeans are heirs of the Greeks and Romans and all coexist within a biblical historical arch. Non-Europeans, including especially Africans and Amerindigenes, are entirely outside this historical frame and its circle of accommodation.[21]

The idea of ancient liberties constitutes a kind of early modern identity politics, articulating strict lines of membership along ethnic, religious, and, gradually, national axes. These different vectors of liberty converge in anti-tyrannical writing, which had at its core an emerging notion of citizens' rights. As David Wootton has explained, citizens' rights in this period were not, of course, about the right to vote, but rather about the right to revolt, the simple idea that all citizens have a God-given prerogative to overthrow a tyrannical government because God created Man free.[22] Imagined as natural and collective, citizens' rights in the Renaissance described the entitlements of the political community, which were always framed by broader entitlements of Christian community. In *A Short Treatise of Politique Power* (1556), for example, John Ponet discusses how the law of nature permits the killing of tyrants. This allowance, he declares,

> is no private Law to a few or certain people, but common to all: not written in Bookes, but grafted in the hearts of men: not made by man, but ordained by God: which wee have not learned, received, or read: but have taken, sucked and drawne it out of nature.[23]

Nyquist describes this as "the principle of collective liberty-preservation": "not the individual, but the political collective stand in need of preservation."[24] Later, in the seventeenth century, this principle would combine with Protestant antipathy toward idolatry to bolster the radical political writings produced in the context of the English Civil War and the execution of Charles I. Consider Richard Overton who insists in *An Arrow Against All Tyrants* (1646) that "Every man by nature" is "a King, Priest and Prophet in his own natural circuite and compasse";[25] or John Milton who asserts, more bluntly, in *The Tenure of Kings and Magistrates* (1649) that "No man who knows aught can be so stupid to deny that all men naturally were born free, being the image and resemblance of God himself."[26] Each of these writers invokes a divine framework to assert baseline rights and liberty. They conjure something we might think of as a commons of personhood, formed by all those living within God's dispensation.

Material Aggregation and Taxonomical Pluralism

There are two different ways to think of *collectivity* in the context of personhood, and fleshing them out will give us an opportunity to extend the discussion beyond anti-tyrannical writing. One is as material aggregation (the assemblage of various human and nonhuman things into a whole); the other is as taxonomical pluralism (the embrace of multiple life forms under a single status). The first category is best exemplified by the Renaissance corporation, which takes a wide variety of forms: parish churches, hospitals, towns, universities, colonies, joint-stock companies, chanceries, guilds, and so on.[27] Corporations have their roots in Roman law and were widespread in England by the sixteenth century. Corporate personhood was cemented in two important cases, *Calvin's Case* (1608) and *Sutton's Hospital* (1612), which are still cited by lawyers today. In his report on *Sutton's Hospital*, Edward Coke defines the corporation as follows:

> A Corporation aggregate of many is invisible, immortal, & resteth only in intendment and consideration of the Law . . . They may not commit treason, nor be outlawed, nor excommunicated for they have no souls, neither can they appear in person, but by Attorney . . . A Corporation aggregate of many cannot do fealty, for an invisible body cannot be in person, nor can swear . . . it is not subject to imbecilities, or death of the natural body, and divers other cases.[28]

This description of corporate personhood evokes what Henry S. Turner calls the "uncanny presence" of the corporation. The corporate person is both one and many, both there and not there, and to this extent "seems like a confusion of categories, if not a grotesque distortion of common sense."[29]

On the other hand, as Turner also points out, Coke's account of corporate personality fits well with Hobbes's model of the person. A corporation is a person that cannot "appear in person," but depends instead on representation for presence. Like Hobbes's actor-character, the corporate person is only materially apprehensible in relational terms. A corporation must be spoken into being by a proxy since it cannot speak for itself, much like "the King" or "a Clown" in a stage play must be spoken into being by an actor. Indeed, the assemblage-like structure of corporate personhood raises ontological questions about voice, presence, agency, and what for lack of a better term we might call "realness" that are as germane to theories of literary character as they are to issues of legal responsibility.[30] Elizabeth Fowler has coined the term "social persons" to describe how character functions in late medieval and Renaissance literature:

> Social persons provide a shorthand notation that gives us enormous leverage in reference. Indeed, literary characters are largely cobbled together out of allusions to a number of social persons. In this way, social persons are like genres: they are abstract conventions that never actually "appear" in any pure form, but are the implied referents by which characters are understood. They are the collective imaginative technology that allows language to make literary character . . ., but, like

chisels, scaffolding, and plans that have left their marks on a monument
but since disappeared, social persons must be inferred from their artifac-
tual traces if characterization is to be understood.[31]

Many elements of the framework Fowler develops for social persons in a literary context could easily be applied to the corporation
in a legal-philosophical context. Both hover between presence and
absence. Both are fundamentally interdependent systems of meaning.
In this sense, too, both have something in common with Renaissance
understandings of Incarnational personhood, the way Christ holds in
suspension, without combining into a single substance, two distinct
natures (human and divine) and three distinct entities (the Father, the
Son, and the Holy Ghost).[32] As Richard Hooker puts it in Book V
of his *Of the Lawes of Ecclesiastical Politie* (1597), "Christ is a person both divine and human, howbeit not therefore two persons," but
rather "two natures, humaine and divine conjoined in one and the
same person."[33] Incarnational personhood does not quite fit the category of "material aggregation" I designated above since it is ultimately
a metaphysical concept. But it shares with corporate personhood a
core sense of multiplicity—a conceptual structure that depends on a
relationship between parts and whole—which is essential to Renaissance personhood more generally.

The other way to think about the collective nature of Renaissance
personhood is in terms of what I have called taxonomical pluralism,
the embrace of multiple life forms under a single status of accommodation. Once we free personhood from the individual (as in the discourse of anti-tyrannism), and once we free it from the human (as in
theories of incorporation), it becomes easier to think of *personation* as
a legal and political capacity afforded to creatures across taxonomical
thresholds. The Lockean inheritance has made nonhuman personhood
a thornier legal and conceptual issue in our own day than it would
have been in the Renaissance. True to their Enlightenment roots, modern theories of personhood tend to be embedded in contract-based
definitions of political life in which rational consent is the engine of
accommodation. Locke provides a good example of this idea in *Two
Treatises of Government* (1689):

> Men being, as has been said, by Nature, all free, equal and indepen-
> dent, no one can be put out of this Estate, and subjected to the Political
> Power of another, without his own *Consent*. The only way whereby
> any one devests himself of his Natural Liberty, and *puts on the bonds
> of Civil Society* is by agreeing with other Men to joyn and unite into

a Community, for their comfortable, safe, and peaceable living one amongst another, in a secure Enjoyment of their Properties, and a greater Security against any that are not of it.[34]

In this passage, personhood—legal accommodation involving both protections and constraints—is an arrangement one arrives at only by passing through the portal of consent. Personhood starts, in other words, with the rational individual who can act and choose; and because the community of choosers is exclusively human within liberal political philosophy (and even then, not automatically inclusive of children, the severely mentally handicapped, or those with advanced neurodegenerative impairments), there is a rhetorical and technical burden placed on those wishing to argue for animal entitlements. Such an argument typically needs to be made in terms of "animal rights," which, as Laurie Shannon has pointed out, derives "awkwardly from '*human* rights'" rather than from any foundational doctrine of cross-species egalitarianism.[35] Nor is there much in the way of an active principle of care in modern theories of personhood for litigants, activists, and policy-makers to draw on.[36]

During the sixteenth century, the imaginative landscape was decidedly different. There was, in Julia Reinhard Lupton's words, "a theological conceptualization of natural phenomena" grounded in scripture, especially Genesis and its related commentary tradition.[37] Viewed from this perspective, justice, law, entitlement, and government were far less anthropocentric ideas than they were in narrowly juridical contexts. Justinian's *Institutes*, for example, which influenced a range of sixteenth-century English theologians and legal theorists, asserts that

> The law of nature is that which nature teaches all animals. For that law is not proper to the human race, but is common to all animals which are born on the earth and in the sea, and to the birds also.[38]

Animals were not, of course, considered equal to humans in everyday contexts, but they possessed personhood to the extent that they were imagined to inhabit a space of shared polity with the other beings of God's Creation. To quote Shannon again, "when early moderns describe relations between humans and nonhumans," they deploy an "unabashedly political vocabulary," referring "to rule and tyranny, liberty and bondage, obedience and rebellion, contingency and negotiation, and transgression and entitlement; they refer to citizenship."[39] Consider, for instance, Guillaume Du Bartas, who in Joshua

Sylvester's 1605 English translation of *The Devine Weekes*, refers to nonhuman creatures as "Sea-*Citizens*," "the *people* of the water," and "slimie *Burgers* of this Earthly ball."[40] We do not need to think that animals possess reason or rights or the ability to consent or make contracts to see them as persons, since personhood for much of the Renaissance depended on none of these things. The sixteenth-century lawyer Christopher St. German maintained that "The lawe of nature . . . is referred to all creatures, as well reasonable as unreasonable: for all unreasonable creatures lyve under a certayne reule to them given by nature."[41] Instead, personhood expressed a natural, God-given liberty held in common with a collective; it denoted a certain relational status to other beings and things; and it ushered the bearer of that status into the ambit of co-dependent justice.

This Volume

If we trace the conceptual itineraries of personhood in the Renaissance, through statutes and legal cases, political philosophy and poetics, theology and theater, a map begins to emerge of a network that stretches far beyond the cloistered spaces of the human, the individual, and the rational mind. This map provides a shared starting point for contributors to this volume, each of whom guides the reader through a more detailed case study of personation in relation to chairs, machines, doors, trees, animals, race, food, the body, or land. Common to all these case studies is an interest in pushing personhood outside the closed perimeter of essence into the embedded world of substance. Starting with the objects, environments, and physical processes that made personhood legible in the Renaissance, the chapters that follow generate a new account of personhood in the sixteenth and seventeenth centuries by re-reading one of our most cherished legal fictions from the outside in rather than from the inside out.

Taken together, the chapters in this book constitute the first sustained materialist study of Renaissance personhood. That said, we also build on important scholarship devoted to law, theater, slavery, ecology, animals, and corporations that address personhood in ways that are relevant to the concerns of this volume. Amanda Bailey and Mary Nyquist, for example, have both explored the relationship between personhood and the body—Bailey in relation to debt law and Nyquist in relation to slavery.[42] Julia Reinhard Lupton has discussed the way a specifically Shakespearean account of personhood emerges at the intersection of thought about politics and life in *The Tempest*.[43] Monique Allewaert, Laurie Shannon, and Henry S. Turner, meanwhile, have commented in various ways on personhood as a form of collective life.[44] This volume extends and develops the insights of these studies, but does so from within a uniquely pluralistic critical framework, one that draws eclectically on animal studies, ecocriticism, and food studies, and models new ways of entering these posthumanist approaches into conversation with legal theory, cultural history, and literary analysis. The result, we hope, is a volume that makes a distinct contribution to both early modern studies and the interdisciplinary humanities by retelling the story of Renaissance personhood as one of material relations and embodied experience rather than of emergent notions of individuality and freedom.

The subsequent chapters are divided into three sections signaled in the subtitle to this book, "Materiality, Taxonomy, Process." Each term offers a different conceptual frame for thinking about personhood in physical and experiential terms. Part I, "Materialities of Personhood: Chairs, Machines, Doors," features chapters by Stephanie Elsky, Wendy Beth Hyman, and Colby Gordon, which together show how the world of objects provided Renaissance men and women with a language for thinking about liberty, agency, and entitlement. Elsky's "Daughters, Chairs, and Liberty in Margaret Cavendish's *The Religious*" zeroes in on the striking centrality of a beloved chair in a little-known seventeenth-century closet drama. Her analysis raises new questions about the conceptual and physical boundaries of moveable goods in the Renaissance, which in turn challenge received understandings of the relationship between person and property. In "The Inner Lives of Renaissance Machines," Hyman recovers various theatrical, intellectual, and rhetorical contexts in which humans and machines shared properties and functionalities, or were otherwise coextensive or inter-animated. By replacing modern notions of agency with something that looks more like automaticity, this archive helps us see more clearly how personhood was understood in mechanistic rather than psychological terms in the Renaissance. Gordon closes the section with "Two Doors: Personhood and Housebreaking in *Semayne's Case* and *The Comedy of Errors*," a chapter that looks for the first time at how domestic space formed an integral component of the lived structure of personhood in the Renaissance. In Gordon's analysis, personhood provides legal scripts for the material and spatial practice of dwelling.

Part II, "Taxonomies of Personhood: Status, Species, Race," offers three test cases in the powerful, but consistently problematic, way in which personhood has developed alongside ideas of humanness. Chapters by Joseph Campana, Holly Dugan, and Amanda Bailey approach the topic from arboreal, simian, and racial perspectives, showing how personhood has both generated and challenged conventional hierarchies of life. Taking Christopher Stone's landmark 1972 essay, "Should Trees Have Standing?," as a jumping-off point, Campana explores the emotionally, and sometimes verbally, responsive trees of the Renaissance literary tradition in his chapter, "Should (Bleeding) Trees Have Standing?" This *topos*, he argues, helps us understand core attributes of personhood—rights, inclusion, protection—beyond the parameters of sentience and anthropomorphism. Moving from trees to apes, Dugan's chapter, "Aping Personhood," presents a fascinating account of the Renaissance sources for modern legal debates about simian personhood. The implications of this neglected legal and natural-historical genealogy are far-reaching, offering new perspectives on the emergence of the idea of "human rights" and the history of species definition. In the final chapter in this section, "Race, Personhood, and the Human in *The Tempest*," Bailey takes up the relationship between personhood and humanness from another perspective: Renaissance conceptions of race. Focusing on Shakespeare's *The Tempest*, Bailey considers personhood in relation to the "genres of the human" in the Renaissance.

Part III, "Processes of Personhood: Eating, Lusting, Mapping," includes chapters by David B. Goldstein, John Michael Archer, and Gregory Kneidel devoted to the way things (food, bodies, land) are re-presented as processes (eating, lusting, mapping). Their collective aim is to show how aspects of personhood that, post-Descartes and post-Locke, we tend to associate with inner life—things like agency, sentience, and even the primordial capacity to feel shame—were for most of the Renaissance viewed in environmentally embedded terms. Goldstein's chapter, "Liquid *Macbeth*," conducts its investigation of Renaissance personhood by means of the *topos* of "liquidity," a motif which is pervasive in Shakespeare's *Macbeth* and indicative of less well-defined ways of conceiving the distinction between subjects and objects than would emerge in the later seventeenth century and beyond. In "Things in Action: Shakespeare's Sonnet 129, *Macbeth*, and Levinas on Shame," Archer draws on literary and philosophical sources to show how shame is both a primordial legal mechanism and a bodily experience. Shame sits at the crossroads of individual physiology and communal ethical norms and, as such, offers a unique starting point for thinking about personhood since it dispenses from the outset with hierarchies of reason and reflection. Finally, Kneidel's chapter, "Edward Herbert's Cosmopolitan State," considers political accommodation as a spatial phenomenon in the Renaissance. At the center of Kneidel's analysis is Edward Herbert's 1608 verse satire, "The State progress of Ill," which, he shows, offers a rich imaginative inventory of how perspectival representation changed ideas about land, property, and personhood.

The mission of this volume is to recover for the first time the way Renaissance personhood was shaped by ideas about the material world, both human and nonhuman. The work presented here should remind us that one of the core legal fictions of liberal modernity, a legal fiction that we now tend to associate with Enlightenment notions of agency, reason, and individuality, has other sources in the physical experiences, creaturely lives, and material encounters of the Renaissance.

Notes

1. "person, *n*." *OED Online* (Oxford: Oxford University Press, February 2019).
2. Marcel Mauss, "A Category of the Human Mind: The Notion of Person, the Notion of Self," in *The Category of the Person: Anthropology, Philosophy, History*, ed. Michael Carrithers, Steven Collins, and Steven Lukes (Cambridge: Cambridge University Press, 1985), 1–25.
3. Mauss, "A Category of the Human Mind," 4–5.
4. Mauss, "A Category of the Human Mind," 9.
5. Thomas Hobbes, *Leviathan*, ed. Richard E. Flathman and David Johnston (New York: W. W. Norton, 1996), 88.
6. Hobbes, *Leviathan*, 90.
7. Hobbes, *Leviathan*, 89.
8. Hobbes, *Leviathan*, 88.
9. Henry S. Turner, *The Corporate Commonwealth: Pluralism and Political Fictions in England, 1516–1651* (Chicago: University of Chicago Press, 2016), 204. See also Paul Kottman, *A Politics of the Scene* (Stanford: Stanford University Press, 2008) and Mónica Brito Vieira, *The Elements of Representation in Hobbes: Aesthetics, Theater, Law, and Theology in the Construction of Hobbes's Theory of the State* (Leiden: Brill, 2009).
10. John Locke, *An Essay Concerning Human Understanding*, ed. Kenneth P. Winkler (Indianapolis, IN: Hackett Publishing, 1996), 138.
11. Locke, *An Essay*, 148.
12. Locke, *An Essay*, 138.
13. For a few examples, see Daniel Dennett, "Conditions of Personhood," in *What Is a Person?*, ed. Michael F. Goodman (Clifton, NJ: Humana

Press, 1988), 145–67; Lawrence A. Locke, "Personhood and Moral Responsibility," *Law and Philosophy* 9 (1990): 39–66; Martha J. Farah and Andrea S. Heberlein, "Personhood and Neuroscience: Naturalizing or Nihilating," *The American Journal of Bioethics* 7 (2007): 37–48.

14. Derek Parfit, "Personal Identity," *The Philosophical Review* 80 (1971): 3–27; John Perry, "The Problem of Personal Identity," in *Personal Identity*, ed. John Perry (Berkeley: University of California Press, 1975), 3–30 and "The Importance of Being Identical," in *The Identities of Persons*, ed. Amelie Oksenberg Rorty (Berkeley: University of California Press, 1976), 67–90.

15. See especially Sir John Baker, *The Oxford History of the Laws of England, Volume VI: 1483–1558* (Oxford: Oxford University Press, 2003), 597–627, on which this paragraph draws heavily.

16. HLS MS 47, ff. 59–60v, 114 (tr.), quoted from Baker, *Oxford History*, 600.

17. *Statutes of the Realm, 1101–1713*, ed. A. Luders et al., 11 vols. (London, 1810–28).

18. See further, Sir John Baker, "Personal Liberty under the Common Law of England, 1200–1600," in *The Origins of Modern Freedom in the West*, ed. R. W. Davis (Stanford: Stanford University Press, 1995), 178–202.

19. Mary Nyquist, *Arbitrary Rule: Slavery, Tyranny, and the Power of Life and Death* (Chicago: University of Chicago Press, 2013), 11. See also Paul Cartledge and Matt Edge, "'Rights', Individuals, and Communities in Ancient Greece," in *A Companion to Greek and Roman Political Thought*, ed. Ryan K. Balot (Chichester: Wiley-Blackwell, 2009), 149–77.

20. Algernon Sidney, *Discourses Concerning Government* (London, 1698), 6.

21. See further, Nyquist, *Arbitrary Rule*, 274–9.

22. David Wootton, ed., *Divine Right and Democracy: An Anthology of Political Writings in Stuart England* (London: Penguin Books, 1986), 40. See also Annabel S. Brett, "The Development of the Idea of Citizens' Rights," in *States and Citizens*, ed. Quentin Skinner and Bo Strath (Cambridge: Cambridge University Press, 2003), 98.

23. John Ponet, *A Short Treatise of Politique Power* (London, 1556), 50.

24. Nyquist, *Arbitrary Rule*, 65.

25. Richard Overton, *An Arrow Against All Tyrants* (London, 1646), in *The Levellers in the English Revolution*, ed. G. E. Aylmer (London: Thames and Hudson, 1975), 69.

26. *The Complete Poetry and Essential Prose of John Milton*, ed. William Kerrigan, John Rumich, and Stephen M. Fallon (New York: Modern Library, 2007), 1028.

27. Turner, *Corporate Commonwealth*, 13–14.

28. *The Selected Writings and Speeches of Sir Edward Coke*, ed. Steve Sheppard, 3 vols. (Indianapolis, IN: Liberty Fund, 2003), I:371–2.

29. Turner, *Corporate Commonwealth*, xi.
30. See further, Barbara Johnson, *A World of Difference* (Baltimore: Johns Hopkins University Press, 1987), 184–222; "Anthropomorphism in Lyric and Law," *Yale Journal of Law and the Humanities* 10 (1998): 549–74; Barbara Johnson, *Persons and Things* (Cambridge, MA: Harvard University Press, 2008).
31. Elizabeth Fowler, *Literary Character: The Human Figure in Early English Writing* (Ithaca, NY: Cornell University Press, 2003), 17.
32. See further, John Parker, "Persona," in *Cultural Reformations: Medieval and Renaissance in Literary History*, ed. Brian Cummings and James Simpson (Oxford: Oxford University Press, 2010), 591–608.
33. Richard Hooker, *Of the Lawes of Ecclesiastical Politie* (London, 1597), 109.
34. John Locke, *The Second Treatise of Government*, 8:95, in John Locke, *Political Writings*, ed. David Wootton (Indianapolis, IN: Hackett Publishing, 2003), 309.
35. Laurie Shannon, *The Accommodated Animal: Cosmopolity in Shakespearean Locales* (Chicago: University of Chicago Press, 2013), 38.
36. See further, Martha C. Nussbaum, *Frontiers of Justice: Disability, Nationality, Species Membership* (Cambridge, MA: Belknap Press, 2006).
37. Julia Reinhard Lupton, "Creature Caliban," *Shakespeare Quarterly* 51 (2000): 1–23, 1.
38. Justinian, *Institutes* I:1.2, qtd. in Jean Porter, *Nature as Reason: A Thomistic Theory of Natural Law* (Grand Rapids, MI: William B. Eerdman, 2005), 346.
39. Shannon, *Accommodated Animal*, 3.
40. Guillaume du Bartas, *Bartas: His Devine Weekes and Workes*, trans. Joshua Sylvester (London, 1605), 146, 145, 208 (emphasis mine).
41. Christopher St. German, *The Dialogues in Englysshe, bytwene a Doctour of Dyvynyte and a Student in the laws of Englande* (London, 1543), fol. 4.
42. Amanda Bailey, *Of Bondage: Debt, Property, and Personhood in Early Modern England* (Philadelphia: University of Pennsylvania Press, 2013); Nyquist, *Arbitrary Rule*.
43. Lupton, "Creature Caliban." See also Julia Reinhard Lupton, *Thinking with Shakespeare: Essays on Politics and Life* (Chicago: University of Chicago Press, 2011).
44. Monique Allewaert, *Ariel's Ecology: Plantations, Personhood, and Colonialism in the American Tropics* (Minneapolis: University of Minnesota Press, 2013); Shannon, *Accommodated Animal*; Turner, *Corporate Commonwealth*.

Part I

Materialities of Personhood: Chairs, Machines, Doors

Chapter 2

Daughters, Chairs, and Liberty in Margaret Cavendish's *The Religious*

Stephanie Elsky

Seventeenth-century England saw significant changes to the meaning of property in the legal and political realm, changes that had profound implications for definitions of personhood in both those realms. This chapter focuses on one particular shift: the unsettling of the long-standing legal hierarchy that placed realty, or land, far above personalty, or personal property, including and especially "moveable goods," a category that encompassed furniture, apparel, money, animals, and household stuff.[1] Feminist scholars have illuminated the close and complex relationship that early modern women had with moveable goods, as the latter could be both a source of power in the household and emblematic of their legal erasure. What, then, were the implications of these changes in property and personhood for women? I argue that Royalist noble playwright and philosopher Margaret Cavendish explores this question in her little-read play *The Religious* (1662).

The plot of *The Religious* has all the hallmarks of Margaret Cavendish's politically minded romances: young lovers, enforced marriages, broken marriage contracts, family quarrels, and political intrigue.[2] The two main characters, Lord Melancholy and Lady Perfection, having been in love since childhood (which they are still in the midst of, since they are thirteen and ten years old, respectively), decide to wed while Lord Melancholy's father is abroad acting as the Emperor's ambassador. Lord Melancholy's uncle gives consent to their marriage, only for his father to angrily insist upon an annulment when he returns because Lady Perfection's father left his family deep in debt upon his death. The annulment is granted, and Lord Melancholy married off to a woman of his father's choosing, the Arch-Prince's niece. Although the niece eventually dies in childbirth, by this point, it is impossible for Lord Melancholy to marry Lady Perfection because she has joined a religious order to escape marrying the Arch-Prince himself. A "Religious Father" comes up with an ingenious solution to their problem: Lord Melancholy and Lady Perfection should institute a new religious order, the Order of Chastity in Marriage, and live out their lives together in a Cloister. As in Cavendish's 1656 prose romances, *The Contract* and *Assaulted and Pursued Chastity*, the conflict over marriage probes the parameters of consent and obligation; the desire for the loved one versus the desire to fulfill the dictate of the father is framed as a conflict between conscience and law; and, unusually for a Royalist, the outcome uniting the two lovers attests to the centrality of "the ongoing consent and affection" to the efficacy of a contract, even one that has been broken by others.[3]

Meanwhile, in the play's subplot, a young woman named Mistress Odd-Humour sits. That is, she spends the entire play in one room in her father's house, sitting in her childhood "little low-wicker armed chair" that she has long outgrown, conversing with her maid, Nan.[4] The subplot and Mistress Odd-Humour's attachment to the chair grows more and more absurd, reaching its apex when a suitor is brought in to meet Mistress Odd-Humour and rejects her on the grounds of laziness: she finally tries to get up from the chair to greet him and finds that she cannot. This structure of high-minded main plot and comic subplot is not an unusual feature of Cavendish's 1662 volume of plays, in which *The Religious* appears. Rather than dramatic unities, which she explicitly rejects, Cavendish uses multiplot plays, which feature "parallel and juxtaposition" to "advance their theme."[5] This structure, Lara Dodds and Margaret Ferguson argue, allows for "heroic narratives to exist alongside other forms of dramatic representation"; together, they "create a double vision in which positive representations of exceptional women [Lady Perfection, for example] are accompanied by representations of women who are constrained by circumstance and negative portraits drawn from the tradition of misogynist satire."[6] Certainly Mistress Odd-Humour would fit into the "Variety" of "Follies, Vanities, Vices, Humours, Dispositions, Passions, Affections, Fashions, Customs, Manners, and practices of the whole World of Mankind" that Cavendish explains she seeks to depict.[7]

In one sense Mistress Odd-Humour functions as a parodic foil for the main plot. Throughout the play, she and Nan anthropomorphize the chair, who becomes far more appealing than any husband could be. It is as if the chair and Mistress Odd-Humour are the play's other star-crossed couple. Even if we allow that all figurative language, including personification, constitutes "a sort of abuse . . . in speech," as George Puttenham described it in the previous century, Mistress Odd-Humour's descriptions of the chair are extreme.[8] At the same time, however, her affection for her personified chair depicts early modern women's multifaceted relationship to "moveable goods," a relationship of which Cavendish was well aware. Women were associated with moveable goods in ways that were both positive and negative. In marriage, they were expected to manage these goods, which gave them a powerful role in the household as consumer goods became more ubiquitous.[9] At the same time, however, to be connected with moveable goods was to be connected to a lesser form of property than land, at least in the legal terms that were most relevant to Cavendish as a noblewoman, those of common law. Finally, moveable goods were emblematic of the losses that accompanied marriage, since, upon being wed, women relinquished their property rights to their goods under the terms of coverture.[10] The attempts made to maintain proprietary connections with these goods—inscribing their names in their books, for example—registered their recognition of their attenuated relationship with that which was paradoxically theirs and not theirs.[11] Cavendish depicts the intensity of this loss when she has Mistress Odd-Humour prefer her chair to marriage. Mistress Odd-Humour recognizes that she will have to choose between continuing to invest her affection in her chair or transferring that affection to her husband. Later in the play, her sense of this choice is confirmed when the chair must be destroyed by her father before she can manage to get betrothed at all.

While we still might interpret Mistress Odd-Humour's preference for her chair as a feminine foible, I argue that it instead brings together the changing legal valence of personal property with emerging political ideas about property, both of which had an effect on understandings of personhood. In the legal realm, the hierarchy of real property and moveable goods was becoming more flexible, to the extent that the possibility of absolute ownership of the latter was becoming a model for possessing the former.[12] This change raises questions about the nature of legal personhood, which was connected to landed property, that early modern and contemporary legal scholars may not have pursued, though it seems that political thinkers were keenly aware of them. The hierarchical flexibility went even farther in the political realm, in part made possible by these legal shifts. For Thomas Hobbes, a major influence on Cavendish's thought, the distinction between moveable and immoveable property was inconsequential.[13] It was the ability to own property and not the type of property one owned that constituted the necessary condition for civil society. As we shall see, as a result of how the sovereign enabled this ownership, the distinction between humans and things for Hobbes diminished as well. While things did not become persons, they did become, like humans, "actors" and, in this way, "reflected" a kind of personhood.[14] In this play, Cavendish takes on Hobbes's political philosophy by personifying the chair. The particular way in which she does so both legitimates Mistress Odd-Humour's attachment to the chair as an inalienable possession and suggests that the chair itself attains a kind of personhood that is not limited in its liberty in the ways that Cavendish, unlike Hobbes, recognized a woman on the cusp of marriage would be. In particular, for Cavendish, a gentlewoman seeking liberty would do well to model herself after her chair.

I

Part of the subplot's joke is Mistress Odd-Humour's confusion of legal hierarchies when she favors her chair, a moveable good, over a desirable marriage, which was associated at the elite social level with the gaining and passing down of land. In this section, however, I argue that Cavendish instead registers the increasing difficulty of distinguishing between the two types of property in both the legal and political realms. She does so not only by characterizing Mistress Odd-Humour's father as a tyrant who wants to separate her from her chair, but also by choosing a chair or seat, a moveable good that has its own longstanding metaphorical associations with land, as the object of Mistress Odd-Humour's attachment. Her use of the chair, an object that metaphorically collapses the boundary between real property and moveable goods, also challenges the boundaries between alienable and inalienable possessions for a marriageable woman. Cavendish, I argue, suggests that Mistress Odd-Humour's attachment to her chair might not be so easily dismissed, and thus demonstrates that it presents a viable alternative to the land for constituting legal personhood.

Mistress Odd-Humour's attachment to her chair changes from a characterological idiosyncrasy to a social problem when it prevents her from getting married. She recounts to Nan the unfortunate tale of her first meeting with a suitor with whom her father had negotiated a marriage contract:

Why, I was sitting in that little Chair you know I take delight to sit in, and was singing of Ballads, not expecting that any stranger would come into my Chamber without my notice; but as I was sitting and singing, in comes my Father and the Gentleman you told me of, that was to be my Husband, whereat I was so surprized, as I forgot the Chair was so little I could not readily part from it; I started up in a fright, and run away, the Chair being so little in the seat, stood so close to me, as it went a-long with me, and my back being towards my Father and the Gentleman, saw the Chair as it stuck to me (2.16, pp. 538–9)

The comic inseparability of Mistress Odd-Humour from her chair leads directly to the suitor breaking off his contract with her father, as he wryly observes that "his Daughter was of so lazy a Nature, that rather than stay or want a seat, [she] would have a Chair tyed to [her] breech" (2.16, p. 539).

Not only the sheer absurdity of this moment, but also the legal status of moveable goods, especially in the context of marriage, might lead us to read this as a parody of feminine affective investment in objects. More specifically, Mistress Odd-Humour privileges the lesser form of property, moveable goods, over land that is negotiated with marriage. Common law was almost entirely devoted to the different forms of land ownership and its transfer, paying scant attention to chattel, which fell largely under the jurisdiction of the ecclesiastical courts. Moveable goods were ultimately incommensurable with real property, which was a key determinant of political power. If, as scholars have long recognized, legal personhood was not a single, monolithic status, but rather a "gradation" in which some legal persons had more rights and duties than others, the possession of land in early modern England placed one at the top of that gradation.[15] The vast temporal difference between land and moveables goods accounts for this legal difference. Land endures; moveables are impermanent. "Goods," David Seipp explains, "could be made and then consumed or destroyed, animals were born and would perish, but the land remained indefinitely."[16] Even further, because they were moveable, chattel could be stolen or appropriated. How could one base economic and political identity and authority on something that, quite simply, could be misplaced?

At times, moveable goods could play a compensatory role for those who would not inherit land: in her examination of early modern wills, Amy Louise Erickson has shown that in cases where there was an attempt to "divide property approximately equally," the testator would balance lands and moveables.[17] For example, a will might specify that profit from the eldest brother's land go toward younger sons' or daughters' cash portion, which they would receive upon their majority. Erickson notes that this was a frequent practice among the aristocracy and gentry.[18] At the "ordinary social level," heirs to real property might receive none of the moveable goods, which instead would go to "compensate his siblings for the lack of land."[19] Yet, even when judges and lawyers recognized the growing importance and value of moveable goods in the early modern period, it was in an attenuated fashion. For example, as early as 1527, Lord Justice Fitzherbert acknowledged that the relationship between land and goods was changing, remarking in one case that "many people who have no lands have goods and money of as great value as land."[20] But the phrasing of this recognition implied that if those "many people" possessed land, it would take precedence, and, as J. H. Baker points out, this recognition did not lead to any real change in common law, which continued its focus on land law.[21] The social and political difference between possessing land and owning moveable goods is one to which Cavendish would have been attuned, especially after the Restoration when she devoted her energies to restoring her husband's estates, Welbecke Abbey and Bolsover Castle.[22]

Mistress Odd-Humour exhibits worrying signs for her future as a wife. Because of objects' impermanence and their consequent existence outside the genealogical aims of land law and inheritance, one's attachment to them was associated with a certain aspect of personhood: individual idiosyncrasy and whim. As Katharine Eisaman Maus puts it, "because they are not inherited from forebears but selected and purchased by the consumer, [goods] can therefore function as markers of individual style."[23] Far from something to be celebrated, individual style was associated with prodigality, "luxurious self-indulgence inevitably tend[ed] to waste and excess."[24] These qualities would not have been considered ideal in anyone, but especially a wife because, as Natasha Korda has shown, despite the fact that most women had to relinquish their ownership of moveable goods upon marriage, the management of "household stuff" was increasingly a wife's domain and responsibility.[25] This management included "not only saving, storing, and maintaining, but marking, ordering, accounting, dividing, distributing, and disposing of household property, including durable and perishable goods."[26] Surely the inability to properly dispose of (or at least repurpose) a chair that has outlived its purpose does not bode well for Mistress Odd-Humour's treatment of other household stuff.

Yet, there is another way to understand this idiosyncrasy. The chair's ignominious fate undermines the developmental narrative implied in the story Mistress Odd-Humour has told: women must grow up and learn to forsake childish attachment to objects and adopt an appropriate investment in the land instead. The chair's ultimate fate, destruction at the hands of her father, transforms her father into a tyrant, a prominent figure in the main plot. Although the play ends with Mistress Odd-Humour preparing herself for marriage, it is not because she has undergone a developmental arc. Instead, her connection to her chair persists and can only be broken by a destructive act. In retribution for the broken betrothal, her father "vow[s]" to "break or burn" the chair (2.16, p. 539). One might have expected that this would be a turning point in the play, leading the mortified Mistress Odd-Humour to mend her ways. Instead, she and Nan scheme to protect her chair. But, at one point Mistress Odd-Humour's father catches her in the act of sitting on it, and it meets a tragic end, which she describes to Nan: "[H]e carried it away in one hand, and led me along in the other hand, causing a fire to be made of the Chair, made me stand by to see the Martyrdome, whereat I was so afflicted, as I lost my fight in tears" (4.31, p. 549). It is only then, once the chair is gone, that Mistress Odd-Humour resigns herself to her future. The narrative is not presented as a natural one, but rather is forced upon her. The characterization of her chair as a martyr invokes the discourse of tyranny.[27] In this moment, Mistress Odd-Humour's father resembles nothing so much as the tyrannical father figures of the main plot—Lord Gravity, who forces his son to marry the Arch-Prince's niece despite his conscience, and the Arch-Prince, who is on the brink of forcing Lady Perfection to marry him, despite the dictates of her conscience.

Moreover, the choice of object, the chair, foregrounds the difficulty of distinguishing between realty and personalty. The word "seat," which is also used to describe the chair in the play (pp. 530, 531, 539), has a dual meaning. It is both the thing *upon which* you sit and the place *in which* you sit. And not just any place, but the place that gives your identity legal and political meaning. In *A New World of Words* (1611), an Italian–English dictionary, John Florio defined the Italian "séde" as "a situation. Also any kind of seat, chair, stoole, bench, or sitting place. Also a place to dwell in, a mansion or resting place."[28] In his manuscript, *A Glossary of Proper First Names* (c. 1626–8), John Dodderidge defined a "sett" as "an habitacion or Seate," leaving unclear whether or not the two definitions are synonymous.[29] Finally Thomas Blount's 1656 *Glossographia, or A Dictionary Interpreting All Such Hard Words* defines "site (situs)" as "the setting or standing of any place, the seat, or situation; a Territory or quarter of a County" and "Principality (principalitas)" as the "estate or seat of a Sovereign Prince." The Louvre is defined as "the royal seat of the Kings of France in Paris, famous throughout Europe."[30] In the case of the chair or seat, the moveable good functions as a synecdoche for real property, underscoring the extent to which the two categories are in fact inextricably linked. Indeed, the chair traveled with the monarch as a symbol of his or her sovereignty.[31]

On a practical legal level, too, determining what counted as a moveable good was not always straightforward. Their nomenclature makes it seem as though the definition should be clear enough. In Henry Swinburne's words, they are "goods both actiuely and pas-siuely moueable."[32] But in practice, it was more complex: what was the status of, for example, fixtures, or artifacts attached to houses or other buildings? In 1493, Justice Fairfax ruled that church pews, for example, were part of a freehold, making the important criterion for a moveable good removeability. Yet, in a sixteenth-century case that long remained important, "the removeability test [was] completely abandoned."[33] In this case, an oven that was cemented to a floor was removed by the will's executors. Yet, despite the fact that it clearly *could* be removed, the heirs won their case that when the executors did so, it constituted trespass.[34] In other words, despite the oven being technically moveable, it had become part of realty.

Finally, and most significantly for my purposes, land and moveables were becoming fundamentally, conceptually intertwined in the law over the course of the sixteenth and seventeenth centuries. Seipp argues that, especially during the seventeenth century, the ownership of moveable goods surprisingly became the paradigm upon which property in land was modeled.[35] In legal treatises and Year Books, the terms "property," "owner," and "ownership" were far more likely to refer to animals and goods than to land itself.[36] In his late sixteenth- and early seventeenth-century *Reports*, Edward Coke usually used "property" in the context of chattel, only starting to include more references to land as property and landholders as owners in his later *Institutes*.[37] Instead of "property," land was described in treatises and Year Books in terms of "right," "possession," and "seisin."[38] What was the significance of this separate terminology? "Property" signified the absolute ownership of moveable goods: "every possession of goods or animals was potentially exclusive," as Seipp puts it.[39] One could have a "unitary interest in a horse or a book or a bolt of cloth."[40] By contrast, "right" and related terms reflected the complex, overlapping set of partial legal connections that different people had to the same parcel of land.[41] Thus, a lord might be seised in "fee simple," while his tenants had rights in common. Yet, over the course of the sixteenth and seventeenth centuries, common lawyers started to include land in their definition of property, "carrying the conceptual trappings of absolute property in goods and animals into the context of land disputes." Even Coke began to generalize about, in his words, "property of lands and goods."[42] In legal disputes regarding the land, rather than referring to different "holders of rights," disputants were referred to as "owners of the soil" or "owner of the land."[43]

The slow process of convergence between land and ownership that Seipp describes came to a head during the English Civil War and Revolution. In particular, the 1646 abolition of feudal tenures and the Court of Wards, which was confirmed in 1660, transformed the legal status of land. No longer did the king have the ability to grant tenures with an array of "feudal incidents" attached to them in order to raise revenue. As the 1660 statute put it, "all Tenures to be created by the King's Majesty, his Heirs, or Successors . . . shall be in free and common Socage only."[44] In other words, landholders no longer held their lands by fulfilling feudal services to the Crown. Land ownership thus went from conditional to absolute, and land owners were free to buy and sell their land just as they would any other commodity.[45] Conversely, as Blackstone observed, "the extension of commerce and trade brought mobile chattels, or personalty, almost to the level of realty."[46] Realty becomes less important because it is not "susceptible to absolute possession," but with legal devices like entail, in which a landowner dictates the line of inheritance, limiting it, for example, to male heirs, realty can become an absolute possession like personalty.[47] With entail, there is a breach of feudal law because of the "metamorphosis of a conditional into an absolute possession." Indeed, as Jonathan Lamb argues, under entail immobile property begins "to function as if it were mobile."[48]

The difference between land and moveable goods was shrinking not only in the legal realm, but also in the intertwined political realm. Michael McKeon argues that in the process of losing its privileged legal status, for political thinkers, land ceased to be a political category and became an economic category[49]—just as moveable goods had always been. But it might be more accurate to say that by redefining realty and personalty, political thinkers like Thomas Hobbes imagined land and objects together have a crucial role in constituting civil society, one in which land looked remarkably like an object. According to Hobbes, the possession of objects, and the need to protect them, forms the basis of civil society. Justice, then, shifts from being "a matter . . . of proportionate or fair relations between people," as Aristotle would have it, to being "a matter of individuals' relations to things."[50] Hobbes's guiding premise is that "the state has point of origin in agreement to unite in a common-wealth, and that its history is an account of how the ends proposed by its foundation, chiefly self-preservation and the securing of action are fulfilled in action."[51] According to Hobbes, while man has a right to all things in the state of nature, which he famously calls a state of war, there is no way to own a particular thing since there is no way to vindicate one's right to own all things.[52] In effect, there is no natural property right, and nothing to call one's own "until a property is made."[53] Hobbes asserts that law and justice do not exist in the state of nature, and therefore neither does propriety, or the ability to own property:

> Where there is no common power, there is no law; where no law, no injustice . . . It is consequent to the same condition that there be no pro-priety, no dominion, no *mine* and *thine* distinct, but only that to be every man's that he can get, for as long as he can keep it.[54]

And propriety emanates not from the labor one puts into it, as Locke and others would have it, but from the authority of the magistrate or sovereign. One renounces his right to all things—or more, precisely, the right to use one's private judgment about how to preserve oneself by acquiring necessities[55]—to the sovereign in order to protect one's rights to some things. And, once you own something, be it land or goods, you own it absolutely; the sovereign sees to the security of that ownership.[56] The question of that thing's mobility, of its perma-nence, is rendered largely irrelevant.

In this context, the choice of the chair as Mistress Odd-Humour's fixation foregrounds the difficulty of distinguishing between real and moveable goods.[57] Cavendish's use of an object that collapses the dis-tinction between legal categories suggests that the boundary between an alienable and inalienable possession is not as clear cut as it might seem. She invites us to consider the implications of these collapsing boundaries for female personhood in particular. In her *Sociable Let-ters* (1664), Cavendish draws a direct connection between the legal status of women and that of moveable goods. One of the two anony-mous female correspondents wonders why two ladies of their mutual acquaintance are "Melancholy . . . for want of Children."[58] Why, the very practically-minded Lady wonders, would a woman "desire Children for her Own Sake?" After all, her family name will not be passed on, nor her estates "according to the Lawes and Customes of this Countrey."[59] Sons will only continue the male line of succession, and with daughters, one is worse off because they cannot pass on even that. "Daughters," the Lady explains, "are but Branches which by Marriage are Broken off from the Root from whence they Sprang, & Ingrafted into the Stock of an other Family, so that *Daughters are to be accounted but as Moveable Goods*, or Furnitures that wear out."[60] Invoking the image of the family tree, the Lady explains that daughters and sons may spring form the same roots, but only daughters can be detached from those roots and attached to another tree through marriage, which she describes as the horticultural practice of grafting, a practice that was often described in terms of and used as a metaphor for procreation.[61] At the same time, daughters are characterized by the same ephemerality as "moveable goods"; they can both "wear out." In the case of a daughter, her connection to her family is fleeting, lasting only until marriage. While the first horticultural metaphor could be read as dismissive, it at least has the virtue of implying renewal and futurity.[62] This second metaphor, by contrast, evokes only attrition and decay. Even while daughters are unmarried, and thus still part of their family, they are always already in the process of eroding. While this letter is parodic in the Lady's utter lack of sentimentality regarding offspring, it nonetheless offers a poignant account of a daughter's status. Daughters are akin to inanimate objects. They are not only robbed of personhood but consigned to a lesser category of property at that, since the metaphor relies on the persistent idea that moveable goods are secondary to land in the law. But what if that is no longer the case? And what if, as a result, the definition of personhood is radically altered as well?

II

Cavendish explores these questions through the ongoing personification of the chair and thus calls attention not only to the similarity between moveable goods and land, but also to that between humans and objects. With this trope, the play legitimates Mistress Odd-Humour's affective attachment to the chair. At the same time, it again summons up and responds to the political philosophy of Cavendish's contemporary Hobbes, especially his influential category of "artificial persons." As Lamb has argued, by endowing things with person-like capacities, Hobbes introduces a potential instability in the relationship between persons and objects, in which property, though it can now be owned more absolutely, can nonetheless exceed a person's control.[63] Yet, for Cavendish, who has her own theory of self-moving objects, this instability introduces yet another possibility, what Karen Detlefsen calls "radical freedom."[64] Ultimately, Mistress Odd-Humour and Nan imagine what liberty might look like if a married woman took as her model the mobile object.

The choice of the chair goes even further than confounding the difference between legal categories. The pervasive personification of Mistress Odd-Humour's arm chair as sexual rival calls our attention to this overlap between person and thing, since it reminds us that the chair, which accommodates the human form, is remarkably close to that form. The "arms" resemble that which rest upon it.[65] Throughout, the chair is figured as a rival to Mistress Odd-Humour's suitors. In a series of exchanges, the two women debate the relative merits of chair and husband. In their first scene together, Mistress Odd-Humour says she would not part from her chair "for anything," to which Nan replies, "Yes, you would part with your little old Chair for a proper young Husband, who would set you on his knee." Mistress Odd-Humour protests: "By my faith I would not, for I should find more trouble and less ease on a young Husbands knees, than on my old Chairs seat" (1.3, pp. 530–1). After Mistress Odd-Humour tells the story of her meeting with her suitor, she worries about the fate of her chair:

> Mistress Odd-Humour. . . . O Nan, what shall I do to save my chair? For to lose both Chair and Husband will be too great a loss.
> Nan: Which had you rather lose, the Gentleman or the Chair?
> Mistress Odd-Humour. O the Gentleman Nan, for he will not do me half so much service as the Chair hath done me; he will never bear me as the Chair hath bore me: and I perceive by his she humour, and Courteous Nature, that he would sooner break my head with a Chair, than ease my hips with a Seat. (2.16, p. 539)

Mistress Odd-Humour responds to Nan in sexually suggestive terms, activating the dual meaning of ease as comfort and as pleasure.[66] She suggests that the chair's sexual prowess outstrips that of her potential husband. Finally, the chair shifts from rival to paramour. Determined to save the chair from her father's wrathful hands, Mistress Odd-Humour explains that she will only sit in it when her father is away, and commands Nan will keep watch to give her warning if he is coming. In this way, she explains, she will "take such times as wives do to Cuckold their Husbands as in their Husbands absence." Nan loyally, though reluctantly, affirms, "So I shall be as the Bawd between the Chair and you" (2.24, p. 545).

One might read this as a parody, but the play goes to some lengths to suggest that we take the relationship seriously. On the one hand, this personification might be another instance of Mistress Odd-Humour not getting the relationship between women and household stuff quite right. Although the affective connection between women and household stuff was recognized and encouraged by early modern prescriptive literature, it was described as a maternal one. Multiple authors likened household management to the process of a bird staying in the nest, sitting on an egg waiting to hatch.[67] Mistress Odd-Humour, by contrast, is more likely to want to marry than mother her household goods. But there is an odd parallel between the main plot of the virtuous, high-minded lovers and the story of Mistress Odd-Humour and her chair that legitimates this romantic attachment. Each follows the familiar plot of falling in love with someone in your household that your father deems unsuitable. The play opens with two maid servants, Kate and Joan, discussing Lord Melancholy and Lady Perfection's desire to marry one another. Kate remarks that the two children "are the kindest lovers, for so young ones, as that ever I knew," and Joan explains that this is because "[t]hey have been bred together, and they have not been acquainted with the Vanitye and Vices of the world, which makes love the more pure" (1.1, p. 527). When Mistress Odd-Humour is first introduced to the audience a few scenes later, her maid Nan similarly wonders about her love for her chair, exclaiming, "Lord Mistris, you take great pains to crowd into that Chair, I wonder you can take delight to sit so uneasily," and Mistress Odd-Humour explains: "O Custom is a second Nature; for I using to sit in this Chair from my Childhood, I have a Natural Love to it, as to an old acquaintance" (1.3, p. 530). Thus, from the beginning of the play, Cavendish emphasizes that the two plots are connected via the love of that with which you've been bred. The play invites us to imagine the suitability of marrying your favorite childhood thing.

In doing so, I argue, it invokes the Hobbesian idea of personation. In Chapter 16 of *Leviathan*, "Of Persons, Authors, and Things Personated," Hobbes distinguishes between natural and artificial persons. Natural persons, who exist only in the state of nature (or whose existence is only significant in that moment), own their own words and actions. Owning one's words and actions is akin to dominion, the right of possession. By analogy, if you have the right of possession over your words and actions, you have "the right of doing any act."[68] In other words, natural persons are "authors." Most significantly for Hobbes, authors possess the right to transfer their rights, that is, "perform the act of authoriz[ing]" someone else to speak or act in their name.[69] That someone (or something) else is an artificial person, known as an "actor." According to Quentin Skinner, Hobbes offers this analysis in service of explaining how "it is possible for a state—or any other abstraction or collectivity—to perform actions and take responsibility of the consequences."[70] On the one hand, then, the primary actor with which Hobbes is concerned is the commonwealth, who can be defined as "One Person."[71] But, on the other hand, when authors cede their ownership, they too become artificial persons, and thus, it is not possible to simply say that authors are the represented and actors are their representatives.[72]

Once the actor or artificial person encompasses the represented and not just representatives, the category becomes almost endlessly expandable. As Skinner puts it, Hobbes believes that "almost anything can count as a person, since almost anything can be validly represented."[73] To quote Hobbes's own words: "There are few things, that are uncapable of being represented by Fiction. Inanimate things, as a Church, an Hospital, a Bridge, may be Personated by a Rector, Master, or Overseer."[74] If there is "some state of Civill Government," inanimate objects do not need to be authors to have actors ("Owners or Governours") represent them.[75] Henry Turner cautions against conflating personation with personhood, explaining that Hobbes is not here attributing actual personhood to things. Instead, "inanimate things may enter into a representational relationship with a human being who acts as artificial person on their behalf," creating a "kind of reflected personhood."[76] At the same time, however, it is crucial to Hobbes's theory of the state as an artificial person that inanimate objects are capable of acting.[77]

In the play's ending, Cavendish invokes objects yet again, but modifies Hobbes's idea of personation in a particularly feminist register that has ramifications for women's liberty. The penultimate scene finds Mistress Odd-Humour weeping because she can no longer escape her fate, her "father will have [her] marry." Despite not knowing future husband, she is sure he will be a "fool." As is typical, Nan instructs her mistress that her problem is actually an opportunity. She points out, "[i]f he prove a foolish Husband you have no reason to cry, for then you will have the more Liberty." Mistress Odd-Humour at first doubts Nan but is eventually to be won over to her way of thinking:

> Mistress Odd-Humour. The more liberty to be a Fool you mean.
> Nan. Indeed liberty to women makes them rather more foolish than wise: for women know not how to use liberty discreetly, for when they have liberty they run beyond the bounds of discretion.

> Mistress Odd-Humour. Faith if I marry this same Gentleman that my
> Father says I shall, I shall run beyond the bounds of Matrimony.
> Nan. That is to run into your Neighbors Bed. (5.36, p. 554)

In their exchange, matrimony is figured as a piece of land, an estate
with borders. While the verb "run" seems to call attention to Mistress Odd-Humour's status as human, it also emphasizes her object-
like mobility. Cavendish similarly objectifies her potential lover by
referring to his bed rather than, say, his arms. In both cases, the
characters highlight what humans and objects have in common that
humans and land do not. Yet, rather than lose agency in marriage,
Mistress Odd-Humour gains it by recognizing her similarity to those
objects she must relinquish in marriage.

For Hobbes, this might represent the nightmare of personation.
The "level of fiction necessary to the conduct of the state," in Lamb's
evocative phrase, created the unsettling possibility that absolute
dominion over things may be impossible: "How can authors of such
fictions draw limits around their inventions and determine their relation to truth when they themselves are creatures of similar fictions,
owning actions that are not theirs?"[78] Hobbes's solution is to distinguish between "good" and "bad" fictions, fictions that serve the
commonwealth and those that create illusions of power that persons
no longer possess.[79] According to Lamb, Hume later explains that
the former "stabilize" relationships between individuals and external
objects, while the latter disturb them; these range from accidents to
war, madness to death.

But it turns out that it is not that easy to separate out the good
fictions from the bad. The prime example Lamb examines is entail,
wherein a landowner dictates the line of inheritance after his death,
which weighed heavily on eighteenth-century authors and legal
thinkers alike; yet, entail had been part of English common law since
the thirteenth century. At the same time, the line of descent "becomes
less and less predictable" as time goes on, "having more to do with
chance or fortune . . . than with the will of the person who set it
in train."[80] Ironically, our desires and attempts to obtain absolute
ownership introduce the "possibility of a thing's appearing to own
and move itself."[81] The vagaries of the entailed estate may even hint
at "the inclinations of the fief itself."[82] More often than not, in a
civil society that depends upon absolute ownership, we are forced to
reckon with, to invoke Hume again, the "looseness" of things.

Yet, indeed, this problem becomes an opportunity for Mistress
Odd-Humour. In the play's conclusion, objects become a model for

Mistress Odd-Humour in a way that land can never be—as much as she herself would prefer to imitate the land and stay put. If wielded correctly, Nan instructs, her status as moveable, which had been so derided in the *Sociable Letters*, ironically can offer Mistress Odd-Humour a measure of "liberty." On the one hand, in the context of marriage, liberty does not possess an entirely positive valence, since it is here associated particularly with sexual liberty, something Cavendish roundly condemns when she advises that

> 'tis more seemly, graceful and becoming, for a wife to have her husband always with her to be a witness to her honest actions, than to give a suspicion to both her husband and the world, as if she desired to be absent from him and out of sight, that she might take more liberty to be wanton . . .[83]

On the other hand, in the context of the play's main plot, the term resonates with Cavendish's political philosophy. Lady Perfection first invokes the term when debating the efficacy of their own marriage contract with paternal or sovereign powers. When the Arch-Prince tries to persuade her that she can marry him because her marriage to Lord Melancholy has been annulled, she replies in seventeenth-century political terms: "'Tis true, I am Chast, and so I will remain, and though the law hath set my person free, my conscience is not yet [a]t liberty" (2.21, p. 540).[84] In Mistress Odd-Humour's case, the law binds her, but she still has the liberty of motion.

Given this context, it is important to grasp Cavendish's definition of liberty and its limits. Detlefsen argues that while Cavendish was deeply influenced by Hobbes's account of civil society, she diverges from his understanding of the nature and role of liberty in that society. Specifically, for Cavendish "the realm of unfreedom is considerably wider" than for Hobbes.[85] Hobbes, as Skinner has shown, distinguishes between two circumstances that render an agent powerless to act; only one of these, in his view, constitutes a lack of liberty or freedom. An "external, physical force" preventing an "agent's intrinsic power" qualifies as an instance of unfreedom.[86] If, however, an "intrinsic (or psychological) impairment" prevents action, this would not be considered a lack of liberty or freedom.[87] This is because our internal wills are not free to begin with, since, in Hobbes's words, the will "is appetite" and "[man can no more] determine his will than any other appetite."[88]

By contrast, as Detlefsen concludes by examining both Cavendish's *Philosophical Letters* and plays published in the same volume as *The*

Religious, Cavendish equates *both* circumstances—external and internal constraints—with a lack of liberty. This difference can be attributed to Cavendish's natural philosophy, in which, unlike Hobbes, she posits that all matter is self-moving, whether animate or not; movement, in other words, does not need to be caused by an external force, and is itself rational. Thus, the human will can be "the free and undetermined source of its own movement." This is the source of what Detlefsen terms Cavendish's notion of "radical freedom," which includes freedom from external *and* internal constraints.[89] The manipulation of humans through fear misuses their internal rational capacity rather than, as Hobbes would have it, their always already unfree wills.[90] In her drama, Detlefsen argues, Cavendish is far more attuned to the internalized constraints placed upon women in particular and suggests that the internal constraints that emerge from external, social constraints are arbitrary, unnatural, and reformable.[91] As a result, despite her Royalist and absolutist leanings, Cavendish disagrees with Hobbes that the sovereign can bind the will of its citizens through the internal constraint of fear.[92] Victoria Kahn argues similarly that in her prose romances, Cavendish "raises questions about what it means to consent under the threat of violence or enslavement and about the relative political value of fear and love in inducing voluntary subjection."[93] Kahn likewise concludes that Cavendish unexpectedly rejects fear as a legitimate basis for sovereign authority.[94]

If we return, then, to the chair's undoing, we might say that Mistress Odd-Humour's father has illegitimately manipulated her liberty through the internal constraints of fear. Nan's advice to run beyond the bound of marriage by running to her neighbor's bed, perversely, represents a reclamation of that liberty through movement.[95] There turns out to be an advantage to being a "branch" that can be "broken off," a benefit to being "accounted but as moveable goods," as Cavendish describes daughters in the *Sociable Letters*. If we begin the play, then, with one moveable object, the chair, we end it with another, Mistress Odd-Humour herself. Yet, over the course of the play, the nature of the moveable object has itself been changed—from the "superfluous" thing[96] that prevents Mistress Odd-Humour's transition into the shared legal personhood of her husband to an integral part of her personhood, and even to something that shares the status of personhood in its own right. Astonishingly for a noblewoman, in this play Cavendish responds to contemporary theories of personhood to redefine it as rooted, so to speak, not in the permanence of land but rather in the mobility of objects.

Notes

1. Henry Swinburne, *A Briefe Treatise of Testaments and Last Wills* (London, 1590), 306, 314.
2. Victoria Kahn, *Wayward Contracts: The Crisis of Political Obligation in England, 1640–1674* (Princeton, NJ: Princeton University Press, 2004), ch. 7, *passim*.
3. Kahn, *Wayward Contracts*, 173.
4. Margaret Cavendish, *The Religious*, in *Plays Written by the Thrice Noble, Illustrious, and Excellent Princess, the Lady Marchioness of Newcastle* (London, 1662), 1.3, 530, <http://gateway.proquest.com/openurl?ctx_ver= Z39.88-2003&res_id=xri:eebo&rft_id=xri:eebo:citation:11861873> (last accessed April 24, 2019); hereafter cited in the text.
5. Lara Dodds and Margaret Ferguson, "Sidney, Cary, Cavendish: Playwrights of the Printed Page and a Future Stage," in *A New Companion to Renaissance Drama*, ed. Arthur Kinney (London: Wiley-Blackwell, 2017), 589.
6. Dodds and Ferguson, "Sidney, Cary, Cavendish," 589.
7. Qtd. in Margaret Cavendish, *The Convent of Pleasure and Other Plays*, ed. Anne Shaver (Baltimore: Johns Hopkins University Press, 1999), 55–6.
8. George Puttenham, *The Art of English Poesy* [1589], ed. Frank Whigham and Wayne Rebhorn (Ithaca, NY: Cornell University Press, 2007), 238.
9. Natasha Korda, *Shakespeare's Domestic Economies: Gender and Property in Early Modern England* (Philadephia: University of Pennsylvania Press, 2002), 26.
10. Krista J. Kesselring and Tim Stretton, "Introduction," in *Married Women and the Law: Coverture in England and the Common Law World*, ed. Tim Stretton and Krista J. Kesselring (Montreal: McGill-Queen's University Press, 2013), 7–8. One exception was "paraphernalia," which usually referred to clothing and jewelry. In this case, as Blackstone put it, "the wife may acquire a property in some of *her husband's* goods" (emphasis mine). See William Blackstone, *Commentaries on the Laws of England*, vol. 2, ed. Simon Stern (Oxford: Oxford University Press, 2016), 295.
11. For a good overview of this scholarship, see Natasha Korda, "Coverture and Its Discontents: Legal Fictions On and Off the Early Modern Stage," in *Married Women and the Law*, ed. Stretton and Kesselring, 45–51.
12. David J. Seipp, "The Concept of Property in the Early Common Law," *Law and History Review* 12.1 (Spring 1994): 31.
13. Hobbes was employed by and enjoyed the patronage of the Cavendish family, particularly Margaret's husband William's first cousins, for most of his adult life. Hobbes's first book of political philosophy, *The Elements of Law*, was likely written at William Cavendish's behest, and he is often associated with the "Welbecke academy," scientists with whom William Cavendish studied and conversed at

his Welbecke estate. See Noel Malcolm, "A Summary Biography of Hobbes," in *The Cambridge Companion to Hobbes*, ed. Tom Sorell (Cambridge: Cambridge University Press, 1996), 22–3. Cavendish herself engages with Hobbes's natural philosophy in her *Philosophical Letters* (1664).

14. Henry S. Turner, *The Corporate Commonwealth: Pluralism and Political Fictions in England, 1516–1651* (Chicago: University of Chicago Press, 2016), 214–15. For an elaboration on these ideas, see pages 33–4 below.

15. Andrea D. Boboc, "Introduction," in *Theorizing Legal Personhood in Late Medieval England* (Amsterdam: Brill, 2015), 2–3.

16. Siepp, "Concept of Property," 44. Katherine Eisaman Maus points out that moveable goods were exceptionally durable during the early modern period—"household goods were manufactured to last for generations"—but even this sturdiness paled in comparison to the permanence of land. Katherine Eisaman Maus, *Being and Having in Shakespeare* (Oxford: Oxford University Press, 2013), 44.

17. Amy Louise Erickson, *Women and Property in Early Modern England* (London: Routledge, 1993), 69.

18. Erickson, *Women and Property*, 69.

19. Erickson, *Women and Property*, 70.

20. Qtd. in Sir John Baker, *The Oxford History of the Laws of England, Volume VI: 1483–1558* (Oxford: Oxford University Press, 2003), 727.

21. Baker, *Oxford History*, 727.

22. As Julie Crawford has shown, Cavendish saw her role as wife as deeply political. See "Margaret Cavendish, Wife," in *Family Politics in Early Modern Literature*, ed. Hannah Crawforth and Sara Lewis (London: Palgrave Macmillan, 2017) and "'Pleaders, Attorneys, Petitioners, and the Like': Margaret Cavendish and the Dramatic Petition," in *Women Players in England, 1500–1660: Beyond the All-Male Stage*, ed. Pamela Allen Brown and Peter Parolin (Aldershot: Ashgate, 2005).

23. Maus, *Being and Having*, 46. Maus offers the example of Prince Hal's association with consumables in Shakespeare's *1 and 2 Henry IV*.

24. Maus, *Being and Having*, 47.

25. Korda, *Shakespeare's Domestic Economies*, 26.

26. Korda, *Shakespeare's Domestic Economies*, 27.

27. Erna Kelly compares Mistress Odd-Humour's father's searching for her chair to "government officials searching for false priests." Erna Kelly, "Playing with Religion: Convents, Cloisters, Martyrdom, and Vows," *Early Modern Literary Studies* Special Issue 14 (May 2014): 20, <https://extra.shu.ac.uk/emls/si-14/kellplay.html> (last accessed April 24, 2019). For more on tyrants and martyrs, see, for example, Mike Pincombe and Gavin Schwart-Leeper, "John Foxe's *Book of Martyrs*: Tragedies of Tyrants," in *The Oxford Handbook of Early Modern Literature and Religion*, ed. Andrew Hiscock and Helen Wilcox (Oxford: Oxford

University Press, 2017). Charles I famously depicted himself as a martyr to tyranny in his 1649 *Eikon Basilike*.

28. John Florio, *Queen Anna's A New World of Words, or Dictionarie of the Italian and English Tongues* (London, 1611), 486, <http://gateway.proquest.com/openurl?ctx_ver=Z39.88-2003&res_id=xri:eebo&rft_id=xri:eebo:citation:99892301> (last accessed April 24, 2019).

29. John Dodderidge, *A Glossary of Proper First Names*, BL Sloane MS 3479, <https://leme.library.utoronto.ca/lexicons/351/details#fulltext> (last accessed April 24, 2019).

30. Thomas Blount, *Glossographia or a Dictionary* (London, 1656), <https://leme.library.utoronto.ca/lexicons/478/details#fulltext> (last accessed April 24, 2019).

31. Florence de Dampierre, *Chairs: A History* (New York: Abrams, 2006).

32. Swinburne, *Treatise*, 306.

33. Baker, *Oxford History*, 736.

34. Baker, *Oxford History*, 736.

35. Seipp, "Concept of Property," 47, 87.

36. Seipp, "Concept of Property," 39.

37. Seipp, "Concept of Property," 80–1. As late as 1651, in his posthumously published *The Compleat Lawyer*, William Noy, who was Charles I's Attorney General, only applied the term "property" to moveables. See G. E. Aylmer, "The Meaning and Definition of 'Property' in Seventeenth-Century England," *Past & Present* 86 (February 1980): 92.

38. Seipp, "Concept of Property," 37, 39.

39. Seipp, "Concept of Property," 46.

40. Seipp, "Concept of Property," 46. See also Baker, *Oxford History*, 748.

41. Seipp, "Concept of Property," 46.

42. Seipp, "Concept of Property," 47.

43. Seipp, "Concept of Property," 85.

44. Qtd. in Charles J. Reid, Jr., "The Seventeenth-Century Revolution in English Land Law," *Cleveland State Law Review* 43.2 (1995): 242.

45. Christopher Hill, *The Collected Essays of Christopher Hill*, vol. 3 (Amherst: University of Massachusetts Press, 1986), 100.

46. Jonathan Lamb, *The Things Things Say* (Princeton, NJ: Princeton University Press, 2011), 8.

47. Lamb, *Things*, 6.

48. Lamb, *Things*, 7.

49. Michael McKeon, "The Secret History of Domesticity: Public, Private, and the Division of Knowledge," in *The Age of Cultural Revolutions: Britain and France, 1750–1820*, ed. Colin Jones and Dror Wahlman (Berkeley: University of California Press, 2002), 179.

50. Lamb, *Things*, 10.

51. Lamb, *Things*, 8.

52. Richard Tuck, "Introduction," in Thomas Hobbes, *Leviathan*, ed. Richard Tuck (Cambridge: Cambridge University Press, 1996), xxvii, xxx.

53. Hobbes, *Leviathan*, 90.
54. Hobbes, *Leviathan*, 90; see also 100–1.
55. Tuck, "Introduction," xxx–xxxi, xxxii.
56. Although this might be the case in Hobbes's theory, multiple scholars have pointed out that even in *The Commentaries*, wherein Blackstone declares property to be "the sole and despotic dominion which one man claims and exercises over the external things of the world, in total exclusion of the right of any other individual in the universe," one "finds . . . at every turn, on every page, less-than-absolute property rights." See Blackstone, *Commentaries*, 1; David B. Schorr, "Community and Property: How Blackstone Became a Blackstonian," *Theoretical Inquiries in Law* 10.1 (January 2009): 107, 107n.6; Daniel Stout, "Uncommon Land: Public Property and the Rise of the Individual," *Victorian Studies* 60.2 (Winter 2018): 271–2.
57. Alison Findlay also sees objects and land as related, arguing that the chair represents Cavendish's "deliberate attempt to manage" the loss of her childhood home, St. John's Abbey Colchester, in the Civil War. The tragic destruction of the chair evinces this loss, while the humorous aspects of Mistress Odd-Humour's relationship to it are a kind of "self-mockery" of her attachment. Alison Findlay, "'I hate such an old-fashioned House': Margaret Cavendish and the Search for Home," *Early Modern Literary Studies* Special Issue 14 (May 2004): 7–8, <https://extra.shu.ac.uk/emls/si-14/findhate.html> (last accessed April 24, 2019).
58. Margaret Cavendish, *Sociable Letters*, ed. James Fitzmaurice (Ontario: Broadview Editions, 2004), 145.
59. Cavendish, *Sociable Letters*, 145.
60. Cavendish, *Sociable Letters*, 145 (emphasis mine).
61. Vin Nardizzi, "Shakespeare's Penknife: Grafting and Seedless Generation in the Procreation Sonnets," *Renaissance and Reformation/Renaissance et Réforme* 32.1 (Winter 2009): 83–106.
62. It should be noted that not all early modern literature embraced this valence of grafting. On Perdita's critique of the unnaturalness of grafting in Shakespeare's *The Winter's Tale*, see Ari Friedlander, "Roguery and Reproduction in *The Winter's Tale*," in *The Oxford Handbook of Shakespeare and Embodiment: Gender, Sexuality, and Race*, ed. Valerie Traub (Oxford: Oxford University Press, 2016), 500–1.
63. Lamb, *Things*, 12–13.
64. Karen Detlefsen, "Margaret Cavendish and Thomas Hobbes on Freedom, Education, and Women," in *Feminist Interpretations of Thomas Hobbes*, ed. Nancy J. Hirschmann and Joanne H. Wright (College Park, PA: Pennsylvania State University Press, 2012), 156.
65. For more on this similarity, see Aaron Kunin, "Marlowe's Footstools," in *This Distracted Globe: Worldmaking in Early Modern Literature*, ed. Marcie Frank, Jonathan Goldberg, and Karen Newman (New York: Fordham University Press, 2016), 64–5, 70.

66. "ease, *n*.," II.2.a. *OED Online* (Oxford: Oxford University Press, July 2018), <http://www.oed.com/view/Entry/59073> (last accessed April 24, 2019).

67. Korda, *Shakespeare's Domestic Economies*, 28–30.

68. Hobbes, *Leviathan*, 112.

69. Quentin Skinner, "Hobbes and the Purely Artificial Person of the State," *The Journal of Political Philosophy* 7.1 (1999): 9.

70. Skinner, "Hobbes," 3.

71. Hobbes, *Leviathan*, 121; Skinner, "Hobbes," 3.

72. Hobbes, *Leviathan*, 111–12, 120; Skinner, "Hobbes," 12.

73. Skinner, "Hobbes," 16.

74. Hobbes, *Leviathan*, 113.

75. Hobbes, *Leviathan*, 113.

76. Turner, *Corporate Commonwealth*, 214–15.

77. Skinner, "Hobbes," 22.

78. Lamb, *Things*, 11.

79. Lamb, *Things*, 11.

80. Lamb, *Things*, 11.

81. Lamb, *Things*, 13.

82. Lamb, *Things*, 11 (emphasis mine). The self-movability of objects would be particularly problematic for Hobbes's mechanistic view of the universe.

83. Cavendish, *Sociable Letters*, 164. This is not to say that Cavendish always finds liberty in marriage problematic. In another letter, she explains that "I am more happy in my home retirement . . . having a noble and kind husband who is witty and wise company, a peaceable and quiet mind, and recreative thoughts that take harmless Liberty" (79), and in another extols the countryside over the city for offering her "more Liberty" (136).

84. Kahn, *Wayward Contracts*, chs. 2 and 7. In the following scene, Lord Melancholy similarly opposes liberty and law. Lord Dorato confronts his forlorn son, encouraging him to spend time with his new wife, the Emperor's daughter:

> *Lord Dorato.* Why how now Son, shall I never find you with Company, but always alone, in a musing Melancholy posture?
> *Lord Melancholy.* I never did love much Company Sir.
> *Lord Dorato.* But methinks in honesty, you might love the Company of your Wife.
> *Lord Melancholy.* Were my liberty equal to my Love, I should not be o[f] ten from her.
> *Lord Dorato.* Why, who bars you from that liberty?
> *Lord Melancholy.* The Laws Sir. (sc. 22)

In his retort to his father, Lord Melancholy replaces the Emperor's daughter for the woman he considers his true wife, Lady Perfection.

85. Detlefsen, "Margaret Cavendish," 149.

86. Detlefsen, "Margaret Cavendish," 157.
87. Detlefsen, "Margaret Cavendish," 157.
88. Qtd. in Detlefsen, "Margaret Cavendish," 155.
89. Detlefsen, "Margaret Cavendish," 156.
90. Detlefsen, "Margaret Cavendish," 156, 155.
91. Detlefsen, "Margaret Cavendish," 156–7.
92. Detlefsen, "Margaret Cavendish," 156–8.
93. Kahn, *Wayward Contracts*, 174.
94. Kahn, *Wayward Contracts*, 185.
95. For another approach to the freedom of furniture via the concept of "affordances," see Kunin, "Marlowe's Footstools," 72; Julia Reinhard Lupton, *Thinking with Shakespeare: Essays on Politics and Life* (Chicago: University of Chicago Press, 2011), 54–5.
96. Shakespeare, *King Lear*, in *The Norton Shakespeare*, 3rd edn., ed. Stephen Greenblatt, Walter Cohen, Suzanne Gossett, Jean Howard, Katharine Eisaman Maus, and Gordon McMullan (New York: W. W. Norton, 2016), 2.4.260.

Chapter 3

The Inner Lives of Renaissance Machines

Wendy Beth Hyman

Over the last several decades, an array of new materialisms has roused into animacy a previously inert world. Resituating objects not quite as subjects *per se*, but as fellow actants, these theorists revise everything we thought we knew about the relationships among living and non-living beings. To cite one now-familiar articulation of an orientation with both philosophical and ethical ramifications, Bruno Latour's thesis that "objects too have agency" and are "*participants* in the course of action" depends on a prioritizing of material effects rather than interior experience. Although such a claim at first seems counterintuitive, many languages' grammars actually corroborate the syntactical difficulty of withholding agency from objects. Latour notes that "kettles 'boil' water, knives 'cut' meat, baskets 'hold' provisions, hammers 'hit' nails on the head, rails 'keep' kids from falling, [and] locks 'close' rooms against uninvited visitors,"[1] all syntactical constructions that relocate subjectivity in surprising ways. Contemporary metaphysical discourses therefore regularly propose that (at least some) objects ought to be recognized as agencial "things," makers as well as made, consequence-producing entities whose effects extend beyond their material forms.[2]

Paradoxically, at the very time in which many scholars have accepted the call to reconsider the ontology of things—what Jane Bennett calls the "vitality of materiality"—we have become less inclined to theorize the "thing power" (again, Bennett's phrase) of personhood.[3] The material world, the new paradigms insist, is not inert. Yet those critical discourses that reveal objects or networks to be agencial tend, inversely, to de-ontologize the human. Within any number of cultural materialist frameworks, personhood—with all the self-directed interiority that that term implies—ceases to be a meaningful category. Positionalities held within discursive strategies of power are taken to be more salient than perceptions of individuality. Foucauldian biopolitics, in this sense, proffers an uncanny return of Hobbesian determinism: for in the pan-optical and clockwork universe alike, human agency is accidental, even a misnomer. Humans are, in both paradigms, effectively "cogs" oper-ated by one or another totalizing superstructure. We thereby trace the continuity between present-day cultural materialism and its Marxist origins. In that earlier era, "the machine" stood in for the supreme monolith, a representative of all that was dehumanizing about capital, about (factory) work, and about the bureaucratic state. The age of industry is ostensibly over. Yet as we continue to manufacture machines (guns, automobiles, fracking drills, etc.) that cause death and even threaten apocalyptic destruction, we surely further cede our own claims to personhood. This sense of profound alienation culminates in post-humanism, a longing for a world absented of ourselves.

But in the early modern era, this chapter argues, human and thing—and especially human and machine—were mutually constitutive rather than antithetical, more situational than existential. Person-hood was (and in many ways remains) a fragile legal fiction, an idea summoned to negotiate interactions among people, processes, posses-sions, and institutions. Renaissance personhood was also, more loft-ily, a humanist fantasy that required ongoing vindicating, curating, and "fashioning." In neither case, however, was personhood a self-evident or uncontested category. Inversely, the early modern concept of "machine" intimated complex, orchestrated acts of making or con-triving, yet the term did not yet signify as a symbol of impersonal automaticity or a political juggernaut. When early moderns *did* rec-ognize analogies between human and machine, those analogies were not only deployed to the denigration of the human. On the contrary, as I hope to show, the operations proper to the early modern machine were believed to resemble something more like a thought process than a production line, and to exemplify qualities of intentionality, perfectibility, and even consciousness. If there is a relevant anach-ronism to deploy here, it is that of Kleist's "Marionette Theatre," which sees in the depersonalized automaton the elegance of divinity, wherein "grace appears most purely in human form which either has no consciousness or an infinite consciousness. That is, in the puppet or the god."[4] To identify forms of kinship is to recover several of the interrelated contexts whereby the human and machine were always already imbricated and inter-animated: such that persons sometimes cultivated their mechanicity, and machines were understood to be in possession of something like an inner life.

As a literary historian, my primary evidence for these claims derives naturally from the proliferating depictions of machine-like men and humanoid machines in early modern literature and art. But my preference for this archive is not just professional *habitus*. Instead, I propose that Renaissance literature emerges as a generative place to observe the mingling of personhood and mechanicity especially because writing—and the writing hand—is so often construed as a specialized kind of thinking machine. This chapter argues that early moderns recognized what I am calling the "inner lives" of machines within themselves, and often figured their own thinking and making in those machines' terms. Writing becomes a flashpoint for ambiguous personhood, as the interiorized self wrests language into shape with the help of what Aristotle paradoxically referred to as the "instrument of instruments": the human hand.[5] Implicit here is both the reflexivity of the creative act and the hard labor of writing, for to compose a text in the Renaissance is to "look in thy heart," as Sidney puts it, but also to be the instrument of the muse. These complexities interpolate the writer in a process both human/e and mechanical, much like Vulcan at his forge: hammering away at resistant material, yet capable of producing the most delicate and ensnaring of filaments. In tracing continuities between human and machine, early moderns reflected a view of personhood that was situational and vulnerable, ingenious and engineered. Personhood was not a transcendent category, but rather something that could be brought into and out of being: or as we might say nowadays, a kind of "fabrication" or social "construct."

Mythological Prehistory

The argument that the categories of human and not-human were not mutually exclusive can be traced back even to Western foundation narratives. In one of the opening episodes of Ovid's *Metamorphoses*, Deucalion and Pyrrha, the only human couple to survive the cataclysmic primordial flood, think in despair about how to repopulate a decimated humanity. Praying for guidance, they receive the injunction to "Go from the temple, / Cover your heads, loosen your robes, and throw / Your mother's bones behind you" (I.379–81). Initially recoiling from the apparent desecration of their ancestors, they come to realize that "those bones the goddess mentions are the stones of earth" (393–4) and obey. Trepidation turns to delight as they witness something miraculous: the stones losing their hardness, and beginning to "look like human beings, / Or anyway as much like human beings / As statues do, when the sculptor is only starting" (395–7).[6]

The story presents, then, a reading lesson—although perhaps not the one we expect. Its message initially seems to be about the importance of learning to read metaphorically, as Deucalion and Pyrrha revolt from the idea of throwing around their mothers' bones; in other words, it first seems they fail to recognize that "bones" are a metaphor for "stones." Yet as the story unfolds, the metaphorical gives way to uncanny literalization: for the stones, tossed backwards to the earth, indeed *are* (or instantaneously become) the bones of the future race. Through human hands throwing inert matter, the goddess actualizes a latent potentiality in the earthly rock, just as a statue, with Venus' blessing of Pygmalion's handiwork, becomes a human wife. Bones, stones, human bodies, sculptures: these entities, we therefore come to understand, are not only metaphors of each other, but are continuous with each other. Their variegated existences are consequent upon specialized actions. By the same token, as Ovidian mythology conversely shows, humans just as readily decompensate (or reassemble) into the natural objects, animals, and material traces out of which they primordially arose, unbecoming persons. In the instantiating myth, that is, Ovidian personhood is not so much a permanent state of being as it is the result of a series of operations. And the potency of these operations—the undertakings of artistic craft, the efficacious results of prayers to deities, and the interactions among natural materials under specialized conditions—reveal the truth of the riddle. Personhood is not anterior to those effects; its latency is actualized through coordinated actions.

That the mythological realm specifically would configure metamorphic transitions among muddled forms of life is, in itself, no surprise. We might say that such ontological permeability is even the *sine qua non* of genres such as classical myth (cf. folklore, magical realism, romance, fairy tale). What might be *less* understood is just how robustly the early modern world even in its proto-scientific discourses validated these complex ontologies between animated objects, human beings, and mechanical process. We see the logics of these conflations everywhere, as in the *Kunstkammern* that collated fossils, statues, complex mechanisms, and lively paintings as mutually illuminating and interrelated, forms of life.[7] As in natural philosophy, so too in political science. Hobbes most famously refers to political systems as automatons, arguing that if "life is but a motion of limbs" and thus that "all *Automata* . . . have an artificial life," then we ought see the entire political system as an "Artificial Man; though of greater stature and strength," and sovereignty in particular as "an Artificiall Soul, as giving life and motion to the whole body."[8] We might think this fantastical, but these metaphors, if they are indeed only metaphors, played out on the microcosmic level as well. As Michael Witmore has uncovered, for example, automatons in civic pageantry did not just imitate human motion: they were, in turn, imitated *by* human beings.[9] The confusion comes in assumptions that superimpose contemporary taxonomies on the past.[10] Today, for example, "we tend to use *natural* and *organic* as synonyms, but in Garrick's day," notes Joseph Roach, in relation to the Enlightenment's most famous actor, "Romanticism, Naturalism, and Darwinism had yet to proclaim that we have more in common with the scum on the pond than with the statue in the park."[11] Each of these critics helps uncover the interchangeability of the living and the mechanic in even the most creative endeavors. This interanimation receives especially poignant expression in early modern figurations of writing, where interiorized self wrangles with technology to turn thought into language. John Wilkins corroborates the impulse in his book on chirography, observing that "Men, that have *Organicall bodies*, cannot communicate their thoughts, so easie and immediate a way [as the angels]. And therefore have need of some corporeal instruments, both for the *receiving* and *conveying* of knowledge."[12] This reaching towards the "instrumental" may identify a longing to express desire without the interference of messy human organicism, or perhaps merely an impulse to augment the organic with the prosthetic. But then, early moderns understood that such instruments do not necessarily diminish the human. In fact, they often make the human possible.[13]

Machine in Your Mind

To begin to make sense of this, it helps to point to a crucial point of origin, when the word "machine" initially entered the English language. According to the *Oxford English Dictionary*, this was in 1450, where it curiously enough begins life as a verb describing forms of mental processing. The *OED*'s example, from the *Life of St. Cuthbert*, is "she . . . machynd in hir mynde . . . Þat it was best for hir to fly."[14] As this quotation reveals, to "machine that" meant something close to "to think," "to contrive," "to resolve," or "to determine." This verbal form, a harbinger of the now-familiar "machination," exists in the language for fully one hundred years before it becomes (c. 1545) a noun meaning, according to the *OED*, an "independently functioning structure," not far from how we might use the term today. Even then, it lacks of the metallic monolith. Instead, this was an act of making, of building, *ideas*, those surprisingly material products of surprisingly technologized minds.[15] The dictionary's examples for this early noun form of "machine" are not, as we would expect, printing presses, military bridges, screw jacks, or milling devices, but rather more abstract formulations such as the "fabric of the world," "a scheme or plot," or a "living body" (1.1a and b; 2).

The world, the universe, the human body: these are the initial "independently functioning structures" from which our contemporary notion of a "machine" derives—which is to say that the machine and body were, in effect, mutually constitutive long before the Enlightenment proposed that one was a reductive analogy for the other. Moreover, to consider the evolutionary trajectory of the word—its beginnings as a verb meaning "to contrive," "to resolve," or "to determine" and its subsequent materialization as a noun meaning a living body or other complex structure—is to acknowledge that for the early modern period, the machine is, above all, a kind of information network, or what we think of as a thing that *thinks*. Thus we read Francis Bacon hoping in his *New Organon* to "transform the 'whole operations of mind' so that 'the thing [is] accomplished as if by machinery.'"[16] And we recognize the theatrical device of *psychomachia* as a performative manifestation of these mutually constitutive categories, externalizing through living actors the conflicted thoughts in a protagonist's mind.

The same hybridity is evidenced in the word "engine," which derives in part from the Old French *engin*, meaning "inborn talent," "intelligence," or "wit."[17] Thus, the ingeniousness of engineering: when we observe that inventiveness reveals ingenuity, we literally mean *engine*-uity. Again, this renders the machine as a thinking thing. Even more telling is "engine's" other etymological origin, the Latin *ingenium*. Meaning "innate or natural quality," this derivation suggests that an engine, like a person, can be possessed of a kind of interiority, a sense of being proper to itself, something like a consciousness. Together, these etymologies construc machines as complex contrivances and mobile infrastructures—some alive, some lively, nuances still very much alive in the early modern period. They suggest that early moderns recognized what I am calling the inner lives of machines, and that, indeed, they figured their own thinking and making in those machines' terms. At least, it was certainly so in the case of the "machine" belonging to Hamlet. If the literature's most exemplary person thought of himself in partly mechanical terms, we begin to get some sense of the extent to which questions of agency, or the limits of a thinking being to exteriorize its will, are brought to a crux around questions of machining. Thus Bosola, the incredibly complex villain/victim in John Webster's *Duchess of Malfi*, refers to the Duchess's having made a nobleman of Antonio by means of "that curious engine, your white hand."[18] The grammatical apposition suggests the equivalence of hand and engine, but not in a Cartesian sense. Instead, "engine" seems to mean, on the one hand, a depersonalized stratagem—the appendage by which she effectuated a plan. But on the other, it refers to the Duchess's power to invest *another* with authority and agency through her own innate qualities. She "makes" Antonio a man not in the mechanical sense, but in the metaphysical sense (we might recall here Aristotle's reference to the hand as the "instrument of instruments"). If we have any residual sense of this, it lies in our construction of an "instrument" as a "tool"—a passive object put to use by an active subject—even as "instrumentality" refers to a process of *effectuating* action. It is no wonder that his replica hand is handed back to her as she loses agency (though not identity) over the course of the play.[19]

In the twenty-first century, the engine or machine is always the product of artifice, and is itself artificial. No oppositional structure feels more self-evident than that of nature versus machine. But this dichotomy clearly needs to be historicized. As for "machine," "engine," and "instrument," so too for "automaton," the word that, more than any other, we use to impugn someone's free will or self-directedness. But the early modern concept of the automaton still retains traces of its original vitality thanks to its etymological origin in the Greek word (αὐτόματος, *neuter*) that means "acting of itself."[20] The paradox, again, has to do with an inscrutable rendering of agency. When a *machine* is an automaton, it is wondrously self-directed, agencial. But in contemporary parlance, if a *person* is an automaton, they are unthinking, externally programmed. These contradictions seem impossible to square. Recalling that "innate or natural quality" that *ingenium* bequeaths to "engine," as well as the thinking, contriving, and determining that once defined the act of "machining," one must ask: where did the inner life of the machine go? Is it we who are correct in seeing machines as soulless objects, or did we at some point lose our sense that widely varied kinds of creatures might be in possession of a kind of interiority?

"Is not thy soul thine own?"

In early modern literature the characters to whom we are quickest to ascribe an inner life or consciousness are often also those who are most interpolated by automaticity. The sense of volition may be especially compromised while writing. Contrary to what we might expect, that part of man's being that was mechanical, or having to do with automatic bodily processes, was *not* necessarily the most dehumanizing. Take, for example, the moment in *Doctor Faustus* when Faustus intends to sign in blood the contract that will bind his soul to Lucifer. Despite his expressed will to sign, Faustus observes that, "my blood congeals, and I can write no more."[21] As Mephistopheles leaves to fetch fire that will "dissolve it straight," Faustus meditates "what might the staying of my blood portend?":

> Is it unwilling I should write this bill?
> Why streams it not, that I may write afresh:
> "Faustus gives to thee his soul." O, there it stayed!
> Why shouldst thou not? Is not thy soul thine own?
> Then write again: "Faustus gives to thee his soul." (2.1.62–7)

A deeply complex negotiation among opposed impulses is represented in this passage, but one that does not correspond with our own sense of ontology. Where, exactly, does agency and will reside here, with its ascription of "will" to Faustus's blood? And who is addressing whom in this complex drama between "it" and "Faustus" and "thou"? The demigod magician seems utterly unable to effectuate any action: try as he would, he cannot write.[22] His body, on the other hand, expresses intentions that thwart those represented as Faustus's. The somatic "unwillingness" trumps the overreaching Faustus's will, such that even this most ambitious of men is overruled by his physicality, indeed is not in charge of his own body. Who is the willing agent, the erstwhile man, and who is the machine? The impotence of Faustus's multiple attempts to direct the action—"then write again"—show that agency does not reside *in* him even before it definitively resides with Satan. Instead, the preeminent agency here lies in the blood that stops his hand, leaving the man a mere witness to the actions of his body. The hand acting separately from the man suggests something approximating *psychomachia*, a conflict of the mind expressed by another (semi-disembodied) entity on the stage. And at the same time, perhaps even more uncannily, it suggests an enactment of *prosopopoeia*, something inside of or beyond Faustus, speaking through the instrument of his hand.[23]

In early modern literature, questions of agency, or the limits of a thinking being to exteriorize its will, are frequently brought to a crisis around moments of writing like these. Take, for instance, the writer's block that Sir Philip Sidney disingenuously complains of in the opening sonnet of *Astrophil and Stella*. Unable to find "fit words" to express his proclaimed "truth," he turns to earlier poets, scanning for inspiration, or even snippets of text to recycle. Yet this, like every previous attempt, purportedly fails. "But words came halting forth, wanting invention's stay, / Invention, nature's child, fled step-dame-study's blows / And others' feet seemed but strangers in my way. / Thus biting my truant pen, beating myself for spite, / 'Fool' said my muse to me, 'look in thy heart and write!'"[24] Sidney, or Sidney's narrator, remains a spectator to this one-act play in which words halt, invention flees a personified step-dame-study, and others' writing trips him up. While the poem ends with a flourish, suggesting that the poet has finally found the key to authentic expression, it also quite literally performs the failure of said authenticity, since the muse—not the poet—dictates the final line. Does the poet express agency, then, or is he merely a transcription machine, ventriloquizing the voice of the muse?

Language Machines

One of the key reasons these questions of agency and automaticity find expression around moments of writing is attributable to the fact that, as the editors of *Language Machines: Technologies of Literary and Cultural Production* put it, "language is now and has always been produced by a variety of *machines*." Some of those "machines," from the perspective of early moderns, were already located within the human body. Looking back to John Bulwer's *Anthropometamorphosis*, for instance, the *Language Machines* editors cite his evocation of "the curious Machine of Speech,"[25] a locution that was later echoed by Thomas Hobbes. To the contemporary ear Hobbes's equation of these disparate communicative technologies approaches zeugma: "The Invention of *Printing*, though ingenious, compared with the invention of *Letters*, is no great matter . . . But the most noble and profitable invention of all other, was that of SPEECH . . . The first author of Speech as *God* himself."[26] The category distinctions we would make, those discriminating biological and mechanical and supernatural processes, do not predominate, if they are operant at all. To his conceptualization, the truly relevant fact is that all three are fundamentally technologies for the processing of language.

In a post-Romantic world, as has often been observed, authorship and writing have been construed as the product of numinous inspiration, ethereal happenings far from the physical world. But most writers rarely admit of such compositional ease. Early moderns had it much closer to correct, it would seem, in construing writing as a laborious process requiring great physical exertion. They frequently deploy mechanical and metallic figures to think about the act of writing, and in ways that indicate just how complexly they thought of their writing process as mechanical—albeit not in a "dehumanizing" way. Shakespeare's poetically gifted but politically condemned Richard II, for example, muses in prison about how he might fill his desolate prison cell with life, despite the factual "impossibility" of doing so:

> I have been studying how I may compare
> This prison where I live unto the world;
> And for because the world is populous,
> And here is not a creature but myself,
> I cannot do it. Yet I'll hammer it out. (5.5.1–5)[27]

In this periodic sentence, the full grammatical force is carried by that unlikely verb "hammer," the action that somehow enables him to do that which—merely on the other side of that brief caesura—he insists he "cannot." Here is not imagination disembodied, but specifically the mechanical metaphor that augments and directs his creative capacity. The doomed, creative king "hammering" out an alternate realm makes sense within this larger framework of understanding we are outlining here, one in which poetry was a kind of technology for "machining" language, operated by the poet-machinist.[28]

The formulation was not unusual. In his dedicatory poem to Shakespeare in the First Folio, "To the memory of my beloved, The Author Mr. William Shakespeare," Ben Jonson evokes the blacksmith's forge as a "metaphor for the poet's rigorous and laborious shaping of his materials." By doing so, as Anthony Miller puts it, Jonson proffers a modest critique of his colleague who might have benefited from more craft. Musing of authorship that he that

> . . . casts to write a living line,
> (Such as thine are), and strike the second heat,
> Upon the *Muses* anvile: turne the same,
> (And himself with it) that he thinks to frame.

Setting aside the grammatical subordination that buries the ostensible compliment ("such as thine are"), the critique rests on the suspect facility of Shakespeare's compositions, which might well have reworked its "metal" (and presumably "mettle") via a "second heat." That is, in contradistinction to Heminge's and Condell's more oft-remembered praise of Shakespeare's ease in composition ("who, as he was a happie imitator of Nature . . . what he thought, he uttered with that easinesse, that wee have scarse received from him a blot in his papers"), Jonson famously wished he had blotted, and revised, more of his work. As Miller points out, Jonson here "partly praises Shakespeare, but also . . . reshapes him in the mould of the true poet" who "hammering away in the poetic smithy . . . must be thorough and meticulous."[29]

In smiting or hammering the palpable material of language into form, poets came surprisingly close to thinking of writing as a kind of machining: a process employing not only *techne* but also technology.[30] We trace these machines of writing everywhere, from the "iron interpreter" that Famiano Strada fantastically imagined in the possession of Pietro Bembo, to the spiritualist's planchette popularized by the Ouija board, from the book wheel invented by Agostino Ramelli to abet multitasking scholars, to the bevy of ingenious instruments invented for the transcription and decoding of secret writing.[31] Moreover, for many early modern authors, writing "technologies" even included such seeming intangibles as line length, meter, and stanzaic shape, all of which honed language into a precise instrument of thought. Thus Thomas Blount's rhetorical handbook suggests that the process of distilling language into its most intense form is much like "forming all her thoughts in a Cone, and smiting with the point, &c."[32] Montaigne agrees that the metrical nature of verse concentrates verbal matter. Deploying a similarly metallic vehicle, Montaigne suggests that

> just as sound, when pent up in the narrow channel of a trumpet, comes out sharper and stronger, so it seems to me that a thought, when compressed into the numbered feet of poetry, springs forth much more violently and strikes me a much stiffer jolt.[33]

The concentrated regularity of poetic verse is analogous to the machined form of the blown trumpet, both of which martial utterance into material form—or rather, take something already presumed to have some degree of materiality and concentrate it. In Jonathan Sawday's formulation, poetry for Montaigne is nothing less than "a kind of hydraulic sound engine."[34] It is an engine whose component parts are iambs, strophes, and troches, arranged in tetrameter, pentameter, and hexameter. While such interlocking precision might strike modern readers as rather bloodless, it yet inscribes poetic rhythm as participatory in larger systems of movement, shape, and form—in other words, making it vital stuff.

Toy Medium

If these constructions seem to encode an implicit theory of poetics in particular, certainly there are scholars who would agree. Daniel Tiffany, for example, identifies a mechanistic quality as peculiar to lyric, given that its "medium" is, in a way distinctive from other modes, the rebus-like alphabet itself. Referring to lyric as "as a veritable 'machine' of literature," he cites Paul Valéry in turn calling poetry "a kind of machine for producing the poetic state of mind by means of words." Valéry here seems to point to an altered or hypnotic consciousness produced, paradoxically, by the regularized features of the short form. Tic tac tock. Tiffany himself goes further still, suggesting that "the lyric poem appears to have a special affinity for the implications of a doctrine of technological determinism."[35] It is a compelling formulation.

Yet perhaps we should not be so sure that lyric has a monopoly on mechanism. For what Tiffany and Valéry ascribe to lyric, other scholars identify instead as a special feature of fiction and, especially, the novel. Joseph Drury's *Novel Machines: Technology and Narrative Form in Enlightenment Britain* traces a long line of post-Shklovskian critics who "argued that literary composition ought to be seen as a form of craftsmanship that involved the artful manipulation of various 'devices,'" forwarding the view that fictional narrative should justly be read as "a kind of machinery."[36] Such a conclusion is hardly far-fetched with an Enlightenment-era author like Eliza Heywood's address to the reader who, "if he has patience to go thro' the following pages, will see into the secret springs that set this fair machine in motion."[37] Looking back to Cervantes, Drury locates a similar tendency in relation to the "ontological status of fictional characters, who seem like autonomous agents but are in fact no more than artificial devices manipulated by the hand of the author."[38] The eighteenth-century novel thus represents the culmination of a kind of mechanistic determinism, a view shared not only by structuralists, but also by social historians.[39]

Finally, others make the case that it is drama, with its stage marvels and automatons and performative iterativity, that is most proximate to the realm of mechanism. Certainly at the most basic level, actors empty themselves of identity in order to voice the words of others, a process whose logical culmination, as Joseph Roach records, finds actors emulating not humans, but statuary.[40] Ben Jonson famously satirized the engineered wonders of his collaborator ("Pack with your peddling poetry to the stage, / This is the money-get, mechanic age!")

but in turn demonstrated his own cynicism about the dehumanizingly transactional nature of the theatrical enterprise. Theorizing the complex forms of ontology represented on the early modern stage, Henry S. Turner proposes "that we approach the early modern theater as a kind of machine with which to fashion or to project artificial life."[41] And to Benjamin Bennett, tragic inevitability itself operates as a mechanism, proposing especially that "the myth of Oedipus, along with its historical descendants, understands each human being as a machine that finds its way automatically to a predetermined goal or fate."[42] In other words, as "this machine is to him, Hamlet."[43] Each of these modes encodes a version of the mechanicity of the literary as dependent upon the formal components of a genre, medium, or mode. All forms of writing show the gears turning: the machinations and aspirations of a person struggling to become itself though the technologies of literary expression.

On an affective level it is therefore no wonder that the difficulty of writing—like the difficulty of existing—may even spur the longing to be a machine. As I have written elsewhere, moments like these recall several instances where poets, in lieu of the conventional desire to sing like Philomel, instead envy unencumbered avian automata.[44] After all, at some level, every invocation of the muse expresses a desire not to invent but to *dictate* poetry, with pneumatic "inspiration" literally taking the place of messy, organic, labored writing. These expressions may even be literalized, such as when the emblematist George Wither writes: "Oh that my Tongue were now with Silver tip't, / Since to yee Ladies I must sing with it: / Nay, I could wish the concave of my throate / Were lin'd with Brasse, since that I the note / Of the sad Knight must sound unto your eares / And with my Verse expresse his mourning teares."[45] Here, the poet indulges in a kind of bionic fantasy, one that imagines that a perfect mechanism will come to the rescue of faltering expression. But these longings recognize not only failures in ourselves, but also potentialities in the things around us. We might look ahead with Timothy Norton to Shelley's *Defence of Poetry*, wherein that poet likens humans to Aeolian harps. Norton poses this question: "If a sentient being is like a wind harp, and if, moreover, sensation and thinking are ontologically similar to one another, then we can invert the image. Wind harps *are like sentient beings*."[46]

Personhood is a cherished fiction, and indeed the fiction at the heart of Renaissance "humanism." Yet as contemporary post-humanists, eco-feminists, and actor-network theorists have urged, personhood is a category that sets us apart from other beings with devastating consequences. Personhood is also, as this chapter has tried to suggest, a fiction that sets us apart from *ourselves*. Although it certainly feels phenomenologically true—we do *experience* personhood—a genuinely humane view of personhood might be one that recognizes the extent that its achievement is an *effect* produced by a complex of factors. Instead of being satisfied with the compelling but misleading fiction that we alone have the right to personhood, we might become more attuned to the ways in which that experience is constructed, and indeed mutually dependent upon machines, things, other beings, and the larger networks within which we exist. Instead of identifying only with what we experience, we might think of personhood as something that is achieved, something is done, something that we can *do*. And in this reformulation of a forgotten idea, we locate a kernel of Renaissance humanism that just might—if we do the right thing—turn towards justice and futurity.

Notes

I want to thank the organizers of the international conference, *L'Automate: Enjeux Historiques, Techniques et Culturels* (Musée d'Art et d'Histoire de Neuchâtel in September 2012), especially Rossella Baldi and Pierre-Alain Mariaux, for inviting me to present an early version of this work; I received helpful feedback from several colleagues there, especially Adelheid Voskuhl. I also appreciate the opportunity to present a piece of this study at the Modern Language Association in January 2011 on "Nonhuman Lives" roundtable with Laurie Shannon, Caryn O'Connell, and David Landreth. The panel was chaired by Natasha Korda and responded to by Jonathan Gil Harris.

1. Bruno Latour, *Reassembling the Social: An Introduction to Actor-Network-Theory* (Oxford: Oxford University Press, 2005), 71.
2. I am alluding to the central distinction between an "object" and "thing" in Martin Heidegger's essay, "The Thing," in *Poetry, Language, Thought*, trans. Albert Hofstadter (New York: Harper & Row, 1971). A thing enacts its ontological potential by compelling the actions that lead to its making. In his example, "the Jug is not a vessel because it was made; rather, the jug had to be made because it is this holding vessel. The making . . . lets the jug come into its own" (168).
3. Jane Bennett, *Vibrant Matter: A Political Ecology of Things* (Durham, NC: Duke University Press, 2010), 10.
4. Heinrich von Kleist, "On the Marionette Theatre," in *Hand to Mouth and Other Essays*, trans. Idris Parry (Manchester: Carcanet New Press, 1981), 9–18.
5. Cited in Katherine Rowe, *Dead Hands: Fictions of Agency, Renaissance to Modern* (Stanford: Stanford University Press, 1999), 5. Compare Michael Tausig: the face is "the figure of appearance, the appearance of

58 Wendy Beth Hyman

appearance, the figure of figuration." Cited in Julian Yates, *Error, Misuse, Failure: Object Lessons from the English Renaissance* (Minneapolis: University of Minnesota Press, 2003), 32.

6. Ovid, *Metamorphoses*, trans. Rolfe Humphries (Bloomington: Indiana University Press, 1955), 14–15.

7. Horst Bredekamp, *The Lure of Antiquity and the Cult of the Machine* (Princeton, NJ: Marcus Wiener, 1993).

8. Thomas Hobbes, *Leviathan*, ed. C. B. Macpherson (New York: Penguin, 1981), 81.

9. Michael Witmore, "Arrow, Acrobat, and Phoenix: On Sense and Motion in English Civic Pageantry," in *The Automaton in English Renaissance Literature*, ed. Wendy Beth Hyman (Farnham: Ashgate, 2011), 109–28. Witmore also argues that to a great extent, Renaissance theater operated upon the assumption of the "automatism of the child," in *Pretty Creatures: Children and Fiction in the English Renaissance* (Ithaca, NY: Cornell University Press, 2007), 8.

10. As Jessica Wolfe notes, "While there indeed exist 'machine men' before the rise of the corpuscular philosophy, they do not necessarily behave in ways sympathetic to a post-Cartesian understanding of what it means for a human being or an animal to be 'like a machine' or, for that matter, what it means for a machine to be lifelike. One of the profoundest and yet most imperceptible legacies of the intellectual and scientific revolutions of the seventeenth century is the way in which new systems of classification and discourses of knowledge alter the perceived relationship between humans and machines." Jessica Wolfe, *Humanism, Machinery, and Renaissance Literature* (Cambridge: Cambridge University Press, 2004), 240.

11. Joseph Roach, *The Player's Passion: Studies in the Science of Acting* (Ann Arbor: University of Michigan Press, 1993), 59.

12. John Wilkins, *Mercury, or the Secret and Swift Messenger: Shewing, How a Man may with Privacy and Speed communicate his Thoughts to a Friend at any distance* (London, 1641).

13. Cf. Elaine Scarry, "The Merging of Bodies and Artifacts in the Social Contract," in *Culture on the Brink: Ideologies of Technology*, ed. Gretchen Bender and Timothy Druckrey (Seattle: Bay Press, 1994), 85–97, 97: "If our artifacts do not act on us, there is no point in having made them. We make material artifacts in order to interiorize them: we make things so that they will in turn remake us, revising the interior of embodied consciousness." See also Walter J. Ong, *Orality and Literacy: The Technologizing of the Word* (New York: Routledge, 1982), 81–2: "Technologies are artificial, but—paradox again—artificiality is natural to human beings. Technology, properly interiorized, does not degrade human life but on the contrary enhances it." These issues are also being taken up by Miriam Jacobson and Julie Park in their forthcoming collection, *Organic Supplements: Bodies, Objects and the Natural World, 1580–1750* (Charlottesville, VA: University of Virginia Press, under contract).

14. According to the *OED*: "sense 1 is < Anglo-Norman and Middle French *machiner* to plot, intrigue (13th cent. in Old French) < classical Latin māchinārī (see machinate v.); later senses are < machine n.) †1. trans. With that-clause or infinitive: to resolve, determine. Also: to contrive or plot (esp. the death or downfall of a person); (occas. intr.) to plot against a person. Obs. ?c1450. Quote: *Life St. Cuthbert* (1891) 523."
15. And as Jessica Wolfe (*Humanism, Machinery, and Renaissance Literature*, 6) notes, "sixteenth-century uses of the word *technologia* . . . carry similar connotations, referring not to mechanical practice but rather to rhetorical or philological methods." Like anyone writing on this topic, I am greatly indebted to her far-reaching study of "the ideational role machines play in sanctioning or condemning instrumentality or artifice" in the early modern period.
16. Cited in Wolfe, *Humanism, Machinery, and Renaissance Literature*, 26.
17. *OED*, "engine," I.3.
18. John Webster, *The Duchess of Malfi and Other Plays*, ed. René Weis (Oxford: Oxford University Press, 1996).
19. "Hands can absorb and register character and identity, even when they are detached. Crucially, the detached wax hand becomes a psychological symbol mediating the relationship between the Duchess and Ferdinand as it passed from one to the other. It simultaneously represents the Duke's desire to literally take hold of his sister's sexual behavior and the Duchess as symbol of devotion, in this case, to her love and her identity." Farah Karim-Cooper, *The Hand on the Shakespearean Stage: Gesture, Touch and the Spectacle of Dismemberment* (New York: Bloomsbury, 2016), 204–5.
20. *OED*, "automaton" (etymology).
21. Christopher Marlowe, *Doctor Faustus (B-Text)*, ed. David Scott Kastan (New York and London: W. W. Norton, 2005). I am grateful to Kaara Peterson for our discussion of this passage.
22. For more on the "effectless hand" in the early modern period, and specifically in *Titus Andronicus*, see Rowe, *Dead Hands*, 52–85.
23. See, for comparison, Random Cloud's curious study of nonsense language ("Chough") in *All's Well that Ends Well*: "Chough is extemporized before our eyes. This language has no past . . . for there need never have been anterior or exterior sounds which these written words evoked. Nor were there necessarily objects or ideas to which they referred . . . It may be best to define Chough as *manguage* rather than language—as *hand* rather than tongue." Random Cloud, "Shakespear Babel," in *Reading Readings: Essays on Shakespeare Editing in the Eighteenth Century*, ed. Joanna Gondris (Madison, NJ: Fairleigh Dickinson University Press, 1998), 1–70, 1.
24. Sir Philip Sidney, *The Complete Poems of Sir Philip Sidney*, ed. Alexander B. Grosart (1877).
25. Jeffery Masten, Peter Stallybrass, and Nancy J. Vickers, eds., *Language Machines: Technologies of Literary and Cultural Production* (New York:

Routledge, 1997), 1. Bulwer not only thought of the voice box, tongue, and mouth as a machine in these terms, but more famously went on to schematize the human hand as an instrument of communication in the paired volumes *Chirologia* and *Chironomia* (1644).

26. Hobbes, *Leviathan*, 100 (Part I, ch. 4).

27. William Shakespeare, *Richard II*, in *The Norton Shakespeare*, 2nd edn., ed. Stephen Greenblatt, Walter Cohen, Jean E. Howard, and Katharine Eisaman Maus (New York: W. W. Norton, 2008). All references to Shakespeare plays are from this edition unless otherwise noted and will appear in the body of the text. I discuss this unlikely relationship between creativity and mechanicity in Shakespeare's history plays in "'For now hath time made me his numbering clock': Shakespeare's Jacquemarts," *Early Theatre* 16.2 (December 2013): 145–58.

28. For a discussion on translation, too, as a kind of mechanical "construction," see Patricia Parker, *Shakespeare from the Margins: Language, Culture, Context* (Chicago: University of Chicago Press, 1996), 108; the larger chapter, "Rude Mechanicals: *A Midsummer Night's Dream* and Shakespearean Joinery," develops the connection between the historical guilds, theatrical making, and unlikely jointures in the world of the play.

29. Anthony Miller, "Ben Jonson and 'the proper passion of Mettalls,'" *Parergon* 23.2 (2006): 57–72, 58. I thank Adhaar Desai for pointing me to this article and its consideration of Jonson's metalworking metaphors. I have cited Jonson's poem as it appears in Miller's essay; he sources it from *Ben Jonson*, ed. C. H. Herford and Percy and Evelyn Simpson, 11 vols. (Oxford: Clarendon Press, 1925–52), 8:392.

30. For a much fuller discussion of "poesy as *techne* rather than aesthetics, and figurative language as framed or tempered matter, rather than verbalized concepts," see Rayna Kalas, *Frame, Glass, Verse: The Technology of Poetic Invention in the English Renaissance* (Ithaca, NY: Cornell University Press, 2007), xi.

31. Gerard Passannante, *The Lucretian Renaissance: Philology and the Afterlife of Tradition* (Chicago: University of Chicago Press, 2011), 2. On secret writing arts, see Wolfe, *Humanism, Machinery, and Renaissance Literature*, 103–6; Lois Potter, *Secret Rites and Secret Writing: Royalist Literature 1641–1660* (Cambridge: Cambridge University Press, 2009).

32. Thomas Blount, *The Academy of Eloquence* (London: for Anne Moseley, 1664), D9v. I discuss this passage at greater length in *Impossible Desire and the Limits of Knowledge in Renaissance Poetry* (Oxford: Oxford University Press, 2019), 22.

33. Michel de Montaigne, *The Complete Essays of Montaigne*, trans. Donald M. Frame (Stanford: Stanford University Press, 1958), 107.

34. Jonathan Sawday, *Engines of the Imagination: Renaissance Culture and the Rise of the Machine* (New York: Routledge, 2007), 53.

35. See Daniel Tiffany, "Lyric Substance: On Riddles, Materialism, and Poetic Obscurity," *Critical Inquiry* 28.1 (2001): 72–98, 77.

36. Joseph Drury, *Novel Machines: Technology and Narrative Form in Enlightenment Britain* (Oxford: Oxford University Press, 2017), 19–20. My thanks to Alice Dailey for pointing me to Drury's work.
37. Eliza Haywood, *The History of Miss Betsy Thoughtless*, qtd. in Drury, *Novel Machines*, 2.
38. Drury, *Novel Machines*, 4.
39. See, for example, Margaret C. Jacob, who argues that mechanistic theories of motion fostered pornography, a realm in which human bodies "became simply, unrelentingly, matter in motion . . . the new erotic narratives quickly embraced mechanistic materialism." Margaret C. Jacob, "The Materialist World of Pornography," in *The Invention of Pornography*, ed. Lynn Hunt (New York: Zone Books, 1993), 157, 159.
40. See Roach, "Nature Still, but Nature Mechanized," in *Player's Passion*, 68.
41. Henry S. Turner, "Life Science: Rude Mechanicals, Human Mortals, Posthuman Shakespeare," *South Central Review* 26.1/2 (2009): 197–217, 204, <http://www.jstor.org/stable/40211296> (last accessed April 24, 2019).
42. Benjamin Bennett, "*The Thinking Machine*," *Revue Internationale de Philosophie* 65, 255.1, *Le Théâtre, de la Renaissance à Aujourd'hui: Une Approche Philosophique* (2011): 7–26, 9.
43. Shakespeare, *The Tragedy of Hamlet* (2.2.123–6).
44. Wendy Beth Hyman, "'Mathematical experiments of long silver pipes': The Renaissance Trope of the Mechanical Bird," in *The Automaton in English Renaissance Literature*, ed. Wendy Beth Hyman (Farnham: Ashgate, 2011).
45. George Wither, "Proem," *The Great Assises Holden in Parnassus by Apollo and His Assessovrs* (1645).
46. Timothy Morton, "An Object Oriented Defense of Poetry," *New Literary History* 43 (2012): 205–24, 205. Other early moderns made similar analogies, as recorded in Sawday, *Engines of the Imagination*; see especially his discussion of Zacharias Heyns, explaining in his 1625 *Emblemata* that "the windmill's dependence on wind power is similar to human dependence on the Holy Spirit for life" (13). Or think of that touching moment in *The Winter's Tale*, anticipating the revivification of Hermione: "what fine chisel could ever yet cut breath?" (5.3.77–9).

Chapter 4

Two Doors: Personhood and Housebreaking in *Semayne's Case* and *The Comedy of Errors*

Colby Gordon

The Comedy of Errors is a story about a door. A man of great wealth and standing arrives home to find his door barred against him, his place assumed by a stranger. Raging against the indignity of his situation, he menaces the servants at the gate, threatening to pry the door from its hinges and abuse everyone he finds inside. When the attempted housebreaking fails, the man experiences his dispossession as a kind of amputation, a loss of self with implications not only for his sense of self, but also for his legal status. Bereft of his home, the merchant is thrust to the margins of personhood, stripped of his rights and reputation along with the relationships that nourish and sustain him. Suddenly subsisting in a state of social death, the householder encounters his domicile as it is experienced by the women, servants, and slaves who also reside there, as a space of captivity, incarceration, and unpredictable violence. In this respect, *The Comedy of Errors* considers the consequences of binding personhood to the material environs of the dwelling, a legal principle that would come to be called the sanctity of the home. As *Comedy* relentlessly demonstrates, this juristic maneuver bolsters the patriarchal power of the householder at the expense of the other forms of life inhabiting the home. Nevertheless, the play is not entirely cynical on this count. Instead, it imagines how collapsing the homeowner's person with the home can also insert him into relationships of care and dependence that can undercut his mastery. As it happens, a decade after *The Comedy of Errors* was first performed at Gray's Inn, the King's Bench issued a decision for *Semayne's Case* that would form the common law wellspring for the sanctity of the home. This chapter argues that *The Comedy of Errors* unfolds the legal futures of the sanctity of the home as established in

Semayne's Case, testing the limits and possibilities of incorporating domestic space into the personhood of its owner.

This too is a story about a door.

In 1604, Peter Semayne approached the London sheriffs for help collecting a debt. Sometime earlier, Semayne had lent money to one George Berisford. Their bond of record had been issued recognizance in the form of a statute staple, a type of security that authorized ferocious measures to secure restitution.[1] In the event of default, a shortchanged lender could proceed to the courts for a writ of extent (*extendi facias*), a civil process that targeted both the person and the property of the insolvent borrower: the debtor would be remanded to custody without bail while the sheriffs and a jury of twelve men appraised or "extended" his lands and chattels. Given the swift and merciless nature of these remedies, it is unsurprising that the process of extent slipped into the popular imagination as an emblem of preda-tory lending, as in Phillip Massinger's grasping villain Sir Giles Over-reach, who threatens Lady Allworth with just such a writ: "When This Mannor is extended to my vse, You'le speake in an humbler key."[2] When the due date passed and payment failed to materialize, Semayne, like a Sir Overreach, set about the process of repossess-ing Berisford's properties. One major obstacle presented itself to this course of action: Berisford was dead, and to complicate matters fur-ther, at the time of his death he had not been in sole possession of the home in which his "divers goods" were still stored.[3] Rather, he and a certain Richard Gresham had "for years" occupied a house in Blackfriars as joint tenants (194). By the time Semayne had secured his writ and taken it to the sheriffs for execution, the house had already passed into Gresham's possession through the right of survi-vorship (*jus accrescendi*).[4] The sheriffs "returned [Berisford] dead," but Semayne was not deterred, promptly acquiring a second writ des-ignating his claim to "all the lands which [Berisford] had at the time of the statute acknowledged, or at any time after, and all his goods which he had at the day of his death" (194–5).

It is at this point that the material structure of the dwelling enters into play. Armed with this second writ, the sheriff and jury marched back to Blackfriars where they planned "to enter the house" and "extend the goods according to the said writ" (195), apparently intending to enter peaceably through an "open door" (*ostio aperto*). The embattled Gresham, however, who was not unaware of their busi-ness there (*praemissorum non ignarus*), bolted his doors to obstruct their entry (*claudebat contra vicecom' & jurator' praed'*). From the plaintiff's perspective, this act signaled that Gresham willfully "intended to disturb the execution" of the writ so that he could retain the use of the goods that "continued and remained" in the Blackfriars home that was now in his sole possession (194–5). Confronted with a barred door, the sheriff had a decision to make: he could return to Semayne empty-handed for a second time, or he could force entry by violently breaching the walls or windows, a practice the common law dubbed "breaking the house." The legality of this procedure must have seemed insurmountably muddled to everyone on the scene: even if Semayne had a valid claim to the goods held in the building, the house itself now clearly belonged to Gresham, who had no part in the suit, and it was not obvious that the sheriff could lawfully exercise such force against a third party's property in pursuit of another's debt. Moreover, Gresham's defiantly barred door fell into the midst of an ongoing jurisdictional dispute between the City of London and the self-policing liberty of Blackfriars, a district equipped with its own constables whose residents passionately resisted interference from the City's officers, particularly in matters of search and arrest.[5] Reluctant to exercise such extreme force in a case where its legality was so unclear, the sheriff retreated, jury in tow, and Semayne, having "lost the benefit and profit of his writ," sued Gresham before the King's Bench (195).

Semayne's Case, significant enough to be recorded by Sir Edward Coke, represented more than a dispute over debt collection. The court was charged with the delicate matter of determining whether, and under what circumstances, the threshold of the home marked a limit to sovereign power. Treading carefully, the justices announced in no uncertain terms that "in all cases where the King is party," that is, all criminal cases, "the sheriff (if the doors be not open) may break the party's house, either to arrest him, or to do other execution of the K[ing]'s process, if he otherwise cannot enter" (195). The King's officers may take whatever measures necessary to apprehend a felon who has taken refuge in a private home, since "in every felony the King has interest," and so "the liberty or privilege of a house doth not hold against the King" (197). The decision goes on to clarify that such breaking and entering was permitted even if the building in question was housed in a liberty like Blackfriars, since "where the King has interest the writ is *non omittas propter aliquam libertatem*," and noted that statutes already permitted bailiffs to "distrain for issues in a sanctuary" (196). Having carefully buttressed the king's privilege to break houses in the interest of the "commonwealth," the court proceeded to rule against Semayne on the grounds that housebreaking was illicit when the writ was pursuant to a civil matter like debt collection, which was merely "for the particular interest" of any mere "common person" (198). Under these circumstances, Gresham had merely "done that which he might well do by the law, *scil.* to shut the door of his own house" (198).

Despite this apparent endorsement of the Crown's unencumbered right to housebreaking, the King's Bench takes great care to enumerate and justify the extraordinary privileges that the common law attaches to the home. The memorable first line of the decision goes so far as to hold, in terms that were to have longstanding significance for the relationship between the property-owning subject and the state, that "the house of every one is his castle" (194). Pressing further, the decision asserts that "the law . . . abhors the destruction or breaking of any house" since everyone's home is their safest refuge or sanctuary (*domus sua cuique est tutissimum refugium*), a space that exists "for the habitation and safety of man" (195–6). The prophylactic nature of the dwelling then authorizes secondary acts of violence in defense of the household: "although the life of a man is a thing precious and favored in law," the decision reads, killing a home invader "is not a felony" and the householder "shall lose nothing" for slaughtering a trespasser (194). Moreover, even though assembling a group of friends and neighbors in a public place normally constitutes criminal activity, even when it is done for the express purpose of personal safety, it is permissible for a man to gather a group "to defend his house against violence" (194). These liberties stem from the essential purpose of the home as a person's best "defense against injury and violence" (195). In other words, *Semayne's Case* asserts that home is an exceptional space, a zone where, under certain circumstances, laws against manslaughter and riot are suspended.[6] The threshold of the home is the threshold of the law itself; piercing or menacing the boundary of the dwelling transmutes murder into justifiable homicide or a mob into a *posse comitatus*.

Given the exceptional status of the dwelling, endowing sheriffs with an unrestricted right to housebreaking, even at the suit of a private citizen, would pose an existential threat to the very idea of home. The decision gravely warns that

> Thence would follow great inconvenience that men as well in the night as in the day should have their houses (which are their castles) broke, by colour whereof great damage and mischief might ensue; for by colour thereof, on any feigned suit, the house of any man might at any time be broke when the defendant might be arrested elsewhere, and so men might not be in safety and quiet in their own houses. (198)

Note that the court was not, or at least not primarily, concerned that an innocent man might watch his home torn apart, even though "no fault is in him" (196). Rather, the key word here is *quiet*. A fear of emotional distress ripples through the decision: the very possibility that "any man" at "any time" might endure such an experience changes the affective texture of the household environment, permanently disrupting the mood of "quiet" that should obtain there. As Dom Birch carefully demonstrates, in early modern England the term "quiet" opened onto a range of different meanings, broadening out from a sense of inner calm to encompass ideas about political and civil harmony, the urban environment and the metropolitan soundscape, religious conformity, marital bliss, and neighborliness.[7] What Peter Semayne wanted—the ability for any private subject with a writ and a grudge to enlist the sheriffs in a campaign of terror against their neighbors—was a danger to quiet in all of its senses. Such license could only degenerate into a perpetual suspicion of one's acquaintances, since "at any feigned suit" they might bring down a whirlwind of violence upon the roof of anyone towards whom they bore ill will.[8] Moreover, the implicit threat posed by the king's officers also factored into the decision: while sheriffs were persons "of great authority and trust" who executed their office with dignity and professionalism, the justices concede that "it appears by experience, that the King's writs are served by bailiffs, persons of little or no value" who were known to take advantage of their license (198). The feeling of restful "repose" that should accompany the spaces and routines of habitation would thus be ruptured by the ever-present possibility of a violent, officially-sanctioned, publicly-staged intrusion. Fear of the neighbor here merged with something like state terror, an anxiety compounded by the possibility that the humiliations and depredations of a rough search could happen not only during the day but at night, a time of particular fear and uncertainty. In other words, *Semayne's Case* understands housebreaking as an assault on the sensorium of the home.

In defining the home as a space of quiet, *Semayne's Case* blurs the lines between selfhood and its material environs. Indeed, the decision seems to define home in phenomenological terms; not just a type of structure, the dwelling is a space of quiet, a zone where particular kinds of sensuous experience should be fostered in an atmosphere that marries creature comforts to a sense of security. As a place consecrated to the restoration and comfort of the body, any disturbance of the home environment impinges upon the psychosomatic well-being of its inhabitant. It is difficult to parse out where selfhood begins and ends: the subject's physical integrity and emotional state bleed out into the object worlds and affective flows of the house. Holding that "the house of every one is his castle" resonates with Eileen Gray's rebuttal of Le Corbusier: "A house is not a *machine à habiter*. It is man's shell, his continuation, his spreading out, his spiritual emanation."[9] In *Semayne's Case*, too, the structure of the home is like an extruded shell, an extension of the subject that collapses person and setting in an environmental manifold. This is the reason that the householder registers an assault on the physical structure of the dwelling as a violation, one that can be redressed with the same retaliatory measures as a threat to his person. The barred doors, stowed chattel, "quiet" atmospheres, conflicting charters, past-due bonds, and multiple writs swirling around the late George Berisford's home contribute to what Kevin Curran calls a legal ecology, a model of distributed selfhood that binds human subjects with nonhuman actors in a juridical context.[10]

Selfhood or subjectivity might not be the most appropriate terms to describe what is at stake in *Semayne's Case*, whose legal futures are oriented towards questions of personhood. In time, the matter of "le shutting del door"[11] and the castle doctrine it established would come to serve as a touchstone Anglo-American jurisprudence, an acknowledgment of the common law's ancient recognition of the sanctity of the home.[12] According to Margaret Radin's influential argument, this reverential respect for domestic space has also factored into a "strand of liberal property theory that focuses on personal embodiment or self-constitution in terms of 'things,'" a "'personhood perspective' [that] corresponds to, or is the dominant premise of, the personality theory of property."[13] The sanctity of the home, she writes, "contains a strand of property for personhood" specifically because it is the space where "one embodies or constitutes oneself," and as such "the home is affirmatively part of oneself."[14] The collapse of personhood and property brokered by *Semayne's Case* has underwritten considerable expansions of personal liberties, including the right to privacy, restrictions on state surveillance and police intrusion, even the decriminalization of contraception and pornography.[15] At the same time, feminists have long recognized that treating the home as a sanctuary dedicated to the intimacies of family life has protected abusers and transformed the household into a space of violence, deprivation, and unpaid labor.[16] Moreover, the castle doctrine underwrites racist self-defense laws like "Stand Your Ground" policies that legitimate the killing of people of color for their mere proximity to domestic space.[17] In this respect, the castle doctrine augments the personhood of the homeowner by empowering him to use violence to maintain the "quiet" and "repose" of his home against disturbances originating from within or without. By contrast, other residents sheltered within the home, including children and animals, women and servants, are remanded to positions of diminished, disabled, or merely potential personhood, reduced to the legal status of chattel whose labor can be extracted for the benefit of the householder. As such, *Semayne's Case* inaugurates a biopolitical mode of dwelling, in that it presses "minor" forms of life to the edges of personhood along a spectrum of social death.[18]

Semayne's Case is a decision populated exclusively by full persons. The King's Bench has nothing to say about how the common law's especial concern for the domicile impacts the other creatures sheltered within the household since, from the court's perspective, the only actions that matter are those undertaken by two landowning men, a creditor, and a sheriff. That there is no mention of women, children, or servants should not suggest that they were not present, merely that the law took no notice of them in considering what kinds of violence, trauma, and damage would be wrought by the sheriff's housebreaking. To fill in the blanks and assess more clearly the multiplex impacts of the sanctity of the home, we have to turn to another story about a door, *The Comedy of Errors*, a contemporaneous literary account of the passages between personhood and property. Just as *Semayne's Case*, with its bumbling sheriff, litigious creditor, and overly-dramatic confrontations, almost edges into city comedy, so too does *The Comedy of Errors*, first staged by law students at Gray's Inn, amount to a particular kind of "legal revelling."[19] Circling around doors that open too easily or close too firmly, *The Comedy of Errors* is a play that thinks through the cluster of legal and theoretical problems raised by *Semayne's Case*: the relationship between personhood and the dwelling; the extended body and distributed selfhood; the divisions between public and private space; the spatial location of sanctuary; and the vicissitudes of quiet within and outside the home. *The Comedy of Errors*, too, is a story about a door, a text that is deeply concerned with the consequences of severing personhood from its material grounding in the home. *The Comedy of Errors*, I will argue, offers an exacting account of the violent consequences that attend elevating the private home to a space of exception and attaching personhood to the ownership of residential property. However, the play also suggests that tethering the dweller's personhood to the extended body of the household, as *Semayne's Case* does, sinks masculine authority into relationships of dependence and care with his immediate environs. This, as we will see, generates opportunities for reversing the hierarchies that scaffold this mode of dwelling.

The Comedy of Errors begins on the very margins of personhood, opening onto a juridical scene that will strip the few remaining rights from Egeon, a merchant hailing from Syracuse who has been captured in Ephesus, flouting the cities' reciprocal travel ban and prohibition against interstate commerce as he seeks his son and wife. Egeon sits upon the cusp of sentencing, even soliciting it in the play's first line, begging the Duke to "proceed" to judgment and "procure" the "doom of death" that will be visited not only on his person, but his property, as the Duke explains: "if any Syracusan born / Come to the Bay of Ephesus, he dies, / His goods confiscate to the Duke's dispose."[20] This injunction is presented to Egeon in terms that are universal and absolute, as if "any Syracusan" apprehended in the city might suffer an equal punishment before the law in courts that "exclude all pity" (1.1.10). Even so, the Duke immediately qualifies this pronouncement, since an ignominious public execution can be neatly avoided if the Syracusan in question can procure "a thousand marks" to "quit the penalty" (1.1.21–2). In the play that, as Richard Strier argues, is Shakespeare's "most wholehearted evocation and celebration of bourgeois life," wealth mitigates the rigors of the law, offering its possessors a legal standing flatly denied to those suffering from poverty.[21] The texture of Egeon's experience of disenfranchisement, then, is more nuanced and fine-grained than the initial framing of his punishment allows. As a person of limited means, a victim of natural disaster and family separation, and an illegal resident in a hostile city, Egeon has existed in a state of impaired personhood since the moment he entered Ephesus, in the sense that he is excluded from the protections of the law while being subject to their lethal disciplinary force. The judgment of execution and property forfeiture merely formalizes the social death that the unlucky merchant has experienced as an ongoing condition. When the sentence is deferred for a day, he returns to that zone of rightlessness, lamenting that "hopeless and helpless doth Egeon wend, / But to procrastinate his lifeless end" (1.1.157–8). Subsisting under the ban, bereft of the support structures that would make his life livable, Egeon is pressed to the outermost limits of legal personhood.

This preoccupation with personhood shapes the play's formal elements as well, particularly its approach to characterization. Among Shakespeare's dramatic works, *The Comedy of Errors* is uniquely difficult to read for its constructions of subjectivity or identity. Flatness rather than depth is the norm in this play. Indeed, the entire plot turns on the utter indistinguishability of the main characters who, despite entire lifetimes of drastically different experiences, have identical personalities, names, appearances, trades, social positions, and tempers. Put differently, we might say that there are no characters in *The Comedy of Errors*, at least if we take the term to mean highly particularized and idiosyncratic figures with distinctive personalities.[22] Neither of the Antipholi express the kind of interiority or depth of feeling we associate with Hamlet or Richard II, nor do they seem exercised by the kinds of epistemological crises occasioned by the division between external display and internal truth so characteristic of Shakespeare's other works.[23] So radically does the play reject the possibility of interiority that Antipholus of Syracuse's first brief monologue entirely frustrates the basic purpose of the soliloquy, the dramatic device that most readily opens onto the emotional authenticity of a character by exposing their affective states and thought processes. Rather than sharpening our sense of Antipholus as an individual, this moment of private reflection makes the twin recede even farther from view:

> He that commends me to mine own content
> Commends me to the thing I cannot get:
> I to the world am like a drop of water
> That in the ocean seeks another drop;
> Who, falling there to find his fellow forth,
> Unseen, inquisitive, confounds himself.
> So I, to find a mother and a brother,
> In quest of them, unhappy lose myself. (1.2.33–40)

What depth does a water drop possess? Rather than unfurl his hidden motives, opening up a gap between his performances and a true self that "passeth show," Antipholus only repeats what we already know: he is a brother seeking his double, a quest that makes him sad and restless. This information, however, arrives second-hand, repeating the expository account Egeon put into circulation a mere fifty lines earlier. These private thoughts, in fact, could not be more public, in that they were already witnessed by a crowd of minor characters and extras as part of Egeon's trial. Emotions, too, are external: Antipholus's "own content" lies outside of himself, since his happiness depends on a reunification with his brother. Even more radically, however, the soliloquy suggests that he is *without content*, an empty vessel, a creature of pure exteriority; like a water drop submerged in an ocean, there is nothing to distinguish him from the crowd.[24] "Confounded" in the flood, Antipholus's self is fluid and mixed, inseparable from others. Both his current situation and his imagined fulfillment turn on a fantasy of abnegation: the lament voices a desire to achieve a state of even less, rather than greater, differentiation, a longing to merge with another "drop." In the meantime, alone on stage and in the world, Antipholus finds himself diminishing until "unseen" and "unhappy," he loses himself altogether.

Although *The Comedy of Errors* rejects interiority and subjectivity, it is deeply invested in personhood. For Hobbes, a person is not necessarily a human at all; rather, drawing on the theatrical roots of the term, Hobbes designates a person as someone "whose words or actions are considered, either as his own, or as representing the words or actions of an other man, or of any other thing," a definition with clear resonances to the slapstick misadventures of *The Comedy of Errors*.[25] A "person naturall" can claim her words as her own, while an attorney, representative, or lieutenant "acteth another" or "beares his Person" (128). Moreover, personation does not require a human referent. Hobbes attests that "there are few things, that are uncapable of being represented by Fiction" (130). A hospital or bridge might be personated, just as "irrational" figures like "Children, Fooles, and Mad-Men" might be represented by guardians, tutors, and curators (130). Personhood is capacious: a "multitude of men" might be represented by a single actor, such as a sovereign or a corporation.[26] Far from representing a singular consciousness, then, the person was an artificial construct flexible enough to represent an assemblage of actors, both human and nonhuman. In Amanda Bailey's evocative description, the person is "a creature whose agency is less a state than a relation," a figure whose transformative potentials she associates with the Pauline corporate body of Christ, a reference with further significance for *Comedy of Errors*' Ephesus.[27]

Antipholus of Ephesus may not be much of a character, but we might well understand him as a person, an Antipholus-assemblage constituted by a collection of actors both human and nonhuman. In fact, even before the arrival of his twin, multiple human bodies contribute to Antipholus as a personage of worth and significance in Ephesus: his own body, to be sure, but also the nonperson of the slave Dromio and the semi-persons of his wife Adriana, his servants, and his mistress. Dromio, for instance, represents or "personates" his master in a strictly Hobbesian sense, in that he performs actions and conveys speech on behalf of an "author" who is not present: Dromio ferries messages, fetches rope, rents rooms, stashes gold, delivers bail, carries dinner invitations, and secures passage (1.1.41). By being subsumed in the person-complex of Antipholus, Dromio extends his master's reach in the fashion of a tool, not unlike the "iron crow" Antipholus sends his slave to fetch so that he can batter down the door to his house (3.1.84). As a person, then, Antipholus is less an individual than an office, an artificial construct roomy enough to house both the Ephesian Antipholus and his Syracusan double, melding them like drops of water. If Antipholus can absorb a multitude of human figures, his person also incorporates a range of nonhuman actors, both material and immaterial, including such intangible things as his reputation and credit. The elusive, discursive quality of Antipholus's repute mediates his relationships with other members of Ephesian society, as Angelo remarks in response to a question about how the man is "esteemed," replying that Antipholus is "Of very reverend reputation, sir, / Of credit infinite, highly beloved" to the extent that "his word might bear my wealth at any time" (5.1.4–8). Affect and gossip congeal into something more solidly material, inserting Antipholus into networks of credit and patronage that allow him to personate others, "bearing their wealth" in order to enrich both parties. This, in turn, feeds into the ever-expanding store of objects that the merchant amasses, goods that do more than simply adorn the figures who collect them. Rather, they become incorporated into the characters themselves, inseparable from the identities of their owners. As Douglas Lanier has noted, character in *Comedy of Errors* has an unmistakably material quality; individuation depends upon the coordination between a given figure and an object world comprised of chains and rings, ropes and purses.[28]

Most significant among all the physical objects that contribute to Antipholus's persona is his home, the Phoenix. The complex ecology of the household sustains Antipholus by providing for his biological needs, freeing him to enjoy a public life. By contrast, the slaves, servants, women bound to the household are reduced to the state of objects or chattel, a diminishment of their personhood that is routinely the source of the play's comedic commentary. The never-ending streams of verbal abuse towards the Dromios, and sometimes their own self-identification, likens the pair to a series of inanimate objects (a post, a football, a basted roast, a scroll of parchment), semi-persons (an idiot, a "mome" or fool, a sot, and a patch), and animalia (a snail, a slug, a capon, a coxcomb, a curtal dog, a malt-horse, an ape, and an ass) (1.2.62, 2.1.82, 2.2.59, 2.2.200, 2.2.204, 3.1.13). Likewise, in describing the "kitchen wench" Nell, Dromio variously casts her as a "beastly creature" like a bear; a collection of grease, from which he might make a lamp; a black shoe; a globe; and a series of continents comically producing additional objects like "rubies, carbuncles, and sapphires" (3.2.85–138). Although she enjoys a higher status as woman of the house, Adriana chafes against her situation, complaining bitterly to her sister, who brushes aside her grievances with quippy commonplaces about women's duties towards their husband. In response, Adriana tellingly remarks that "A wretched soul bruised with adversity, / We bid be quiet when we hear it cry" (2.1.34–5). The threat to marital quiet in the Phoenix is premised on a situation in which Adriana is remanded to the home while her husband moves freely through the city, doing as he pleases: "Why," she asks her sister, "should their liberty than ours be more?" (2.1.10). Luciana replies in an answer that binds political hierarchy to spatiality: "Because their business still lies out o'door" (2.1.11). As the passage between *oikos* and *polis*, home and city, private and public, the door also marks the threshold of personhood, the material boundary between the full suite of rights and privileges afforded to the householder at the expense of his wife, servants, and slaves.

Nevertheless, the distributive personhood sketched by *Comedy*'s household economy does not simply elaborate a negative biopolitics of patriarchalism. The mastery that Antipholus too readily assumes inserts him into relationships of support, care, and mutuality with the object world of the home that threaten to displace the head of the household himself. The conflicts that drive a wedge between Antipholus and his wife have to do with precisely where and how Antipholus's physical needs are being met or, more specifically, where he is having dinner. Adriana bemoans how, like a "too-unruly deer," her husband "breaks the pale / And feeds from home," leaving her a "poor stale" (2.1.99–100). Even as she heralds Antipholus as the "master of my state," the metaphor unbalances the division of power in the household (2.1.94). The pun in "deer" animalizes Antipholus while also defining him by reference to the biological processes that he cannot escape: his sexuality and the urge to "feed" (not dine, which would be more appropriate to a human subject). The comparison also, paradoxically, enhances her stature: her labor elevates her to the status of the sovereign of the "pale" to which her hapless husband belongs. This is not an escapist fantasy; as Adriana understands intuitively, Antipholus is not the master of himself, a bounded and self-sufficient individual. He consumes and metabolizes the labor of the wife, servants, and slaves whose toil is necessary to satisfy the needs of his body, maintain his social status, and execute his business. That is, the "minor" members of the Phoenix are not only legally incorporated with Antipholus; they are part of his physical body and social persona as well, and this can ultimately be turned against the master of the household himself.

Adriana is the first to realize this, and as the play progresses, she leverages the language of corporate personhood against Antipholus with ever greater success. First assaying out of her home to confront her philandering husband, she launches into a remarkable discourse on personation:

> I am not Adriana, nor thy wife.
> The time was once when thou unurged wouldst vow
> That never words were music to thine ear,
> That never object pleasing in thine eye,
> That never touch well welcome to thy hand,
> That never meat sweet-savoured in thy taste,
> Unless I spake, or looked, or touched, or carved to thee.
> How comes it now, my husband, O, how comes it,
> That thou art then estranged from thyself?
> Thyself, I call it, being strange to me
> That, undividable, incorporate,
> Am better than thy dear self's better part.
> Ah, do not tear away thyself from me!
> For know, my love: as easy mayst thou fall
> A drop of water in the breaking gulf,
> And take unmingled thence that drop again
> Without addition or diminishing,
> As take from me thyself, and not me, too. (2.2.106–23)

With an uncanny echo of Syracusan Antipholus's meditations on dissolving selfhood, Adriana doubles down on the "one-flesh model of marriage" that is profoundly carnal, beginning not with an abstract, legalistic definition of incorporation, but in the register of sensory experience.[29] No part of Antipholus is proper to himself; his hands, eyes, tongue, and ears blend together with Adriana's touch, voice, glances, and face in an indivisible haptic admixture. Although the doctrine of coverture, which absorbs the wife into the legal person of her husband, is part of a broader patriarchal apparatus that generally tends to confine women to the household, Adriana invokes it to strikingly different ends. By leaning into her "undividable" and "incorporate" union with Antipholus, she is able to take her own "business out o'door" to render a very public account of her husband's failings in the middle of the mart. Adriana not only understands the deeper logic of the play's attitude towards personhood as compromised, fluid, and flexible, she also showcases how dexterously she can use that knowledge to clear space for her own speech and actions.

When Adriana steers the man she assumes to be her spouse back to the Phoenix, she inadvertently reveals both how central the dwelling is to her husband's person and also how easily replaceable he is. The physical environs of the home serve as a nexus of reputation, rumor, affect, and credit as well as the stores of objects that support and sustain Antipholus's person. These material and immaterial components of personhood blur together in the greatly belabored build-up to Antipholus's frustrated entrance into his home. Antipholus's goal is to entertain his goldsmith and merchant companions in a scene of hospitality that will maintain his relationships with these men, "cheering" the "sad" Balthazar by enlisting the support of the "dainties" and "cates" tendered by a gentle hostess (3.1.19, 21, 28).[30] Handled well, this domestic display should generate an atmosphere of "good welcome" that "answers" the love Antipholus bears towards them, externalizing his "good will" and "heart" in an ambiance that his guests can feel (3.1.20, 29). When his own door is barred against his entry, Antipholus finds himself disjointed and displaced, separated from the supposedly internal qualities of his own "good will" in several registers: his will, in the sense of authority or sovereignty, has been diminished; the affection he bears toward his colleague Balthazar cannot be substantiated; and his specifically "good" intentions rapidly evaporate as he loses his cool and variously screams at the help, beats on the door, and finally orders Dromio to fetch an "iron crow" to "break ope the gate" in a temper tantrum that appalls his friends (3.1.73, 84).

As in *Semayne's Case*, housebreaking amounts to an attack on both body and property at once, but the play clarifies that it is the household staff that will sustain the injurious force of the assault. Antipholus imagines abusing the physical structure of the door as a prelude to beating Luce, assuring her that she will "cry for this, minion, if I beat the door down" (3.1.59). The Dromios, no strangers to their masters' assaults, will also be exposed to violence if the door gives way: "Break any breaking here," Syracusan Dromio offers, "and I'll break your knave's pate" (3.1.74). Such violence, however, threatens to redound onto the householder, as Balthazar clarifies to the enraged merchant:

> Herein you war against your reputation,
> And draw within the compass of suspect
> Th'unviolated honour of your wife . . .
> If by strong hand you offer to break in
> Now in the stirring passage of the day,
> A vulgar comment will be made of it;

> And that supposed by the common rout
> Against your yet ungalled estimation,
> That may with foul intrusion enter in,
> And dwell upon your grave when you are dead;
> For slander lives upon succession,
> For ever hous'd where it gets possession. (3.1.86–106)

Balthazar clarifies the extraordinary dependence of Antipholus's persona on his home's integrity. Material and immaterial blend together in Balthazar's admonition: reputation, itself like a home, is subject to the invasive force of slander which is "for ever hous'd" in the space where it enters with precisely the kind of "foul intrusion" that Antipholus intends to make with his bad mood and iron crow. Turning a "strong hand" against his own home, particularly at the bustling hour of noon, could only generate a "vulgar comment" from the "common rout" that would wound both his own "ungalled estimation" as well as his wife's as-yet inviolate honor. There is nothing feminist about Balthazar's decision to urge restraint or Antipholus's eventual retreat. Under normal circumstances, the home serves as a legal refuge for the disciplinary violence that Antipholus engages in behind closed doors. The routine predictability of his brutality is gestured at in Act 4, when he sends Dromio to purchase a "rope's end" to sharpen the pain and terror of the beating he intends to "bestow" upon Adriana and "her confederates" in the household (4.1.15–16). From his friend's perspective, Antipholus's reflexive resort to domestic violence is not in itself a problem, only that his viciousness threatens to spill over to the wrong side of the door. In light of this possibility, Antipholus relents, agreeing to "depart in quiet" and maintain the integrity of his public persona by abandoning, rather than pursuing, his ugly show of force (3.1.107). The home is not simply a cate that he can enjoy, consume, and dispose of at his leisure; rather, it is a part of himself that he cannot alienate or abuse without consequence. In this respect, the essentially plural nature of the Antipholus-assemblage comes into sharpest focus when the Ephesian merchant returns home to find himself locked out while his seat is occupied, dinner eaten, and sister-in-law seduced by another Antipholus.

Ensconcing Syracusan Antipholus in his twin's household secures him more than the creature comforts afforded by a grand estate; he is also vested with his brother's status and reputation. "There's not a man I meet but doth salute me / As if I were their well-acquainted friend," he wonders, noting how

> Some tender money to me; some invite me;
> Some other give me thanks for kindnesses;
> Some offer me commodities to buy.
> Even now a tailor called me in his shop,
> And showed me silks that he had bought for me,
> And therewithal took measure of my body.
> Sure, these are but imaginary wiles,
> And Lapland sorcerers inhabit here. (4.3.1–11)

Technically this is a soliloquy, but like Antipholus's earlier speech it registers the exteriorization of subjectivity. Indeed, by floating the possibility of enchantment and dark magic, the speech gestures towards the loss of a consistent sense of self, an inability to square internal identity with external reality. In work on *A Midsummer Night's Dream*, Amanda Bailey affiliates such extreme feelings of befuddlement and disorientation with entering into the aggregative state of personhood, which entails a "phenomenological impossibility of self-possession."[31] Absorbed into the person of his twin, Antipholus exchanges interiority for a form of distributed selfhood manufactured from the assortment of objects he accumulates as he makes his way through Ephesus, the various silks and chains that he pulls into his ambit simply by virtue of his presence in the streets. Less solidly material elements also factor into this Antipholus-assemblage too, like the invitations and showy displays of gratitude that wrap the merchant into social networks of exchange that run on influence, credit, and debt. Antipholus's progress through Ephesus tracks the spatial dispersal of personhood across the city, radiating outward from the palatial dwelling he exits through the streets, markets, taverns, and liberties of the port town.

The recently displaced Ephesian Antipholus, by contrast, learns feelingly what happens when the legal fabric of the cityscape warps into a spatial field of social death, risks that coalesce around the purchase and exchange of a chain. The instability of the early modern credit system is here on full display. Everyone's hand is in someone else's pocket: the goldsmith who fashioned the chain for the conspicuous consumption of the Ephesian elite has borrowed money from Angelo, who is in turn indebted to an unnamed merchant whose ships are bound to Persia. While Syracusan Antipholus, unwittingly personating or "representing" his brother in a Hobbesian sense, accepts the chain from the goldsmith, the bill is forwarded to his downwardly mobile brother. Unable to stretch his credit any farther and physically prevented from accessing the money he stores

at home in a desk covered with a "Turkish tapestry," Antipholus
is swiftly arrested or "attached" by the officer who accompanies
Angelo, the goldsmith, and the unnamed merchant as they prowl the
streets of Ephesus, looking for satisfaction (4.1.73, 104–5). Stricken
with a blighted reputation and separated from his emergency fund,
the erstwhile householder finds himself suddenly susceptible to the
rough handling of the law enforcement officials, those "persons of
little or no value" who essentially work as the merchants' enforcers.
This fraying of his legal person is not abstract or conceptual; it also
changes the way the merchant experiences urban space, as Dromio
frantically describes to Adriana:

> No, he's in Tartar limbo, worse than hell:
> A devil in an everlasting garment hath him . . .
> A fiend, a fairy, pitiless and rough;
> A wolf, nay worse, a fellow all in buff;
> A blackfriend, a shoulder-clapper, one that countermands
> The passages of alleys, creeks and narrow lands. (4.2.32–40)

In Dromio's accounting, it is as though his master has been thrust
outside the political order altogether, such that Ephesus has been
transformed into a wilderness or a hellscape in which the bailiffs
hunt like devils or wolves. From Antipholus's customary position
of immense privilege, the juridical and phenomenological texture
of the city has warped beyond recognition. For the first time, the
rich landowner must encounter Ephesus as it is experienced from the
margins, a dangerous terrain where the bailiffs might at any moment
"clap" the "shoulders" of debtors, vagrants, and migrants with a
staff of office to initiate their detention. For Syracusan Antipholus,
Ephesus is an expansive space of possibility and material comfort,
but for his immiserated twin, the city claustrophobically contracts
into alleys, creeks, and narrows where passage is constricted and
countermanded.

As Antipholus discovers, impaired personhood transforms his
relationship to both urban and domestic space. Where the Phoenix had once been a site of refuge, indulgence, consumption, and,
at least ideally, of quiet, the household mutates into a space of
captivity and confinement. Initially, imprisonment does not especially bother Antipholus, who promptly sends a Dromio to drum
up bail while he nurses more fantasies of wife-beating. However,
his instrumental mastery over the "minor" persons in his ambit
has been compromised by his damaged reputation, as he learns
when Adriana, Luciana, and the Courtesan arrive on the scene. In a

surprising display of femme solidarity, the three women collectively secure custody of the frothing Antipholus, the man who has tormented them for the entire duration of the play. Between the arrest, the screaming match outside his home, and the daylight theft of his mistress's ring, the narrative circulating about Antipholus is that he has fallen "mad" and, "being lunatic," requires wardenship (4.3.82, 94). In her capacity as caregiver, Adriana is the logical repository of that trusteeship. Previously, Antipholus's temper was a sign of his patriarchal mastery; now, in a swift turn of events, it serves as a sign of his mental incapacity. Beating Dromio and threatening his wife signify an "incivility" and "ecstasy" that "confirms" his madness past doubt (4.4.46–7, 52). Thus, in her role as helpmeet, Adriana is able to inhabit the position she had imagined for herself, sovereign of the pale. In a perfect reversal of patriarchal logic, according to which the violence of the father-king is necessary to check the impulses of his unruly subjects, Adriana undertakes a bold course of action that is coercive but cloaked in the language of care: "What wilt thou do, thou peevish officer? / Hast thou delight to see a wretched man / Do outrage and displeasure to himself?" (4.4.115–17). Mastery comes easily to Adriana, who summarily orders Antipholus bound and then "safe conveyed / Home to my house" (4.4.123–4). The kinds of support Adriana intends to provide for her husband are multiplex, embodied in the person of Doctor Pinch, who is at once a schoolmaster, a physician, and an amateur exorcist. The door that had been barred against Antipholus's entry now traps him inside, while under Adriana's management the Phoenix is reborn as a space of internment, re-education, spiritual instruction, and medical treatment.

As *Semayne's Case* established for a long line of liberal thinkers, the home is not just a castle, but a sanctuary or refuge (*refugium*), a secure a place to retreat to when confronted with a threat of violence. *The Comedy of Errors* fleshes out just how slender that promise of refuge is, its uneven application to the forms of life sheltered there, the ease with which the home becomes a zone of informal incarceration and casual violence even for the people it is explicitly designed to protect. It is no surprise, then, that Antipholus has to claim sanctuary from his home, which has become for him, as for so many marginalized persons, an unlivable space of deprivation and terror. The cord Antipholus had requested a few scenes before has slipped into the hands of the women he intended to assault. When he meets with Adriana and her colleagues equipped with ropes, the Syracusan Antipholus heeds Dromio's call to "take a house" in "some priory" rather than submit to the women who hope to "bind him fast / And bear him home" for a "recovery" that sounds menacing and invasive, a far cry from the "repose" that *Semayne's Case* associates with domestic space (5.1.36–7, 40–1). The Abbess asserts the priory as a space beyond the jurisdiction of the Duke and the claims of family government in unqualified terms: "Not a creature enters my house," she tells the cadre of armed women, since Antipholus "took this place for sanctuary, / And it shall privilege him from your hands" (5.1.92, 94–5). The possibility of a legally recognized refuge from the volatile environs of the home and the brutal police powers of the city-state, however, is derailed almost as soon as it is introduced, shunted aside by the revelations and recognitions that clear a path towards comic resolution. Forgiveness abounds: the Courtesan is restored her pricey ring; the goldsmith is paid, so the second merchant can make his way to Persia; Adriana and Ephesian Antipholus are reconciled; Syracusan Antipholus is free to court Luciana; the Abbess, now simply Emilia, is reunited with her long-lost husband; Egeon is pardoned, although it is not entirely clear why; and the sets of brothers fall into one another's arms. The pity that radiates from these disclosures is not a function of sanctuary's exceptional jurisdiction, in which the rigors of the law are suspended in favor of a higher power.[32] Rather, mercy flows from the dissolution or profaning of sanctuary itself, the moment when the secularized Abbess becomes Emilia again, a mother and wife who can return to the household.

For better or worse, in *The Comedy of Errors*, there is no escaping the home. The door that was briefly barred against Antipholus reappears, closing behind the entire cast as they file inside, one happy couple trailing another. Despite this blandly copacetic ending, however, *The Comedy of Errors* lingers over the costs of awarding domestic space exceptional status in the law by dissolving the physical environs of the home into the person of the householder. Personhood is a zero-sum game in the Phoenix, where the amplified rights and privileges of one actor come at the expense of the women, slaves, and servants whose labor he consumes and instrumentalizes. Even so, Shakespeare imagines how this distributive personhood can serve dual ends. If possession of the home magnifies Antipholus, it also reduces him to a state of dependence that can be weaponized against him, as the assembled effort of the play's women to bind and capture him in the name of his "recovery" demonstrates. The two doors of *Semayne's Case* and *Comedy of Errors* thus open onto the doubled futures of the sanctity of the home, in which personhood is parceled out according to access to property.

Notes

1. On the evolution of statutes staple and the process of extent, see Thomas Campbell Foster, *A Treatise on the Writ of Scire Facias* (V&R Stevens and G. S. Norton, 1851), ch. 7. 13 Eliz. C.4, "An Acte to make the Landes Tenem[en]tes Goodes and Cattalles of Tellers Receavers &c. lyable to the payment of their Debtes," *Statutes of the Realm, 1101–1713*, ed. A. Luders et al., 11 vols. (London, 1810–28), vol. 4.
2. Philip Massinger, *New Way to Pay Old Debts*, v. i. sig. L2v.
3. *Semayne's Case*, 5 Co. Rep. 91a, 194. Hereafter cited in the text.
4. On joint tenancy and the right of survivorship, see Co. Inst. 1, L.3 C.3 Sect. 280–7.
5. On the jurisdictional antagonism between Blackfriars and London, see A. P. House, "The City of London and the Problem of the Liberties, c1540–c1640," diss. Trinity College (2006), 132–40.
6. I do not mean to suggest that home is an absolute zone of exception like Agamben's camp, which he names the *nomos* of the modern, only that it exists on a spectrum with this and other such extra-legal spaces. On extrajudicial spaces, see Giorgio Agamben, *Homo Sacer: Sovereign Power and Bare Life*, trans. Daniel Heller-Roazen (Stanford: Stanford University Press, 1998).
7. Dom Birch, "'Silence! I have made my decision!': Quietness as Ideology in Early Modern England," unpublished dissertation chapter.
8. This was a real risk, given the incredibly litigious culture of early modern England. On this point, see Christopher Brooks, "A Law-Abiding and Litigious Society," in *The Oxford Illustrated History of Tudor & Stuart Britain*, ed. John Morrill (New York: Oxford University Press, 1996), 139–55.
9. Qtd. in Andrew Ballantyne and Chris L. Smith, eds., *Architecture in the Space of Flows* (Abingdon: Routledge, 2012), 3.
10. Kevin Curran, *Shakespeare's Legal Ecologies: Law and Distributed Selfhood* (Evanston, IL: Northwestern University Press, 2017).
11. Moore KB 971.
12. Twenty years later, Coke would return to *Semayne's Case* as to erect legal defenses against state intrusion into domestic space, arguing that the privacy and security of the home were inviolable rights established in the Magna Carta. Sir Edward Coke, *The fourth part of the Institutes of the laws of England: concerning the jurisdiction of courts* (London: M. Flesher, W. Lee, and D. Pakeman, 1644), 176–7. William Blackstone advanced the thesis that "the law of England has so particular and tender a regard to the immunity of a man's house, that it styles it his castle, and will never suffer it to be violated with impunity." William Blackstone, *Commentaries on the Laws of England*, vol. 2 (San Francisco: Bancroft-Whitney, 1915–16), 4.16.258.2, 2430–1. The sanctity of the home entered US constitutional law by way of John Adams who, as the

plaintiff's attorney in *King v. Stewart*, merged the language of *Semayne's Case* with an almost Hobbesian scene of covenanting: "An Englishmans dwelling House is his Castle. The Law has erected a Fortification round it—and as every Man is Party to the Law, i.e. the Law is a Covenant of every Member of society with every other Member, therefore every Member of Society has entered into a solemn Covenant with every other that he shall enjoy in his own dwelling House as compleat a security, safety and Peace and Tranquility as if it was surrounded with Walls of Brass, with Ramparts and Palisadoes and defended with a Garrison and Artillery.—This covenant has been broken in a most outragious manner." John Adams, *Legal Papers of John Adams*, ed. L. Wroth and H. Zobel (Cambridge, MA: Belknap Press, 1965), 137.

13. Margaret Radin, "Property and Personhood," *Stanford Law Review* 34.5 (May 1982): 958. On the sanctity of the home and personhood, see 991–1000.

14. Radin, "Property and Personhood," 992.

15. *Payton v. New York* struck down statutes authorizing warrantless entries, citing *Semayne's Case* as evidence of the "overriding respect for the sanctity of the home that has been embedded in our traditions since the origins of the Republic," 445 US 573 (1980), 601. *Kyllo v. United States* held that the warrantless use of thermal imaging technology on private residences violates the "Fourth Amendment sanctity of the home," 533 US 27 (2001), 37. Sanctity of the home reasoning animates *Stanley v. Georgia*, 394 US 557 (1969), which decriminalized pornography for use in the private home. Similar language contributed to the decision that decriminalized contraception in part because the kind of police search necessary to find evidence of its use would violate the "sacred precincts of the marital bedroom," *Griswold v. Connecticut* 381 US 479 (1965), 485–6.

16. "The problem is that while the private has been a refuge for some, it has been a hellhole for others, often at the same time. In gendered light, the law's privacy is a sphere of sanctified isolation, impunity, and unaccountability. It surrounds the individual in his habitat. It belongs to the individual with power. Women have been accorded neither individuality nor power." Catharine MacKinnon, "Reflections on Sex Equality Under Law," *Yale Law Journal* (1991): 1311.

17. See, for instance, Christine Catalfamo, "Stand Your Ground: Florida's Castle Doctrine for the Twenty-First Century," *Rutgers Journal of Law & Public Policy* 4.3 (2006): 504–45.

18. The classic work on impaired personhood is Orlando Patterson's *Slavery and Social Death: A Comparative Study*, 2nd edn. (Cambridge, MA: Harvard University Press, 2018). For a necessary and harrowing update of Patterson that considers contemporary forms of racism, incarceration, and illegality, see Lisa Marie Cacho, *Social Death: Racialized Rightlessness and the Criminalization of the Unprotected* (New York: New York University Press, 2012).

19. Bradin Cormack, "Locating *The Comedy of Errors*: Revels Jurisdiction at the Inns of Court," in *The Intellectual and Cultural World of the Early Modern Inns of Court*, ed. Jayne Archer, Elizabeth Goldring, and Sarah Knight (Manchester: Manchester University Press, 2011), 264.
20. *The Comedy of Errors*, ed. Kent Cartwright (London: Bloomsbury, 2016), 1.1.1–2, 19–20. Hereafter cited in the text.
21. Richard Strier, *The Unrepentant Renaissance: From Petrarch to Shakespeare to Milton* (Chicago: University of Chicago Press, 2011), 153.
22. This is not the only definition available; drawing on seventeenth-century character manuals, Aaron Kunin offers a reading of character as a formal device that "collects every example of a kind of person," in his *Character as Form* (London: Bloomsbury, 2019).
23. On subjectivity and interiority in Shakespeare, see, among many others, Katharine Eisaman Maus, *Inwardness and the Theater in the English Renaissance* (Chicago: University of Chicago Press, 1995).
24. Will Stockton reads this passage as a "hyperbolic rejection of interiority" that stems from Reformation ideas about sexuality, polyamory, and the corporate body of Christ in *Members of His Body: Shakespeare, Paul, and a Theology of Nonmonogamy* (New York: Fordham University Press, 2017), 21.
25. Thomas Hobbes, *Leviathan* (New York: Continuum, 2005), 128.
26. On corporate personhood in early modernity, see Henry S. Turner, *The Corporate Commonwealth: Pluralism and Political Fictions in England, 1516–1651* (Chicago: University of Chicago Press, 2016).
27. Amanda Bailey, "Personification and the Political Imagination of *A Midsummer Night's Dream*," in *The Oxford Handbook of Shakespeare and Embodiment: Gender, Sexuality, and Race*, ed. Valerie Traub (Oxford: Oxford University Press, 2016), 414. On Ephesus and the corporate body of Christ, see also Stockton, *Members of His Body*.
28. Douglas Lanier, "'Stigmatical in Making': The Material Character of *The Comedy of Errors*," *English Literary Renaissance* 23.1 (Winter 1993): 81–112.
29. Stockton, *Members of His Body*, 34.
30. As Julia Reinhard Lupton has argued, the scripts of hospitality enlist both the labor of the household and its object world into a scene of display and performance that presses the pre-political space of the home into a site of political speech. Julia Reinhard Lupton, *Thinking with Shakespeare: Essays on Politics and Life* (Chicago: University of Chicago Press, 2011).
31. Bailey, "Personification," 413.
32. On pity and the jurisdictional exceptionality of sanctuary, see Elizabeth Allen, "A Once and Future King: Sanctuary, Sovereignty, and the Politics of Pity in the Histories of Perkin Warbeck," *Journal of Medieval and Early Modern Studies* 47.2 (May 2017): 327–58.

Part II

Taxonomies of Personhood: Status, Species, Race

Chapter 5

Should (Bleeding) Trees Have Standing?

Joseph Campana

Claims ripen, claimants stand. To insist upon relevance, to articulate injury, and to seek redress is, perhaps, to be at least part tree. Of course, in the literary imagination, trees could do all these things. If a tree appears in a text, we tend to read it. Habits of interpretation descend, at least in part, from strategies of allegorical reading prevalent in the Middle Ages and persistent in the Renaissance that teach us how to read nature like a book by stripping the *integumentum* (literally, the husk or bark) to reveal various shades of ever more rarefied meaning. But if a tree cries out in the woods, does anyone hear it? It seems writers have been asking this question for thousands of years if the venerable epic topos of the bleeding tree is any indication. Somewhere in a shadowy forest or in a small stand of trees, from a thicket of bushes or from a crowd of twisted branches, a voice cries out. Someone reaches out to pluck a stem from a tangle of branches, to slice open with knife or sword the flesh of the tree, or to tear away the bark with bare hands. Miraculously, the tree bleeds; then, it speaks. The tree is the source of a voice that echoes in the woods, sending its assailant, who is also its witness, into states of amazement and horror, grief and sympathy. The members of this memorable topos spring up on a hillock on the coast of Thrace in Virgil's *Aeneid* or on the banks of the river Po in Ovid's *Metamorphoses*.[1] They appear in a monstrous, archaic wood outside the Jerusalem of Torquato Tasso's *Gerusalemme Liberata*, on an enchanted isle somewhere in the world of Ludovico Ariosto's *Orlando Furioso*, or even in the bowels of Dante's *Inferno*. Edmund Spenser recreates the topos in *The Faerie Queene*, in an allegorical exploration of pain, masculinity, and embodiment in the wake of the Reformation.[2] William Shakespeare's Ovidian *Titus Andronicus* creates an even-more damaged bleeding tree in the figure of the violated Lavinia.

A topos is not just a theme but most literally a place, a place to stand, one might say, and to explore the dark forest constituted by these mysterious, living figures is to find embedded in the roots and branches of the literary imagination a series of revelatory *hallucinations*. The encounters feel hallucinatory both to the characters within the narrative and to the readers of the narrative as witnesses to the bleeding tree are seized by a state of bewildered contemplation. But more importantly for my purposes here, they are *hallucinations of personhood and standing*. These tenuously sensory, inoperative moments of failure amidst action illuminate rifts and paradoxes that arise in the extension of human legal and political prerogatives to other-than-human lives. The articulate, bleeding tree approximates human personhood, either as the mysterious implantation or trans-formation of a person into vegetative form or as the awakening of vegetative life within the human. And yet, as hallucinations of stand-ing these trees reveal that occupying the ground of relevance requires an injury to create an approximation of personhood, the possibil-ity of voice, and the viability of redress. Moreover, these fascinating articulations of human–plant entanglement also then constitute cau-tionary tales about the impulse to assume interconnectivity across species that necessarily is desirable or necessarily encourages salu-brious and new forms of association. Bleeding trees indicate how important imagination and figuration are to ecological thought, in showing where legal and political categories fail to accommodate life's myriad forms and exposing fantasies of ecological redress as being all-too-human.

*

In its basic parlance, the law tracks time through vegetative growth, suggesting that it is perhaps the case, as Shakespeare intimated some four hundred years ago in sonnet 15, "that men as plants increase" (15.5).[3] If, for Shakespeare, ripeness really is all, perhaps that is because vegetative figurations track bodily time and human mortality. Where else but in the fragile flesh, and in the view of all, does "wasteful time debateth with decay?" (15.11). In a legal context, ripeness refers to readiness or maturity, as when litigation becomes possible or when litigation becomes sufficiently advanced to be ready for judgment, often because of the manifestation of injury or harm.[4] "The question of ripeness," that is, "often arises in cases where the harm asserted by the plaintiff has not yet occurred."[5] Standing, or *locus standi* (literally, a place to stand), refers to a basic relevance with respect to a claim.

It is "a position from which one has the right to prosecute a claim or seek legal redress" (*OED*, s.v. "standing") or "a right to appear in a court or before any body on a given question: a right to be heard" (*Merriam Webster*, s.v. "standing"). More broadly, standing is both a position of relevance from which a claim may be articulated and the very ability to stand in a position, perhaps upright, as a human or tree might stand. It would be easy to dismiss the vegetative implications of legal language as merely metaphorical. The idea of plants as plaintiffs is relatively recent in legal history. How much easier it is to imagine a man or a woman speaking, addressing a judge, a jury, or a crowd. But if claims ripen and claimants stand, why should not plants, too, be persons? Figuration and metaphor, as is often the case, run far ahead of legal rights. But perhaps too a series of internal contradictions— about personhood, injury, and voice—obstruct the extension of pre-rogatives to an ever-wider array of life forms.

In the eyes of the law, to use yet another bodily figuration, to be a person is primarily, and perhaps not surprisingly, to be "a human being—Also termed *natural person*."[6] So, at least, we learn from *Black's Law Dictionary*. If a person is also defined as "the living body of a human being," it is primarily distinguished from an "artificial person" defined as "an entity (such as a corporation) that is recognized by law as having most of the rights and duties of a human being."

Centuries ago, Thomas Hobbes focused the prerogatives of personhood in the capacity to represent, which is to say to speak for oneself or on behalf of another. "A PERSON," he argues, "is he *whose words or actions are considered, either as his own, or as representing the words or actions of an other man, or of any other thing to whom they are attributed, whether Truly or by Fiction*." As such the distinction between natural and artificial persons concerns the basic, representative function of speaking on behalf of another. "When they are considered as his owne," Hobbes says, "then is he called a *Naturall Person*: And when they are considered as representing the words and actions of an other, then is he a *Feigned* or *Artificiall person*."[7]

To be a person may be to speak as or to speak for, but to be a person is also, rather decidedly, not to be property. Persons maintain ownership over property, which is a state that does not require membership in some category called humanity. How capacious an idea that might be and yet how much easier it has been historically for corporations to be recognized as legal persons relative to the more limited success of other entities. That ease seemed to increase substantially after the 2010 *Citizens United* decision of the U.S. Supreme Court to recognize corporations as persons qualified to intervene in elections through financial contributions. How much harder to recognize the personhood of trees, despite Christopher Stone's landmark essay "Should Trees Have Standing?" which argued for "legal rights for natural objects." Those rights emerged in response to various forms of environmental destruction *on behalf of* otherwise apparently mute objects. Stone assesses the right of natural objects, like trees, with comparisons to slaves and fetuses, which he argues were similarly disadvantaged with respect to different moments in history and yet gradually became the recipients of greater standing. And yet it is on the model of the guardianship of "legal incompetents" that Stone proposes "a system in which, when a friend of a natural object perceives it to be endangered, he can apply to a court for the creation of a guardianship."[8] Thus trees might be persons but only so long as they are spoken for.

Stone's essay gained immediate notoriety because of the 1972 *Sierra Club v. Morton* decision, which pitted environmental activists against resort developers. The decades that followed Stone's influential essay witnessed advances not only in environmental law more generally but in respect to the designation of numerous so-called "natural objects." Stone's argument depends on the recognition that it has not been the case that "only matter in human form . . . has come to be recognized as the possessor of rights. The world of the lawyer is peopled with inanimate right-holders: trusts, corporations, joint ventures, municipalities." And, as such,

> throughout legal history, each successive extension of rights to some new entity has been, theretofore, a bit unthinkable . . . the fact is, that each time there is a movement to confer rights onto some new "entity," the proposal is bound to sound odd or frightening or laughable. This is partly because until the rightless thing receives its rights, we cannot see it as anything but a *thing* for the use of "us"—those who are holding rights at the time.[9]

Claims for the personhood of natural objects persist, most recently in the Lake Erie Bill of Rights, proposed by the citizens of Toledo, Ohio to render Lake Erie a person on behalf of whom the citizens could sue polluters.[10]

Stone's essay makes clear the fractures of personhood related to who or what we imagine can have standing and make a claim. Such perceived insufficiencies motivated a range of thinkers to question, despite Stone's strenuous arguments for nonhuman personhood, the utility of law. Luc Ferry's appreciation of Stone in *The Ecological Order* stops short of agreeing with the core thesis. There he argues that

> nature is not an *agent*, a being able to act with the reciprocity of an *alter ego*. *Law is always for men*, and it is for men that the trees or whales can become objects of a form of respect tied to legislation—not the reverse.[11]

Thus it is perhaps no surprise that some would call for more radical possibility, as does Michel Serres in *The Natural Contract* who seeks a more fundamental transformation, the supersession of an original social contract, "a new pact, a new preliminary agreement" to govern the relationship between human and planet, a "natural contract of symbiosis and reciprocity in which our relationship to things would set aside mastery and possession in favor of admiring attention, reciprocity, contemplation, and respect; where knowledge would no longer imply property, nor action mastery."[12]

Bruno Latour more expansively calls for a renovation of the very idea of a political ecology, one that would supersede Serres's natural contract, and in so doing he famously calls for a new Constitution that radically reorients the terms of political discourse not by merely "inserting nature into politics" but rather by creating a new alignment of politics and the sciences so as to "socializ[e] nonhumans."[13] The result would be a Parliament of Things, which Julian Yates and Garrett Sullivan describe in a special issue of *Shakespeare Studies* on "Shakespeare and Ecology":

> only humans would have seats in this Parliament, but those seats would be merely for our comfort—in case we needed a quick sit-down or break. For our role would not be to speak on our own behalf or that of our fellows but to serve as mouthpieces or as some other variously sonifying, visualizing, or animating prostheses for the non-human entities whose existence and whose concerns we hope to make present or knowable.[14]

The result is a thorough renovation of core political and disciplinary terms to reposition the human within broader networks of relation. Thus,

> while policies might remain written or authored by human persons, there is every possibility that those persons will now, in truth, exist merely as factors or occasions by which the interests of the ozone layer, the coastline, sea lions, lichen, and so on, come to serve as co-authors in a collective writing of the world.[15]

A realignment of humans and nonhumans depends throughout Latour's work on a realignment of politics and the sciences, particularly the latter, which must trade "their objectivity, their truth, their coldness, their extraterritoriality" for "their daring, their experimentation, their uncertainty, their warmth, their incongruous blend of hybrids, their crazy ability to reconstitute the social bond."[16] Symbiosis, reciprocity, and co-authorship, all articulated with a heady dose of self-abnegation, may sound encouraging in the wake of millennia of anthropocentrism. But it remains hard not to notice to what extent Latour's real subject is the reconstitution of human institutions. "And yet," as Frédéric Neyrat argues, "it's always the humans that benefit from this lack of distinguishability, as if it were impossible for nonhumans to exist without humans and to create links between themselves, nonhumans with nonhumans."[17] Perhaps the most coercive aspect of Latour's expansive account of distributed agency, networked humans, and a Parliament of Things is the requirement that creatures, objects, and environs have social bonds with humans. What if separation, as Neyrat argues, or indifference or non-relation come to the fore? Perhaps, in the zeal to accommodate at least two decades of invocations of an increasingly mandatory sense of networked life reaching beyond individual figures, we find ourselves with unresolved questions about personhood, standing, and the capacity to make claims.

To return more elaborately to that core term, standing refers to

> a party's right to make a legal claim or seek judicial enforcement of a duty or right. To have standing in federal court, a plaintiff must show 1) that the challenged conduct has caused the plaintiff actual injury, and 2) that the interest sought to be protected is within the zone of interests meant to be regulated by the statutory or constitutional guarantee in question.[18]

About this notion Joseph Vining claims:

> The word *standing* is rather recent in the basic judicial vocabulary and does not appear to have been commonly used until the middle of our own century. No authority that I have found introduces the term with proper explanations and apologies and announces that henceforth standing should be used to describe who may be heard by a judge. The word appears here and there, spreading very gradually with no discernible pattern. Judges and lawyers found themselves using the term and did not ask why they did so or where it came from.[19]

The term seems to refer to appropriate legal relevance that contains several premises. To have standing one must both speak and be able to be heard. To be able to be heard is to be injured and in search of redress. The term suggests that this relevance, which depends on being heard and being injured, also alludes to the capacity to stand, as if in front of or in proximity to another body. And just as we imagine the system of justice to have a body, or at least organs of sense, so too do we imagine that to participate in the law is to have a body that can stand before, proximate to, powers that determine who is injured and who may be heard.

My intent is not to posit a clear origin for the legal notion of standing or for the arboreal implications of legal language. Origins are, as Vining indicates, sometimes mysterious. And yet, a series of relevant and recognizably related fractures of personhood at the border of human and vegetative life appear in the history of figurations that bind literary and legal language in the Renaissance. While they may not be the sole root from which such various pathways branch, the two great charters signed by King John in 1215 provide an initial place to stand and attempt to see the forest for the trees. And, indeed, Roderick Frazier Nash's classic account of the transition from natural rights to the rights of nature starts there as well:

> It began, appropriately enough, outdoors—in a June-green meadow called Runnymede alongside the River Thames. The English barons who gathered there in 1215 forced King John to accept a lengthy list of concessions which came to be known, in the Latin in which it was written, as *Magna Carta*. Although the barons hardly thought of it in such terms, they were in fact dealing with ethical dynamite that revolutionaries five centuries later would call "natural rights." The tendency of this concept to take on expanded meaning is one of the most exciting characteristics of the liberal tradition. Whether this tradition should expand to include nonhuman interests—perhaps even nature as a whole—is the proposition under examination in the present volume.[20]

The anniversary of the Magna Carta arrived in 2015 with invocations of "800 years of liberty" on the elaborate website of the Magna Carta Trust, as well as a series of events and ceremonies to accompany easily circulated truisms about the origins of individual rights in the meadow of Runnymede. Shakespeare's Globe was rather decidedly not above the fray, announcing their very first staging of Shakespeare's *King John* with the implausible claim that it is "the play that naturally attaches itself to the Magna Carta."[21] The play,

while intensely political, rather notably never mentions the document
or its primary concerns, which have sparked some debate amongst
scholars.[22] A review of that very production of *King John* corrects
then artistic director Dominic Dromgoole's assertion, clarifying that
"Even though Shakespeare's King John doesn't show us his capitu-
lation before his rebellious barons at Runnymede in 1215—it's not
even a footnote—James Dacre's revival could hardly be more timely:
we get the context in which Magna Carta came into being." In the
process, reviewer Dominic Cavendish describes the Magna Carta as
"that hallowed document which so crucially set down an insistence
on the need for individual freedom under law."[23]

Yet as Peter Linebaugh argues in *The Magna Carta Manifesto*, "we
must ask *who* traces rights to the Magna Carta? There is a conser-
vative interpretation restricting it to the elite, and there is a popular
interpretation that includes free people and commoners."[24] Even more
importantly he reminds his reader that

> there were two charters forced on King John at Runnymede. Beside the
> great charter with which we are still vaguely familiar, there was a second
> charter known as the Charter of the Forest. Whereas the first charter
> concerned, for the most part, political and juridical rights, the second
> charter dealt with economic survival.[25]

Linebaugh's bracing, progressive manifesto—subtitled *Liberties and
Commons for All*—calls for both a reinvigorated concept of shared
resources under the rubric of the commons and a consequent equi-
table distribution of those resources. It is then no surprise that he
would take up both the "Great Charter of Liberties" and the accompanying "Charter of the Forest" in imagining a commons. The forests of King John's era were not old-growth wonders untouched by
human hands but rather preserves under monarchical or aristocratic
control and upon whose bounty commoners depended. The rights
to graze animals, cut turf or collect branches for fuel, or gather food
were the stuff of survival. Indeed, the Charter of the Forest primarily
concerned the processes of afforestation and disafforestation, which
concerned human access to wooded lands. A document economically
progressive with respect to human access is not likely to be progressive from the point of view of forests, which holds true for a charter
that considers trees and forests to be property, not persons. Despite
his invocation of the tradition of natural rights, even a historian of
environmental ethics like Nash does not mention the Charter of the
Forest at all.

Nash does, of course, treat Stone's "Should Trees Have Standing?" which advanced what even a small sampling of recent authors reveals to be an only ever more complex conversation about law, personhood, and ecology. For Nash, Stone intimated "an ethical system that personified the environment to an unprecedented extent."[26] Recent ecological advocacy still witnesses the core fracture between personhood and property that dates back at least to the Magna Carta and the Charter of the Forest with respect to vegetative life. Advocacy for animal rights may not yet as expansively treat other life forms, like trees, but the fervor for change is palpable. Gary Francione's 2008 *Animals as Persons* diagnoses human "moral schizophrenia" with respect to animals, which can only be corrected if humans "accord animals one right: the right not to be treated as our property."[27] David R. Boyd's 2017 *The Rights of Nature* extends such longstanding arguments for animal rights to a broader range of natural phenomena, joining

> a growing global movement to recognize non-human animals as legal persons, a radical change that would endow them with a variety of legal rights. Animal rights advocates are not saying primates, cetaceans, or elephants are people. They are saying that the law should recognize them as legal persons.[28]

Boyd follows Sue Donaldson and Will Kymlicka's 2011 *Zoopolis*, which more complexly attempts to redress longstanding contradictions in the advocacy for animal rights by adapting the "multiple, qualified, and mediated forms of citizenship" to nonhuman creatures.[29] The result would be a more richly variegated set of relationships. "Some animals," they argue, "should be seen as forming separate sovereign communities on their own territories . . . some animals are akin to migrants or denizens who choose to move into areas of human habitation . . . and some animals should be seen as full citizens of the polity."[30]

How different these arguments for nonhuman rights or citizenship are from Maya K. Van Rossum's equally impassioned 2017 *The Green Amendment*, which takes inspiration for political action from the state constitution of Pennsylvania, which states:

> The people have a right to clean air, pure water, and to the preservation of the natural, scenic, historic and aesthetic values of the environment. Pennsylvania's public natural resources are the common property of all the people, including generations yet to come. As trustee of these resources, the Commonwealth shall conserve and maintain them for the benefit of all the people.[31]

Van Rossum wonders, then:

> Imagine if we passed a federal constitutional provision to our bill of rights—a Green Amendment to the Constitution—guaranteeing that the government has no more ability to harm your environment than it does to deny you due process or overturn your right to free speech.[32]

The consequence, she hopes, would be:

> We would all take it personally when companies destroyed the forests and wetlands around us, or when they polluted our air or water. We'd feel outraged, perceiving that industry wrongfully took something of ours to which they had no right. And we'd feel more of an obligation to protect the earth for others.[33]

Van Rossum suggests people should be offended when companies, which are in fact legal persons, infringe upon the rights of human persons to take advantage of "natural resources." Although ownership may be up for grabs, forests and wetlands are merely property. Like some recent advocates of a Green New Deal, decidedly human economics (with decidedly outsize ecological impacts) come to the fore in Van Rossum's argument.

But imagine for a moment that the Charter of the Forest might be understood to accomplish for forests what some imagine the Magna Carta accomplished for at least some people, which is the establishment of a set of rights or liberties associated with personhood. What would such a document look like? It would not look like the current document, which can offer what some consider a progressive account of the commons only by insisting upon the forest as property and as such the constitutive other of legal persons. The key difference is the distribution of that property to a wider array of peoples. Early modern works of husbandry and forestry were works of management that also describe the wonders of vegetative life, to be sure, but they were primarily works that described the cultivation and health of various forms of plant life in the interest of human comfort and profit. John Manwood's 1598 *A Treatise and Discourse of the Laws of The Forrest* concerns itself primarily with ownership and rights, particularly royal rights, and while John Evelyn's 1662 *Sylva, or a Discourse of Forest-Trees and the Propagation of Timber* may effuse about the wonders of trees, each depiction ends with an account of that tree's use, while the treatise concludes itself with an argument that "our forests are undoubtedly the greatest magazines of wealth, and glory of this nation."[34] Were there other places in which one might sense a more expansive understanding of personhood, one that might include forests and trees? What I propose here is that the woven branches of a literary topos, that of bleeding, voluble trees, might best serve as a hallucination of a Charter of the Forest never written and still yet to be written because only in the tangled thickets of literary figurations of plant life can standing, the capacity to articulate a claim, and even personhood, be granted to trees. If a tree cries in a solitary forest, does anyone hear it? What, to take a page from Vinciane Despret, might trees say if we asked the right questions?[35] Would they talk at all? What would it sound like? Would they want to talk to us?

The thrust of recent writing about vegetation has tried to answer that question by advancing an increasingly uncontroversial proposition—that there is more to know about (and from) plants than has been dreamt of in our philosophies. Increasingly popular titles like Peter Wohlleben's *The Hidden Life of Trees: What They Feel, How They Communicate* reveal a series of profound and to some unexpected capacities for perception and sociality including, as the title indicates, affect and communication.[36] The work of Michael Marder extensively reconsiders Western philosophy from the point of view of plants. "Despite its widespread conceptual allergy to vegetable life—indeed its phytophobia," he argues, "the philosophical tradition of the West could not skirt the issue of plants altogether."[37] Marder refines a notion of "plant thinking" to redress a longstanding bias that "robs the living of their immediate life, promising, in return, their resurrection in the ideal world of its chimeras—the Ideas, substance, Spirit."[38] Matthew Hall similarly draws from the history of philosophy in the attempt to reimagine our "plant-dominated biosphere" and resist the general truism of "plants as passive resources."[39] Outside of predominantly zoocentric Western philosophical traditions, Hall identifies ways to think of plants as persons absorbed in networks of respect, care, and even kinship with humans. Jeffrey T. Nealon assesses this recent vegetative turn in light of recent theories of animality and biopower and primarily with respect to the works of Michel Foucault, Jacques Derrida, and Gilles Deleuze and Félix Guattari, arguing for the need to reconsider such theories from the perspective of plants and to remind ourselves that "discourses of contemporary biopolitics may just need a little water and sunlight, and we likewise need to do some turning of the theoretical soil in which the biopolitics debate originally grew."[40] Scholars of early modernity have been no strangers to such developments and in fact have elaborated the many uses, the putting-to-work, of woods. Jeffrey Theis examines contradictory attitudes towards forests in the era, the trees of which provoke as much anxiety about environmental damage as they did about resource scarcity.[41] Vin Nardizzi considers "the theatre's constitutive woodenness" in the Renaissance, "in an age of this resource's perceived and real shortages . . . In London's theaters, consumers paid the price of admission to experience the pleasures and the frights of being inside virtual woods."[42]

If on the one hand recent work in what tends to be called a turn toward plants or critical plant studies enables us to appreciate the complex capacities of vegetative life, recent work at the intersection of literary and legal studies also significantly impacts the attempt to understand a notion of personhood consistently encroached by vegetative growth in early modernity. While a great deal of fine work focuses on intention, motivation, evidence, and jurisdiction in early modernity, recent scholarship on the fictional and associational nature of personhood remains particularly relevant here. Victoria Kahn champions the potent intersection of literary and legal fictions, arguing that "a person is a theatrical and legal fiction, a disguise or outward appearance, a matter of convention rather than incarnation."[43] For Kahn, the legal fiction offers a way out of the contradictions of political theology and sovereignty that plagued Europe from early modernity to the mid-twentieth century as witnessed in the writings of Kantorowicz, Schmitt, Benjamin, Arendt, and others. For Kahn, legal fictions enable new political formations. "Whereas fascism and religious fundamentalism," she argues, "attempt to give society a body, the usefulness of the category of fiction is that it complicates any attempt to locate power in one particular body or one particular place."[44] While Kahn does not here invoke personhood, it is hard not to see that concept as yet another localization of power from which other scholars too have turned in an attempt to understand broader networks of association. Henry Turner's powerful intellectual history of association in early modernity considers a "rich legal history of corporation as both person and group, taking up the nature of fiction as a rich resource for thinking about corporations."[45] Indeed, this study not only emphasizes the ubiquity of various forms of corporations but also understands them to offer a sense of the "diversity of corporate associational life," the implication of which would be that "the crisis of twenty-first century political life is not that we suffer from an excess of corporations of an authentically public type. We suffer, in short, from a *corporate monoculture* of the for-profit, commercial form."[46] Moreover, Kevin Curran's recent work understands the works of Shakespeare and his era through a concept of legal ecology that witnesses a distributed and connective notion of self. "Law," he argues, "afforded Shakespeare a conceptual language through which the self could be portrayed as part of a vital and interdependent world of things."[47] While Curran distinguishes legal ecology from its broader environmental sense, the now-common invocation of net-worked interdependencies, across many cultural domains and with reference to a wide array of phenomena and objects, raises questions about the compatibility of personhood and an "interdependent world of things." But where, in such a world, are trees?

Like a proverb, a topos acquires force through iterability, potency through distribution. While topoi may leave room for greater varia-tion on the core theme, they distill central queries into the singularity of an image that arrests episodes of action. In this chapter I seek to speak with and for these iterations of the topos, finding in each para-doxes that inform the knot of personhood, standing, and interdepen-dency we still find ourselves still seeking to untie centuries after King John surrendered at Runnymede.

*

In the third book of the *Aeneid*, Aeneas narrates, for Dido, the travels and travails that have taken him from the rubble of Troy to the splendor of Carthage. Carthage, like its alluring queen, is no more than a rest stop on a journey from crushing defeat and exile to resounding triumph and empire. Early on, however, Aeneas and his crew wander, they remain haunted by reminders of the wreck of the past they have yet to convert to triumph. Though Aeneas and his men launch their ships in search of empire, Aeneas' party lands "in a far away land, in vast fields consecrated to Mars and tilled by Thracians, reigned by the bitter Lycurgus" ("Terra procul vas-tis colitur Mavortia campis, Thraces arant, acri quondam regnata Lycurgo" [III.15–16]).[48] Both the deity of war and this king renowned for his savage rule signal the character of the land Aeneas is about to encounter. Still Aeneas attempts to establish a city named after himself: "Aeneadasque meo nomen de nomine fingo" (III.18). The choice of *fingere* here is notable, preserving both the sense of found-ing and finding, perhaps signaling a certain naïveté, as if a new city, a new empire, a new order could be founded without re-finding some uncanny fragment of past experience.

To consecrate his founding act—consolidating masculine subjec-tivity and political identity all at once—Aeneas sacrifices a bull to Jove and then builds an altar to Venus, seeking leaves and branches from a myrtle grove to shade it. Yet as he plucks bristly branches and tender shoots from the trees, he witnesses "a thing terrible and wondrous to see or speak of" ("horrendum et dictu video mirabile monstrum" [III.26]). Drops of black blood pour from the branches and roots torn up by Aeneas, staining the land he has sought to make pure ("et terram tabo maculant"). Aeneas, witnessing these unexpected wounds, relates to Dido a terrifying encounter with someone else's pain: "I was frozen in horror, my limbs quaking, and frigid blood congealed about my heart in fear" ("mihi frigidus horror / membra quatit, gelidusque coit formidine sanguis" [III.29–30]). Following this irruption of unsanctified blood, Aeneas tries force, dragging harder at the roots and branches, only to see the blood gush harder. When brutality fails, Aeneas appeals to the sacred, praying to local Nymphs and father Mars, to re-establish a violent, sacred order in the face of inexplicable recalcitrance. Aeneas continues his bizarre tug of war with the tree, pulling at it a third time, "kneeling on the ground to struggle against it" ("adgredior genibusque adversae obluctor harenae" [III.38]).

Aeneas struggles to wrench free portions of the tree for the sake of their use in his ritual of consecration, attempting to transform a living body into dead, useable matter, rendering land no more than a resource, these trees no more than an obstacle to imperial clearing. And yet, in attempting to found a new city free of the damaging failures of the past, Aeneas collides with the uncanny return of a painful history, figured here as a speaking, bleeding tree. The voice he hears is not found but re-found. After protesting Aeneas' rude treatment and stressing the impiety of an act committed by his otherwise pious hands, the voice reveals its identity and its proximity to Aeneas in a moment closely resembling Aeneas' earlier attempt to found a city by identifying it with himself. Justifying its request for mercy, the voice cries, "I am not born foreign to you of Troy" ("non me tibi Troia externum tulit" [III.42–3]). The intimacy of the address to Aeneas stresses individual likeness as well as family or kin relation, as the suffering "I" displaces Aeneas' name: "For I am Polydorus" ("nam Polydorus ego" [III.45]).

Whereas Aeneas attempts to construct, from the catastrophic fall of Troy, a new sacrificial and social order, Polydorus represents the anti-type of Aeneas' violent consecration. Polydorus becomes the site of the failure of sacred and national order to be established. Fostered with Lycurgus by Priam, Polydorus, we learn, was slain for material and political reasons. Not only did he carry a great deal of gold, but Polydorus was an untrustworthy Trojan in a time of war. While Aeneas attempts to mark the landscape with his name, making himself a signifier rather than a man, Polydorus represents the consistent return of materiality as a variety of suffering that epic masculinity cannot beat back. The very spears that fix Polydorus to the earth seem to return in the horrid and bristly thicket of vegetation that Aeneas hacks into; Polydorus becomes the fertilizing soil in which violence begets violence. And while he may serve as the Thracian scapegoat, the material lust for Polydorus' gold remains most memorable and elicits moral commentary: "what will not gather in the human heart for the sake of the unholy hunger for gold!" ("quid non mortalia pectora cogis / auri sacra fames!" [III.56]). The double sense of *sacer*, which refers to both the polluted and the sacred, orbits a lump of desirable matter.

Polydorus' standing depends upon his injury. He speaks from and about his violation. That is the condition of speech. There is no hope of redress, only appeasement. The imperial logic bolstered by heroic masculinity renders land property, trees resources. Polydorus, as tree, speaks of necessary interconnections—*do not wound me, I am of you*. But such a call to kinship would interrupt the devices by which Aeneas establishes himself as a person with standing and a capacity to act, not suffer. All Polydorus can say is do not wound me. All Aeneas can hear is the call of the sea and the narrative drive of empire. The scions of Troy thus decide to leave the land polluted by the murder of Polydorus, returning to their highly useable ships from the useless suffering of a bleeding tree. All Aeneas can do in attempt to appease the ghosts of suffering and defeat is to rebury Polydorus, build another altar, and make further offerings in the hope of laying to rest this voice. A. Bartlett Giamatti argues that, "[w]ith Aeneas, we learn to look forward, not back; forward to the new city, the new hope—not another Troy, not even a new Carthage, but Rome."[49] It is only by clearing the growth of the past, as Aeneas unwitting attempts to clear Polydorus, that epic thrives and along with it, as Giamatti analyzes, "the explosive, anarchic ways in which new growth means forcible tearing and sundering from the old."[50] Aeneas can only be a person— indeed, a Person—by discarding interconnection for singularity, suffering for action, injured speech for assertive self-nomination.

How seemingly unlike Virgil's tree is Ovid's in the second book of *The Metamorphoses*, where the Heliades undergo a spectacular transformation. Indeed, the lesser-known end of the story of Phaeton concerns his mother and sisters, the Heliades, and it turns away from the masculine terror of suffering and interconnection to the enduring pain of women living in the wake of great violence. Phaeton's mother, Clymene, laments the pain of her loss, in a wild display that follows "all / that can be said when such disaster falls" (II.330–1).[51] She weeps, wails, tears her clothes, and attempts to warm the cold tomb with her bared breasts (II.330–9). More extreme is the grief of Phaeton's sisters. For four months, the girls join their mother in grief, and, in so doing, the narrative stresses, turn a singular practice into custom ("nam morem fecerat usus"). As the grief of the sisters solidifies into habit, so too does that grief change the shape of the sisters' bodies. Their limbs grow stiff as they are transformed into trees—feet becoming roots, arms turning to branches, hair to leaves. Bark slowly grows over the surface of their bodies. Their mother, hearing their cries of dismay and wonder, attempts to rip the bark from their flesh, at which point blood flows from these wounds and the daughters cry:

> "parce, precor, mater," quaecumque est saucia, clamat,
> "parce, precor! nostrum laceratur in arbore corpus.
> iamque vale"

> "O spare me, I pray you, mother," and each one is wounded and cries
> "Spare me, I pray, you! It is our body torn in this tree. And now farewell." (2.361–3)[52]

The mother, here, attempts to save her daughters from suffering transformation. Yet she lays hands upon them violently, and in the process fails to recognize what her daughters have become as George Sandys's translation makes painfully clear: "she strove to take, / Them, from themselves" ("truncis avellere corpora temptat / et teneros manibus ramos abrumpit" [II.358–9]).[53] There is no difference, anymore, between human and tree—trunk and branches have been utterly identified with one another. And yet the mother, perhaps like Aeneas, cannot recognize that interdependency. It is unavailable to her. The daughters are now foreign to their own mother. And their plea is for separation—to be left alone and to be spared human touch.

One tree seems to cry "I am of you" while the other cries "we are no longer you." If Virgil disavows the forms of suffering and interconnection that would interrupt the pinnacle of personhood—active, masculine self-assertion—the sisters of Phaeton offer a cautionary tale of a related variety, one concerning interconnection, about which the recent work of Frédéric Neyrat cautions skepticism:

> Then there is the idea, repeated as a mantra, according to which everything is interconnected. This is what we will call the *principle of principles* of ecology and environmentalism . . . today the notion of interconnection constitutes a kind of theoretical, economic, and political trap that reveals itself in the following way: Since everything is a network linked together, interconnected, then there can be no distance possible in relation to the world in which we live, so we should simply accept the world as it is.[54]

He calls, instead, for "an ecology of separation" that works against "the madness of generalized interconnection . . . When everything is considered to be continuous and connected without a rift or outside, automated reactions replace decisions."[55] The mother of Phaeton sustains the bond of human kinship that Virgil fails to recognize. But she disavows the more-than figural hybridity of human and tree in this episode. Once tree, her daughters are neither person nor kin. Easy assumptions about kinship within or across life forms seem as disastrous as paranoid rejections of such kinship. What these trees seem to indicate is a paradox of interconnectivity. The dubious insistence upon human singularity relies on violence. And yet, interconnection and interdependency provide no simple antidote. In fact, personhood and interdependency might very well be mutually exclusive notions, meaning that the easy extension of personhood to other life forms and the insistence upon interdependence might be two sides of that same problematic coin.

*

Bleeding trees appear not in the infamous *selva oscura* in which Dante finds himself at the beginning of *Inferno* but rather in the wood of suicides, where the souls of the despairing, who have committed violence against themselves, fall as seeds into the seventh circle. There, they grow into plants fed on by vicious harpies. Or so Dante discovers when Virgil encourages him to pluck a branch from one of the trees and encounter a marvel that would be unbelievable unless experienced. From the bloody wound issues a voice crying, "Why do you tear me? Have you no spirit of pity? We were men, and now are turned to stocks" ("Perché mi scerpi? / Non hai tu spirito di pietade alcuno? / Uomini fummo, e or siam fatti sterpi" [13.35–7]).[56] The encounter is understood to be a wonder at the edge of reality, and the perpetrator of violence finds himself accused of injury in a commingling of blood and speech. In this case, the trees insist on their former humanity; their current status as living beings remains ambiguous since they are now "stocks" or dried-out twigs. Most remarkable, however, is Dante's focus on the quality of voice:

> Come d'stizzo verde ch'arso sia
> da l'un de' capi, che da l'altro geme
> e cigola per vento che va via,
> sì de la scheggia rotta usciva insieme
> parole e sangue.

As from a green brand that is burning on one end, and drips from the other, hissing with escaping air, so from that broken twig came out words and blood together. (13.40–5)

Voice is not smooth or immediate but full of gaps, static, and the sound of matter pressed into speech. Ariosto too foregrounds the materiality of voice although in a humorous iteration of the bleeding tree in *Orlando Furioso*, where the captive knight Astolfo has been turned into a tree by the Circe-like enchantress Alcina. His former compatriot hears a mysterious sound and "Rogero mased looked round about / If any man or woman he might see." He sees instead a tree:

> And as an arme of tree from bodie rent
> By peasants strength with many a sturdie stroke
> When in the fire the moisture all is spent
> The emptie places fild with aire and smoke
> Do boile and strive and find at last a vent
> When of the brand a shiver out is broke,
> So did the tree strive, bend, writhe, wring, and breake
> Till at a little hole it thus did speake. (6.27)[57]

Reduction is part of Ariosto's cynical game, as a formerly glorious warrior now speaks haltingly through a tiny hole, but Dante's portrait is far more devastated. The souls of suicides receive a special punishment. They are tormented by the bodies they cast aside in despair:

> Come l'altre verrem per nostre spoglie,
> ma non però ch'alcuna sen rivesta,
> ché non è giusto aver ciò ch'om si toglie.
> Qui le strascineremo, e per la mesta
> selva saranno i nostri corpi appesi,
> ciascuno al prun de l'ombra sua molesta.

> Like the rest we shall come, each for his cast-off body, but not, however, that any may inhabit it again; for it is not just that a man have what he robs himself of. Hither shall we drag them, and through the mournful wood our bodies will be hung, each on the thornbush of its nocuous shade. (13.103–8)

The heft of the body fascinates Dante throughout *Inferno*. Here, bodily resurrection implies a reunion of body and soul at the final judgment, a reunion forbidden those who despairingly cast off their flesh. If injury makes standing and the capacity to make a claim possible, the voice might be one we cannot recognize because of its thickened materiality. It might speak a language we do not understand. It might be a voice choked with blood. It might be an imposition to require it to have a voice at all since the voice seems to be, primarily, for our benefit. Even the recent insistence on the communicative capacities of plants might be more grist for the mill of an anthropological machine into which vegetation is fed and out of which emerge forests and woods designed for human use. Perhaps, too, these trees complicate a notion animating so much ecologically oriented criticism that advocating for shared materiality or embodiment will moderate the exceptionality of the human. In Dante's bleeding forest, it seems more likely we remain too fascinated by injury, too mystified by hybridity, and too ambivalent about our own flesh to think so expansively.

*

When Tasso took up the topos of the bleeding tree, the problem of its irreality became the signature theme as did the living status of the trees in question. Early on, we learn that the trees are one of many obstacles to the core telos of the poem, the reclamation of Jerusalem. The sorcerer Ismeno enchants the forests to resist Christian progress, calling upon legions of demons to aid him:

> "Keepe you this forrest well, keepe euery tree,
> Numbred I giue you them and truly tould;
> As soules of men in bodies cloathed be,
> So euerie plant a sprite shall hide and hould,
> With trembling feare make all the Christians flee,
> When they presume to cut these Cedars ould" (13.8)[58]

And yet as he does so, Tasso embeds what might seem like two unnecessary details. First, he describes the trees as inhabited by spirits, a detail noteworthy in an age that still sustained the Aristotelian idea that all living bodies, including human, were understood to be inhabited by a vegetative soul or spirit, which described the nutritive or basic living functions of the body. Second, Ismeno relies on both the terror-provoking nature of these infernal spirits *and* the status of the Cedars, as if the trees themselves by virtue of their age or by virtue of containing a living spirit would inhibit human interference.

Tasso stages multiple encounters with the trees, each of which renders more ambiguous their status as life forms. First, the army faces a synesthetic cacophony of environmental terror. They approach the woods,

> When from the groue a fearefull sound out brakes,
> As if some earthquake hill and mountaine tore,
> Wherein the southren winde a rumbling makes,
> Or like sea waues against the craggie shore,
> There lions gromble, there hisse scalie snakes,
> There howle the woolues, the rugged beares there rore,
> There trumpets shrill are heard and thunders fell,
> And all these sounds one sound expressed well. (13.21)

Sound alone is enough to terrify and more importantly to confuse the soldiers who become dislocated—do they face soldiers, spirits, or animals? Are they on land or sea? Following the failure of the army in general, the heretofore implacable Switzer knight Alcasto encounters the ensorceled forest, which appears to be both a conflagration and an enemy fortress:

> The fire encreast, and built a stately wall
> Of burning coales, quicke sparkes, and embers hot,
> And with bright flames the wood enuiron'd all. (13.27)

The odd castle is not only made of contrary materials—wood and the very fires that Godfrey's army could use to clear a route to the city— but it is also garrisoned by "strange monsters on the battlement / In loathsome forms" (13.28). Alcasto cannot bear the odd intensity of the forest, which is both infernally shaped and shapeless all at once. Thus "fled the man and with sad feare withdrew, / Though feare till then he neuer felt nor knew" (13.28).

Of all those who approach the infernal blockade that is this forest, Tancred seems most attuned to the irreality of the scene. He passes easily the fires, which do not burn, and he passes the strange monsters, who disappear. But in an episode that has resonated across the centuries, Tancred appears to encounter the spirit of his beloved and enemy, the Saracen Clorinda whom he has recently and inadvertently slain in battle, in the body of a tree he attempts to cut down:

> He drew his sword at last and gaue the tree
> A mightie blow, that made a gaping wound,
> Out of the rift red streames he trickling see
> That all bebled the verdant plaine around,

His haire start vp, yet once againe stroake he,
He nould giue ouer till the end he found
    Of this aduenture, when with plaint and mone,
(As from some hollow graue) he heard one grone.

"Enough enough" the voice lamenting said,
"Tancred thou hast me hurt, thou didst me driue
Out of the bodie of a noble maid,
Who with me liu'd, whom late I kept on liue,
And now within this woefull Cipresse laid,
My tender rinde thy weapon sharpe doth riue,
Cruell, ist not enough thy foes to kill,
But in their graues wilt thou torment them still?

"I was Clorinda, now imprison'd heere,
(Yet not alone) within this plant I dwell,
For euerie Pagan Lord and Christian peere,
Before the cities walles last day that fell,
(In bodies new or graues I wote not cleere)
But here they are confin'd by magikes spell,
So that each tree hath life, and sense each bou,
A murdrer if thou cut one twist art thou." (13.41–3)

Tancred's approach to the infernal forest is legendary in its reception inasmuch as the episode triggered a wide range of art works,
especially opera, and critical conversations. In a rather brief moment
to which later scholars have had frequent recourse, Sigmund Freud
evokes Tancred's wounding of Clorinda as "the most moving poetic
picture" of the force of unbidden and compulsive repetition.[59] Cathy
Carruth influentially expands this reading to encompass not just the
compulsion to repeat but a broader sense of traumatic experience:

> The voice of his beloved addresses him and, in this address, bears witness
> to the past he has unwittingly repeated. Tancred's story thus represents
> traumatic experience not only as the enigma of a human agent's repeated
> and unknowing acts of repetition but also as the enigma of the otherness
> of a human voice that cries out from the wound, a voice that witnesses a
> truth that Tancred himself cannot fully know.[60]

Ruth Leys, more recently, in a broader a corrective to Carruth's
theories of trauma, disputes this reading of Tasso, insisting that both
Tancred and Clorinda remain painfully "knowing" about the tragic
and inadvertent slaying. Moreover, she argues, Carruth makes a
victim out of the aggressor thus ignoring the masculine violence of

Tancred by bestowing on him the diagnosis of a sufferer of traumatic neurosis. Leys is certainly right to point out the way that Carruth seems to allow the wound to circulate from Clorinda to Tancred, with little mention of the role of the former in the whole drama and perhaps to disastrous ethical effect. "For if," Leys argues, "according to her analysis, the murderer Tancred can become the victim of the trauma and the voice of Clorinda testimony to *his* wound, then Carruth's logic would turn other perpetrators into victims too."[61] More recently, Kathleen Biddick reads the episode and histories of trauma in light of "the theologico-political vicissitudes of pleasure and pain, flesh and body at stake in the cult of martyrs, then and now."[62] Despite a series of weighty invocations of pain, trauma, and martyrdom, in none of these readings does voice or injury attach to the tree—only to the supposed spirit within, which the narrative already revealed is not, in fact, Clorinda, but a hallucination provoked by a demonic spirit summoned by Ismeno, confirming one principle these readings share, which is that some varieties of damage do go unnoticed.

The stunning not-so coincidence of Tancred's slaying of his beloved captivates the attention, to be sure, as the operatic legacy of this episode testifies. But what proves even more remarkable for my purposes here is the conclusion Tancred draws from the encounter. For he, unlike these readers of Tasso, is mindful of the tree he wounds. Amid both heart-wrenching grief and the terror of supernatural events, Tancred remains coolly aware of the irreality of the scene: "So feard the knight, yet he both knew and thought / All were illusions false by witchcraft wrought" (13.44). Tancred enters a structure of disavowal, as if to say, "I know very well that Clorinda is dead and in fact converted to Christianity and therefore not really in this tree because this is the product of witchcraft but I will respond in terror and flee nonetheless." While trauma offers one answer why this disavowal might take place, another explanation concerns the trees themselves, and this answer he gives to Godfrey when he reports his failure. He speaks of the false fires and the illusory demons on the battlement but then oddly makes no mention of Clorinda:

"What would you more? each tree through all that wood
Hath sense, hath life, hath speech, like humaine kind,
I heard their words, as in that groue I stood,
That mournfull voice still, still I beare in minde:
And (as they were of flesh) the purple blood,
At euery blow streames from the wounded rind,
    No, no, not I, nor any else (I trow)
    Hath powre to cut one leafe, one branch, one bow." (13.49)

The position Tancred takes is not that he is too weak to face an evil sorcerer or a Saracen knight or even his dead beloved. The claim he makes is that the trees—these old Cedars—represent living entities that ought not be harmed. The trees have sense, life, and speech "like humaine kind." They are, in other words, persons capable of speech by virtue of their injuries. The lack of "powre" Tancred imagines that he "or any else" has in the face of these trees is not a lack of might but a lack of will to wound these living figures. Rather remarkably, Tancred's "trauma" might also be described as a concern for the living localized in the vulnerable bark of trees whose violability inhibits Christian heroic endeavor with a different ethical claim. That claim is only more clear in contrast to the real ambition of the Christian army, whose goal of reclaiming Jerusalem requires not only access to the city but the materials to build engines of war. As Godfrey explains to Rinaldo, who eventually succeeds where Tancred failed,

> That aged wood whence heretofore we got
> (To build our scaling engins) timber fit,
> Is now the fearfull seat (but how none wot)
> Where ougly feends and damned spirits sit. (18.3)

Although Rinaldo does face temptations in the forest—pleasure being his obstacle, not pain or trauma—he easily dispatches the spirits. Then,

> Sent were the workmen thither, thence they brought
> Timber enough, by good aduise select,
> And though, by skillesse builders fram'd and wrought,
> Their engins rude and rammes were late erect,
> Yet now the forts and towres (from whence they fought)
> Were framed by a cunning architect,
>   William, of all the Genoas Lord and guide,
> Which late rul'd all the seas from side to side. (18.41)

Conquest requires that a forest be denuded of any status, natural or supernatural, that indicates the capacities of a living form that must be regarded and that would inhibit resource extraction and martial use. Tasso's disenchanted forest perhaps evokes yet another Ovidian forest violated in the eighth book of *The Metamorphoses* as by "Leud Erisichthon . . . Who Ceres groues with steele profan'd."[63] He strikes down a grand oak, which "sigh'd and trembled at the threatening stroke" and "then wounded by his impious hand, the blood / Gusht from th' incision in a purple flood" (8.758, 761–2). No voice requests a cessation of his brutality because it cannot be expected. He is, instead, warned by a voice: "A Nymph am I, within this tree inshrin'd, / Belou'd of Ceres. O prophane of mind, / Vengeance is neere thee" (770–1). Vengeance comes in form of famine, as Erisichthon receives a curse of insatiable hunger. In Ovid's tale, an insatiable lust for resources finds its poetic justice in a deadly famine. But the core crime is desacralization. In Tasso's iteration, any remaining spirits in the trees—be they fallen heroes, woodland sprites of pagan lore, or demons conjured by the black arts—must be driven forth. The forest is denuded of any figure, even dubious figures, who might articulate claims. Plants cannot be persons because they must be property as certainly as the Christians must reclaim Jerusalem. Tasso's bleeding tree places the logics of conquest and resource extraction, which render forests property, in tension with Tancred's hallucination of personhood and his subsequent disavowal of the irreality of what he experiences. The paradox of pathos is that arboreal personhood, anchored in vulnerable sensation, may be experienced only as a hallucination because standing is, despite some shared morphology between person and tree, yet another all-too-human institution.

*

Amidst the often-confused, woodsy wanderings of Edmund Spenser's Redcrosse knight in *The Faerie Queene*, the would-be paragon of Holiness has his own experience in a dark forest of a bloody spectacle. In yet another example of his less-than perfected virtue, Redcrosse travels in the company of the disguised enchantress Duessa, who we will soon discover has a penchant for turning former lovers into trees. The knight attempts to fashion a garland for his beloved and in so doing unleashes a torrent of blood and voice:

> He pluckt a bough; out of whose rift there came
> Small drops of gory bloud, that trickled downe the same.
>
> Therewith a piteous yelling voyce was heard,
>   Crying, O spare with guilty hands to teare
>   My tender sides in this rough rynd embard,
>   But fly, ah fly far hence away, for feare
>   Least to you hap, that happened to me heare,
>   And to this wretched Lady, my deare loue,
>   O too deare loue, loue bought with death too deare.
>   Astond he stood, and vp his haire did houe,
> And with that suddein horror could no member moue. (1.2.30–1[64])

The tree, formerly the man Fradubio, tells of his captivation by the evil Duessa, who eventually transforms him and his beloved Fralissa into trees. Fralissa, notably, never speaks while the words of Fradubio wash over the Redcrosse knight without providing the suitable moral warning. The knight of holiness should see himself in the weakness of Fradubio since he now travels with Duessa. Instead, Redcrosse imagines the possibility of repair:

> When all this speech the liuing tree had spent,
>   The bleeding bough did thrust into the ground,
>   That from the bloud he might be innocent,
>   And with fresh clay did close the wooden wound. (1.2.44)

And yet, reparation here really aims at rendering Redcrosse "innocent" of injury. But injury did, in fact, happen. There is no undoing it, even as a "wooden wound" is stopped with clay. If the fantasy of standing is that one many establish relevance and register a claim based on injury, a particularly pernicious aspect of this complex is that voice is a product of injury, making restoration an elusive fantasy.

Perhaps no bleeding tree more volubly speaks of the impossibility of repair than the figure into which Lavinia is so cruelly fashioned in Shakespeare's *Titus Andronicus*. Marcus, uncle to the raped and mutilated daughter of the Andronici, discovers her hiding in the wake of her violation in a forest. Although he does not break a branch from any tree, and although Lavinia is not literally implanted within or transformed into a tree as in these other narratives, the virtual signatures of the topos seem to overlay her body. Marcus addresses her:

> Speak, gentle niece, what stern ungentle hands
> Have lopp'd and hew'd and made thy body bare
> Of her two branches, those sweet ornaments,
> Whose circling shadows kings have sought to sleep in,
> And might not gain so great a happiness
> As have thy love? Why dost not speak to me?
> Alas, a crimson river of warm blood,
> Like to a bubbling fountain stirr'd with wind,
> Doth rise and fall between thy rosed lips,
> Coming and going with thy honey breath.
> But, sure, some Tereus hath deflowered thee,
> And, lest thou shouldst detect him, cut thy tongue.
> Ah, now thou turn'st away thy face for shame!
> And, notwithstanding all this loss of blood,
> As from a conduit with three issuing spouts,

Yet do thy cheeks look red as Titan's face
Blushing to be encountered with a cloud.
Shall I speak for thee? shall I say 'tis so?
O, that I knew thy heart; and knew the beast,
That I might rail at him, to ease my mind! (2.4.16–35)[65]

Marcus insists, here, on familial connection—she is first called his "cousin" and then in this speech his "gentle niece"—although later when he presents her to Titus he says, "This was thy daughter." Titus's reply, "Why, Marcus, so she is," provides limited comfort. Her injury and transformation threaten to denude her not only of speech but of recognizable social or familial identity. Jennifer Munroe has argued that this is a pivotal moment for considering what it means to represent others, a critical issue for understanding human entanglement with the nonhuman world, whether one takes up Stone's guardianship model (in which humans speak for trees) or Latour's Parliament of Things (in which humans somehow transcribe and co-author the world with mute things but without speaking for them). As Munroe puts it, Marcus's perhaps compassionately-intended act resonates uncomfortably, since "speaking for nonhuman Nature often goes hand in hand with speaking for or on behalf of women and non-dominant Others."[66] As disturbing as this supplanting of voice is the prospect that this figure is damaged not only beyond repair but so utterly that when she does speak for herself, later in the play, her only subject is her injury. Lavinia eventually identifies her assailants, assists in her father's revenge plot, and dutifully dies at his hands to spare herself, her father, and her line the shame of her violation. The paradox of voice, here, is not only that there is no getting out of the problem of speaking for others but that, even if there is, the identification of a capacity to make a claim with the fact of injury suggests both that there is no speaking beyond injury and consequently that there is no space outside of a damage that is irreparable.

*

Perhaps it would be best to admit that we still live in an age of bleeding trees, even as environmental law grows ever more sophisticated and environmental advocacy grows ever more urgent. Plants may seem closer and closer to being persons, at least in theory, and yet we live still with hallucinations of rights and personhood because the only way trees gain standing is to be under some form of guardianship, which requires speaking for not only individual trees but also whole environments, both of which constitute complex ecosystems that include far more than trees. The complexity of adjudicating needs and protections with respect to legal standing depends on the attribution of fundamentally humanoid forms, which may or may not be analogous to arboreal functions. And yet, the assertion of some affinity for or interconnection with vegetative life is not likely to prove adequate. Trees may stand, suffer, and communicate but do they do so in a way that makes sense with respect to human capacities and institutions? Or, if they do, do the trees benefit as much as we might from such analogies? Might, in fact, "person" really be just another stand-in for "human"? Moreover, can we only hear, or imagine we hear, such voices when trees bleed or forests burn? If injury is the precondition for voice, it is perhaps already too late to listen. A *topos* like the bleeding tree remains important because it carries centuries of contradiction and this signals a fundamental need for imaginative forms of figuration to convey what will not quite fit when we extend existing categories, like personhood, to nonhumans or to some idea of nature itself, when we assume, and even enforce, interconnection or interdependency without a sufficient understanding of separation and nonrelation, when we validate the notion that voice can only emerge from violation, or when we assume the only way to make a claim, and therefore also the only way to stand, is as a person.

Notes

1. For a general treatment of the topos, see Shirley Clay Scott, "From Polydorus to Fradubio: The History of a Topos," *Spenser Studies: A Renaissance Poetry Annual* 7 (1986): 27–57. In a series of articles, William Kennedy treats various instances of the topos with respect to the workings of irony, allegory, and rhetoric; see "Rhetoric, Allegory, and Dramatic Modality in Spenser's Fradubio Episode," *English Literary Renaissance* 3 (1973): 351–68; "Irony, Allegoresis, and Allegory in Virgil, Ovid, and Dante," *Arcadia* 7 (1972): 115–34; "Ariosto's Ironic Allegory," *MLN* 88 (1973): 44–67; "The Problem of Allegory in Tasso's *Gerusalemme Liberata*," *Italian Quarterly* 15–16 (1972): 27–51.
2. I treat this subject at greater length although in primarily non-ecological terms in "Reading Bleeding Trees: The Poetics of Other People's Pain," which is the first chapter of *The Pain of Reformation: Spenser, Vulnerability, and the Ethics of Masculinity* (New York: Fordham University Press, 2012), 47–74.
3. All references (to sonnet and line) are to William Shakespeare, *The New Oxford Shakespeare: Modern Critical Edition*, ed. Gary Taylor, John Jowett, Terri Bourus, and Gabriel Egan (Oxford: Oxford University Press, 2016) and will appear in the body of the text.

4. With thanks to Laurie Shannon for an illuminating conversation about "ripeness" and the law.
5. *Wex Legal Dictionary*, s.v. "ripe," <https://www.law.cornell.edu/wex/ripe> (last accessed April 24, 2019).
6. *Black's Law Dictionary*, s.v. "person."
7. Thomas Hobbes, *Leviathan*, ed. Richard E. Flatham and David Johnston (New York: W. W. Norton, 1997), 88.
8. Christopher Stone, *Should Trees Have Standing? Law, Morality, and the Environment* (Oxford: Oxford University Press, 2010), 7.
9. Stone, *Should Trees Have Standing?*, 2–3.
10. Daniel McGraw, "Fighting pollution: Toledo residents want personhood status for Lake Erie," *The Guardian*, February 19, 2019.
11. Luc Ferry, *The Ecological Order*, trans. Carol Volk (Chicago: University of Chicago Press, 1995), 139.
12. Michel Serres, *The Natural Contract*, trans. Elisabeth MacArthur and William Paulson (Ann Arbor: University of Michigan Press, 1995), 15, 38.
13. Bruno Latour, *Politics of Nature: How to Bring the Sciences into Democracy* (Cambridge, MA: Harvard University Press, 2004), 235.
14. Julian Yates and Garrett Sullivan, "Introduction," *Shakespeare Studies* 39 (2011): 23.
15. Yates and Sullivan, "Introduction," 25.
16. Bruno Latour, *We Have Never Been Modern* (Cambridge, MA: Harvard University Press, 1993), 142.
17. Frédéric Neyrat, *The Unconstructable Earth: An Ecology of Separation*, trans. Drew S. Burk (New York: Fordham University Press, 2018), 103–4.
18. *Black's Law Dictionary*, s.v. "standing."
19. Cited in *Black's Law Dictionary*, s.v. "standing."
20. Roderick Frazier Nash, *The Rights of Nature: A History of Environmental Ethics* (Madison, WI: University of Wisconsin Press, 1989), 13.
21. Mark Brown, "Shakespeare's Globe to stage King John for 800th anniversary of Magna Carta," *The Guardian*, November 21, 2014.
22. See Richard Wilson, "A Scribbled Form: Shakespeare's Missing Magna Carta," *Shakespeare Quarterly* 67.3 (Fall 2016): 344–70.
23. Dominic Cavendish, "*King John*, Shakespeare's Globe: 'could hardly be more timely,'" *The Telegraph*, June 7, 2015, <https://www.telegraph.co.uk/culture/theatre/theatre-reviews/11658067/King-John-Shakespeares-Globe-review-could-hardly-be-more-timely.html> (last accessed April 24, 2019).
24. Peter Linebaugh, *The Magna Carta Manifesto: Liberties and Commons for All* (Berkeley: University of California Press, 2008), 22.
25. Linebaugh, *Magna Carta Manifesto*, 4.
26. Nash, *Rights of Nature*, 129.
27. Gary L. Francione, *Animals as Persons: Essays on the Abolition of Animal Exploitation* (New York: Columbia University Press, 2008), 25.

28. David R. Boyd, *The Rights of Nature* (Toronto: ECW Press, 2017), 48.
29. Sue Donaldson and Will Kymlicka, *Zoopolis: A Political Theory of Animal Rights* (Oxford: Oxford University Press, 2011), 13.
30. Donaldson and Kymlicka, *Zoopolis*, 14.
31. Qtd. in Maya K. Van Rossum, *The Green Amendment: Securing Our Right to a Healthy Environment* (Austin, TX: Disruption Books, 2017), 9.
32. Qtd. in Van Rossum, *Green Amendment*, 12.
33. Van Rossum, *Green Amendment*, 13.
34. John Evelyn, *Sylva, or a Discourse of Forest-Trees and the Propagation of Timber* (London, 1664), 112.
35. Vinciane Despret, *What Would Animals Say if We Asked the Right Questions?* (Minneapolis: University of Minnesota Press, 2016).
36. Peter Wohlleben, *The Hidden Life of Trees: What They Feel, How They Communicate* (Vancouver: Greystone Books, 2016).
37. Michael Marder, *The Philosopher's Plant: An Intellectual Herbarium* (New York: Columbia University Press, 2014), xiv.
38. Marder, *Philosopher's Plant*, xvii.
39. Matthew Hall, *Plants as Persons* (Albany, NY: State University of New York Press, 2011), 3, 5.
40. Jeffrey T. Nealon, *Plant Theory: Biopower and Vegetable Life* (Stanford: Stanford University Press, 2016), xv.
41. Jeffrey Theis, *Writing the Forest in Early Modern England: A Sylvan Pastoral Nation* (Pittsburgh: Duquesne University Press, 2005).
42. Vin Nardizzi, *Wooden Os: Shakespeare's Theaters and England's Trees* (Toronto: University of Toronto Press, 2013), 20. See also his recent special issue "Premodern Plants," *Postmedieval* 9.4 (November 2018).
43. Victoria Kahn, *The Future of Illusion: Political Theology and Early Modern Texts* (Chicago: University of Chicago Press, 2016), 37.
44. Kahn, *Future of Illusion*, 81.
45. Henry S. Turner, *The Corporate Commonwealth: Pluralism and Political Fiction in England, 1516–1651* (Chicago: University of Chicago Press, 2016), xvi.
46. Turner, *Corporate Commonwealth*, xv, xiii.
47. Kevin Curran, *Shakespeare's Legal Ecologies: Law and Distributed Selfhood* (Evanston, IL: Northwestern University Press, 2017), 11.
48. All references (to book and line number) are to Virgil, *Eclogues, Georgics, Aeneid I–VI*, trans. H. R. Fairclough (Cambridge, MA: Harvard University Press, 1999) and will appear in the body of the text. Translations, unless otherwise noted, are my own.
49. A. Bartlett Giamatti, *Play of Double Senses: Spenser's* Faerie Queene (Englewood Cliffs, NJ: Prentice-Hall, 1975), 17.
50. Giamatti, *Play of Double Senses*, 18.
51. Unless otherwise noted, all references (to book and line number) are to Ovid, *Metamorphoses: Books 1–8*, trans. Frank Justus Miller, rev. G. P. Goold (Cambridge, MA: Harvard University Press, 2014).

52. Translation mine. As translated by Miller: "Oh, spare me, mother; spare, I beg you. 'Tis my body that you are tearing in the tree. And now farewell."

53. George Sandys, *Ovid's Metamorphosis: Englished, Mythologized, and Represented in Figures*, ed. Karl K. Hulley and Stanley T. Vandersall (Lincoln, NE: University of Nebraska Press, 1970).

54. Neyrat, *Unconstructable Earth*, 12.

55. Neyrat, *Unconstructable Earth*, 14–15.

56. All references (to canto and line) are to Dante Alighieri, *The Divine Comedy: Inferno*, trans. Charles Singleton (Princeton, NJ: Princeton University Press, 1970) and will appear in the body of the text.

57. All references (to canto and stanza) are to Ludovico Ariosto, *Orlando Furioso: Translated into English Heroical Verse by Sir John Harington*, ed. Robert McNulty (Oxford: Oxford University Press, 1971) and will appear in the body of the text.

58. All references (to canto and stanza) are to Torquato Tasso, *Godfrey of Bulloigne: A critical edition of Edward Fairfax's translation of Tasso's Gerusalemme Liberata, together with Fairfax's Original Poems*, ed. Kathleen M. Lea and T. M. Gang (Oxford: Clarendon Press, 1981) and will appear in the body of the text.

59. Sigmund Freud, *Beyond the Pleasure Principle*, trans. and ed. James Strachey (New York: W. W. Norton, 1989), 17.

60. Cathy Carruth, *Unclaimed Experience: Trauma, Narrative, and History* (Baltimore: Johns Hopkins University Press, 1996), 3.

61. Ruth Leys, *Trauma: A Genealogy* (Chicago: University of Chicago Press, 2000), 247.

62. Kathleen Biddick, "Unbinding the Flesh in the Time That Remains: Crusader Martyrdom Then and Now," *GLQ* 13.2–3 (2007): 198.

63. Sandys, *Ovid's Metamorphosis*, 8.738, 741.

64. All references (to book, canto, and stanza) are to Edmund Spenser, *The Faerie Queene*, ed. A. C. Hamilton (New York: Longman, 1977) and will appear in the body of the text.

65. All references (to act, scene, and line number) are to Shakespeare, *New Oxford Shakespeare* and will appear in the body of the text.

66. Jennifer Munroe, "Is it Really Ecocritical if It Isn't Feminist? The Dangers of 'Speaking For' in Ecological Studies and *Titus Andronicus*," in Jennifer Munroe, Edward J. Geisweidt, and Lynne Bruckner, eds., *Ecological Approaches to Early Modern English Texts: A Field Guide to Reading and Teaching* (New York: Routledge, 2015), 38. For an account of how early modern women writers understood their relationship to nature and to the prospect of speaking for nature, see Sylvia Bowerbank, *Speaking for Nature: Women and Ecologies of Early Modern England* (Baltimore: Johns Hopkins University Press, 2004).

Chapter 6

Aping Personhood
Holly Dugan

"We are most definitely not asking the court to redefine the term 'human-being.'"

—Steven Wise, Nonhuman Rights Project

In December 2013, Steven Wise and the Nonhuman Rights Project filed a petition for a common law writ of habeas corpus on behalf of their client, Tommy. The petition was an important step for animal rights, testing the expansiveness of the legal category of personhood: was Tommy, an animal, a chimpanzee, their client, the plaintiff and subject of the suit, and, subsequently, the appellant in its appeal, also a person under the law? If so, was Tommy being imprisoned unlawfully and thus subject to immediate habeas relief?

A writ of habeas corpus is an important legal protection, one that guarantees due process before imprisonment. Stemming from ideals articulated in chapter 39 of the Magna Carta, and then codified in the Habeas Corpus Acts of 1640 and 1679, habeas corpus protects personal liberty, especially against capricious sentencing and unlawful imprisonment.[1] But imprisonment of whom and by whom?

Such questions sometimes serve as rhetorical provocative, but in this instance, the court aimed to provide a clear answer. Article 70 of New York State's Civil Practice Law and Review, CVP § 7002 (a) and (b) clearly defines "to whom" and "by whom" such a petition can be made: it is a writ made to a judge by a "person." Steven Wise and the Nonhuman Rights Project argued that, although a chimpanzee, Tommy was a person under this statute. Justice Joseph M. Sise, of the New York State Supreme Court, Foulton County, ruled that he was not, denying the writ.[2]

The New York State Supreme Court, Appellate Division (third district), and the New York Court of Appeals concurred with the lower court's decision, though it acknowledged that the case raises "ongoing" questions about the status of animals like Tommy under the law.[3]

More than mere property, but not quite a person, Tommy does not fit neatly within either category. As Steven Wise, founder of the Nonhuman Rights Project and lead attorney, made clear in the initial hearing with Justice Sise, the Nonhuman Rights Project was not seeking to change the definition of "human-being," but rather to expand the concept of "legal person," a proxy of humanity to include Tommy. Human, he argued, is not a legal term of art; person is. As he argued: "human-being is not a synonym for person and person is not a synonym for human being."[4] It constitutes one end of a continuum of legal rights, extending from innate things (property) towards personhood, whether legal or natural.[5] Animals, even sentient and talented animals like Tommy, are deemed things and thus property; Tommy's petition directly challenged his categorization as a thing under the law.

Chimpanzees, though recognized as exceptional in their capacity to mimic humanity both in scientific studies and in entertainment arenas, are unremarkable in terms of their legal status: they are defined either as a wild animal or as animate personal property, owned by humans. As property, their owners can do with them as they see fit. Tommy has had a number of owners during his short lifetime: during the trial, Tommy remained in the custody of Peter Lavery, who inherited him in 2008 from David Sabo, a chimpanzee breeder who had owned Tommy since he was born in the mid-1980s.[6] He is now the property of Bud and Carrie De Young, who run a family zoo and animal sanctuary in Michigan. He is currently not on display to the public and because of this animal-rights activists fear that he may be dead.[7]

In this instance, however, the court was not asked to decide whether or not Patrick Lavery had neglected Tommy or if his treatment of him constituted cruelty; rather, the court was asked to decide if Patrick Lavery had unlawfully imprisoned Tommy. Caged in a small cement block room with only a television set for company, Tommy and the conditions of his care and those of other chimpanzees like him were under scrutiny: were his rights were being violated, both in terms of his unique status as a petitioner and in terms of his species, a species deemed to be highly advanced when compared with other animals? The petition asked the court to recognize "that chimpanzees have what it takes for legal personhood within the meaning of habeas corpus statute, which is autonomy, self-determination, self-agency, the ability to choose how to live their lives."[8]

In making this case, Wise argued for an expansive theory of personhood, one rooted in case law and statutory protections based upon legal precedent, social and political theory, and scientific study. Using fundamental human concepts associated with liberty, Wise applied them to animals defined by genetics to be our closest relatives. His argument structured around both prongs: in terms of historical precedent about humans' fundamental liberties, Wise argued that the case was comparable to eighteenth-century petitions brought by escaped slaves seeking similar writs of protection, petitioners who, at the time, entered the court as legal things and exited as persons; this precedent, Wise argued, shows that not all humans have had the protections associated with legal personhood. Judge Sise rejected the analogy, cutting Wise off at the start of the argument, deeming it to be offensive and not at all comparable to the present situation. Tommy's lawyers then made strategic, strenuous legal arguments that drew upon scientific data about how chimpanzees are "like" us in social, genetic, and cognitive ways. Wise argued that chimpanzees were proximate to humans, perhaps more so than any other animal, including other species of great apes: "These, Your Honor, are essentially us. They're so extraordinarily close to us."[9]

In this chapter, I explore this "extraordinary closeness" as a history that defines human–chimpanzee interaction, one that has its roots in the Renaissance. Renaissance chimpanzees are few and far between: the first chimpanzees were imported and displayed in Europe only in the mid-seventeenth century, though early modern travelogues report of monstrous animal–human hybrids. Chimpanzees, as Renaissance objects of scrutiny, were defined as both human and animal; both were linked in Europeans' racist framing of monstrous African others. The twenty-first-century fight for their legal rights thus revisits old ground. Renaissance understanding of chimpanzee bodies is relevant to unpacking more recent engagements with animal rights. Its very posthuman legal challenge connects to both the history of habeas relief (and its role in defining human rights) and the history of species definition for chimpanzees.

Valued for his likeness to us but deemed a thing under the law, Tommy was bred to mimic humanity with skill and aplomb, without any rights afforded to him. Though Tommy is a twenty-first-century simian, Renaissance concepts of science, politics, and law shape his history, and indeed chimpanzee history, while also troubling the evolving line between property and personhood, animal and human. Tommy's case thus reframed a very old paradox about our legal system in a novel way: who is—and is not—entitled to fundamental legal rights?

Habeas History: Having and Owning a Body

Chimpanzees trouble the two poles of the spectrum that currently categorizes legal rights. Viewed from our contemporary vantage point, the Nonhuman Rights Project's writ on behalf of Tommy seems novel in that it made an expansive claim to redefine chimpanzees from property into personhood, using one of the most established and protected legal rights in United States law: habeas corpus.[10] Tommy thus became part of a very long history of habeas corpus relief, a history that is about bodies, biology, and science as much as it is about politics and law. Legal personhood has been seen as a twenty-first-century fight for fundamental rights for the proto-human (fetuses), artificially human (robots and AI), and nonhuman (animal) entities.

First and foremost, a writ of habeas corpus is about power: both a sovereign's power to detain a subject and, linked to that power, a person's right to be protected from abuse of it. The writ of habeas corpus as an instrument of liberty has its roots in both medieval and early modern theories of political power. Legal historian Amanda Tyler summarizes that habeas corpus protection has always been rooted in protecting power, even as it has been unevenly invoked to protect subjects from abuses of power. Its common law roots protected the king's subjects from unlawful seizures of life or property, rooting it in an extension royal power; whereas its statutory history protected subjects from royal tyranny. Its history is itself paradoxical, rooted in both abuses and protections of state power.

This secondary aspect developed in the seventeenth century through English statutory law, reflecting both the political climate of the Restoration as well as seventeenth-century philosophical and political theories of personhood and property rights. As John Locke articulated in his *Second Treatise of Government*, man had a "natural right" to his body (as property), owning his *persona* and preserving rights, famously, to life, liberty, and property.[11] Therefore, to be and to own are linked, at least in terms of one's property right in the "self," and to the bodily labor one performs. The question of sovereignty, however, emerges when that right to property extends to include other kinds of bodies: women, children, slaves, and, importantly, animals. Such property rights require theories of sovereignty; in Locke's famous formulation, "the preservation of property" is "the end of government," and the reason why men surrender personal liberty in order to be governed by laws that protect "peace, quiet, and property."[12]

This legal history emphasizes the many ways that legal person-hood and physical personhood were not aligned: case law documents the contested expansion of personhood to include "natural" persons (yet legally disenfranchised people), such as slaves, Native Americans, women, disabled people, prisoners, and children, as well as expanding the category of "legal" persons to include corporations, rivers, and governments, and animal, fetuses, and robots. United States case law, for instance, already provides for an expansive category of legal personhood to nonhuman entities, recognizing corporations, ships, and governments; outside of the US, courts have awarded legal personhood to religious books, Hindu idols, and rivers.[13] That the law recognizes some legal persons over some natural persons only intensifies the paradox of personhood.

Read one way, these examples seem to provide a historical development of personhood, one that maps from a very limited definition (white, property-owning, married, and male) towards an expansion of rights in both progressive and posthuman ways. And yet these are questions that reach backwards to the Renaissance, raising questions not only about our legal categories but also about our scientific ones. Did Tommy have the right kind of body? Was caging him an act of unlawful imprisonment? And, if so, what would "liberty" mean for him?

If writs of habeas corpus are about power, they are also about language, both in terms of what we might describe (*pace* Foucault) as the philosophical foundations for the discursiveness of power, or (*pace* Chomsky) as a human cognitive capacity for language. More than one scientist filed an affidavit about chimpanzees' capacity for language acquisition and communication (though the court focused more on human language and its written forms). They did so because language has been the philosophical litmus test of personhood since the Enlightenment, since Thomas Hobbes's famous articulation of "persons, authors, and things personated," as those who can speak on their own behalf. For Hobbes, a person is defined by his words: "When they are considered as his owne, then is he called a Naturall Person: And, when they are considered as representing the words and actions of an other, then is he a Feigned or Artificial person."[14] As Jacques Derrida argued, "the animal" has been constructed as outside of language; it can never respond, only react to human difference.[15]

Tommy's case put pressure on this claim: chimpanzees do more than "ape" our words. The scientific data entered in affidavits sought to argue that such cognitive and social capacities for communication rose to the level of a response. Furthermore, they may also rise to the level of autonomy and social duties. Their ability to speak to one another and to us may change their legal status, as numerous scientists reported in their affidavits. But the *writ* part also mattered, both in terms of the legal arguments that Tommy's lawyers tried to invoke and in terms of the court's scrutiny of the law as a human domain. Semantics mattered as well. Animal, adolescent, chimp, chimpanzee, client, plaintiff, subject, appellant, person: there were many nouns used to describe Tommy in the proceedings. These words were important, defining his body in lieu of his physical absence in court. As an adult male chimpanzee with five times the strength of a male human, Tommy posed a physical risk to those in the courtroom including his lawyers.

Tommy's body carries no "natural" right to its property and its disjunction with the history of habeas relief may have been thought to be too wide a valley for a judge to cross, even for just an hour while in court. Though habeas relief is rarely about these kinds of semantics or semiotics, in this instance it emphasized the writ's Latin roots: what did it mean to "have" a body like Tommy's not just in terms of physical restraint but also in terms of embodied subjectivity? It is often noted that the writ itself—*habeas corpus ad subjiciendum et recipiendum*—requires that a jailor "has the body [of the prisoner], to submit to" the judgment of the court on the legality of the restraint; such a requirement provides for due process and halts any imprisonment that flouts the laws of the land (*contra legem terrae*).[16] Tommy's imprisonment was not deemed to do this, though the judge noted that it did speak "to our relationship with the life around us," life that cannot continue to be ignored. These, however, were deemed ethical issues, or issues of public policy rather than fundamental liberty.[17]

Severely endangered in the wild, chimpanzees' future as a species is uncertain: as Jane Goodall concludes, "unless we act soon, our closest relatives may soon exist only in captivity, condemned as a species, to human bondage."[18] Chimpanzee evolution, Goodall argues, is now severely hindered by human intervention and what she terms bondage. Goodall's work has been key to Tommy's case and she is a board member on the Nonhuman Rights Project; her affidavit, filed as an appendix to Tommy's writ in September of 2015, outlines what she has observed as the "responsibilities and duties" of chimpanzee life: these include mothering, sibling care, fostering or adopting orphans, patrolling and ensuring safety of the troop (including humans), mourning the loss of loved ones, and performing for observers. We might deem these actions social and political behavior.

Chimpanzees have been confused with humans since ancient times. Their history, as a species, is defined by this resemblance, whether genetic, morphological, or cognitive. But the question facing the courts was whether this resemblance was also social, legal, and thus, political. Law and politics are explicitly human domains; whether we invoke Aristotle, Hobbes, Foucault, or Agamben, the animal as a category exists as a starting point for human self-reflection. It defines both the anthropological and the anthropolitical.[19]

As the New York Superior Court judge acknowledged, the political ramifications of acknowledging human–chimpanzee resemblance are deeply troubled and troubling. Comparing humans to animals is part of a long history of racism, misogyny, colonialism, slavery, and violence, the first step in denying humans dignity and legal rights. Chimpanzee–human resemblance specifically has been used to justify scientific racism, legal slavery, and colonialism; it has been a tool of power wielded by humans against humans. It continues to be so. More recently, as legal theorist Richard Cupp argued in an affidavit filed against granting the writ, the analogy Wise makes here about the intellectual resemblance between humans and chimpanzees also raises ethical questions about human intellectual capacity and its role in structuring rights. If we argue that chimpanzees deserve rights because they are intellectually superior to other animals, then what will the impact be for humans with developmental difficulties?

Framed in this way, the court emphasized philosophical questions about personhood rather than historical ones. But these thought exercises relied upon metaphors for comparison: are chimpanzees "like" humans? If so, how? These were framed in terms of both their bodily reality and their social behavior: in terms of cognition, is Tommy "like" a human fetus, a three-year-old toddler, or an adult person who has a cognitive disability? In terms of social behavior, is he like a neglected child, a retired actor, or an introvert? What is his body capable of? The resemblance comes in and out of view. It is perhaps not an overstatement to say that this resemblance is one of the most important comparisons in Western human intellectual history, structuring both scientific advancement about evolution and cognition, and social justifications of violence to marginal and subaltern communities.[20] Trenchant and mobile, intuitive and vexed: comparison defines our approach to the species.

Species History: Naming Chimpanzees

Tommy is a chimpanzee (*Pan troglodytes*), a species of great ape defined by its similarities to humanity in genetic, social, and cognitive ways.[21] Human recognition of this similarity has shaped the history of their species and of ours. Since their "discovery" in the seventeenth century by Renaissance European scientists, chimpanzees have been compared and conflated with humans, and this comparison has been used by those in power to justify colonialist expansion, chattel slavery, and segregation, and to justify denying the rights and protections of legal personhood.

Is a chimpanzee a person? The answer, from a legal point of view, is clear: no. Yet the very name of Tommy's species suggests a different answer, mapping discourses about human power, race, and geography onto animal bodies and animality onto humans as a tool of subjugation. Their scientific species name—*Pan troglodytes*—hints at how these associations worked even as it erases this premodern history through the development of binomial nomenclature. Pan, the Greek god of the wild, was often depicted as human–animal hybrid, more caprine than simian. Known for both terrorizing humans and entertaining the gods, Pan was associated with both violence and delight, inspiring a powerful affective response in the humans that perceived him.[22] "Panic," as a verb ("to affect with panic; to scare into a hasty or rash action"), connects to its previous iteration as a noun ("of, relating to, characteristic of, or associated with the Greek God Pan"). Pan emphasizes that these are "wild" creatures, even if the term now describes a species whose population in captivity vastly outnumbers those in the wild.

Great apes, including chimpanzees, are prevalent in travel accounts from the premodern world, including ancient, medieval, and Renaissance sources, though it is hard to know how to interpret these accounts, given their stark racism. In them, European travelers to Africa confused these creatures with humans who shared their habitats, grouping them together into schemas of monsters (usually as satyrs or pygmies) that erased human/animal categories as salient. Troglodytes, satyrs, nymphs, cynocephalus: these terms defined hybrid creatures, whose bodies were believed to be comprised of both human and animal parts. What linked them was a terrifying wildness. Yet these creatures were also deemed to be unnatural; within Aristotelian schemes of science, they were aberrations that were unique and idiosyncratic rather than systemic or natural.[23]

Premodern monsters, however, were embedded within modern scientific classification systems during the Enlightenment through scientific naming practices. These ancient terms for hybrid monsters now classify simians via their scientific names: chimpanzees (*Pan troglodytes*), orangutans (*Pongo pygmaeus*), baboons (*Papio hamadryas*) and yellow baboons (*Papio cynocephalus*). Only gorillas are unique among great apes in having no premodern etymological history (*Gorilla gorilla*). This shift, from literary discourses about monsters to scientific ones, changed the relationship between humans and apes in the seventeenth century; it was during this period that the first few great apes were captured, chained, and shipped to Europe to serve as royal pets (or as scientific specimens once they died, usually a few weeks after arrival).

We know very little about these creatures, though Tommy's history provides some clues. All great apes on display in Europe in the seventeenth century were infants and adolescents; given the danger and logistics of capturing and transporting adult great apes, European traders most likely shot and killed the mother in order to capture the infant.[24] These infant animals rarely lived long in captivity. Not much is known about them after their death, though later the cadavers were likely studied by anatomists.

Pan troglodytes as a scientific term to describe chimpanzees solved Enlightenment naturalists' contradictions about whether the creatures were human or not. The species' scientific name stems from a nineteenth-century reassignment of two previous eighteenth-century iterations, which categorized chimpanzees in contradictory ways: as *Simia troglodytes*, or "cave-dwelling monkey," and as *Homo troglodytes* or *Homo nocturnus*, or "cave-dwelling man."[25] These terms emphasize that chimpanzees emerged in modern science as what Christina Skott describes as a "composite figure," comprised of contradictory sources that conflated "information about higher apes" (*Simia troglodytes*) with "individual reports" of humanoid monsters (*Homo troglodytes*) and monstrous (and racialized) humans.[26] The controversy was erased in favor of new category both classical in theme and all-encompassing in scope: "Pan."

The debate continues: some scientists recently argued that the striking genetic relatedness between humans and chimpanzees warrants a reclassification of the species as *Homo troglodytes*, replacing classification systems that were based more on human perception of morphological traits than genetic evidence.[27] Others argue the opposite, citing recent genetic data that reveals our fundamental difference from chimpanzees: though it is true that we share almost 99 percent of genes with chimpanzees, human genes differ in an important way, or rather in forty-nine important ways, which constitute "human accelerated regions" of our genome that stimulate brain growth and gestational development in the first and second trimesters of pregnancy.[28] This growth is what makes us human: chimpanzee brains are different than human brains in terms of size (human brain size has almost tripled since we shared a common ancestor), systems, and complexity, as well as in their patterning and layout (or folds).

But genetic information is only one piece of this puzzle; it is how we perceive those differences as a species that also matters. These perceived similarities and differences—between animals and between humans, and between humans and animals—comprise both the scientific and legal precedents that shape this case, as well as the species history.

Chimpanzees have long been confused by European observers with the humans that shared their habitats. Racism saturates these histories. Chimpanzee history, as a species, includes racist histories of science and colonialism; it is also embedded in the medieval and Renaissance natural histories about African "monsters," in eighteenth-century developments of scientific schema to categorize the world and its inhabitants, and in nineteenth-century legal cases about which humans do and do not count as persons under the law. It is in many ways a history of human perception of embodied difference and verisimilitude.

Early editions of Linnaeus's *Systema Naturæ* famously grouped humans, primates, and sloths together into a shared order: this earlier category drew upon late-seventeenth-century work by John Ray and Edward Tyson who identified the genus *Anthropomorpha*, or clawed, anthropoid beings who were "human-like," including man. In early editions of *Systema Naturæ*, Linnaeus divides the species "Homo" into four groups that emphasized race and geography: *Homo Europaeus albescens* (whitish European), *Homo Americanus rubescens* (reddish American), *Homo Asiaticus fuscus* (dark-colored Asian), and *Homo Africanus niger* (black African).[29] This system was replaced in the tenth edition of *Systema Naturæ* (1758), which debuted a much more expansive and complete system of binomial nomenclature. In this edition, *Anthropomorpha* becomes the order "primates," which includes three species of humans: *Homo sapiens*, *Homo troglodytes*, and *Homo caudatus*.[30]

Troglodytes were monsters, but human, linked to giants, pygmies, and Amazons; Herodotus describes them as forest-dwelling creatures, swift of foot and communicating in an unrecognizable language that sounded like screeching.[31] They were also African, positioned on medieval maps in the region southwest of the Nile.[32] Medieval sources describe a range of monsters, animal–human hybrids, who are linked to both human and animal histories. Satyrs, wodewose or wildmen, and cynocephali are perhaps fictionalized accounts of real encounters with animals in contact zones or perhaps racist literary fantasies about human others. Images of simians from this period tend to depict what we would now term monkeys.

Great apes are largely absent from Renaissance accounts, with a few notable exceptions including two English sources about Africa both of which were reported to Samuel Purchas as part of his editorial work on *Purchas His Pilgrim* (1613).[33] Andrew Battell's "Strange Adventures" details Battell's time in Angola in central Africa (as a Portuguese prisoner); Richard Jobson's *Golden Trade* outlines his travels on the river Gambra in West Africa and his encounters with the Malinke tribe of the Gambia.[34] Though these men traveled in very different parts of Africa, both describe large forest-dwelling animal creatures who resembled humans in morphology and in social behavior.

Jobson names them as "baboons," detailing behavior that he interprets as political: "But to speake of the Babowne, I must say, is a wonderful thing, to observe a kind of common-wealth that is among them."[35] Traveling in "heardes" with between three thousand and four thousand in company, the creatures are orderly; "they goe in rancke," following a clear leader. They also have patrols, who defend the herd; Jobson goes so far as to call these guards "master constable." Finally, they have dedicated spaces in the forest, "places they use trees and plants, wound and made up together in that artificially manner . . . kept for their dancing and recreation."[36] He concludes by noting that it is the opinion of the Spanish that they are a "race and kind of people, who . . . will not bee brought to worke, and live under subjection . . . ."[37] Jobson's text is one of the earliest accounts of sixteenth-century slave trading in European Renaissance accounts of the Gambia; his assessment of baboon politics notes both animal and human bondage, even as he notes that these are a creature that refuse both.

It is unclear what kind of animal Jobson is describing; the scale of the herds suggest that these were not chimpanzees, though they are native to this region. Most sources cite instead Andrew Battell's Renaissance account of forest-dwelling monsters in Angola as the first European eye-witness description of great apes in the wild. Early editions of *Purchas His Pilgrimage* merely recounted Battell's tale in the segments on Africa, including his reports of "a kind of greate Apes, if they might so be termed." These creatures were "the height of a man, but twice as bigge in feature of their limmes, with strength proportionable, haire all ouer, otherwise altogether like men and women in their whole bodily shape."³⁸ But Purchas also reports other kinds of "apes" in the area, including "satyrs, with feete like goates, and sphynges, with breasts like women."³⁹

Both Jobson's and Battell's texts seem to describe great apes, even as they frame these accounts with fictive elaboration. That an early modern English source on Africa misrepresents the region is hardly surprising. Purchas aimed for a comprehensive political and religious argument in his text and he asked both Jobson and Battell to report their tales for their value within his literary project.⁴⁰ But we now value Battell's tale for its ethnographic claims about the region, even as we recognize its limited perspective.

Battell was an English soldier and neighbor of Samuel Purchas, who traveled to Brazil with English traders in the late sixteenth century, where he was captured and sold to Portuguese traders.⁴¹ They took him to western Africa, where he lived for a year (1600–1) as a prisoner of the Portuguese, observing the Jaga (Imbangala) tribe of Angola (as it was forming in the early seventeenth century), and reporting on their fierce warrior tactics.⁴² The full account of his "strange adventures" is first included in the 1625 edition of *Purchas His Pilgrim*. It is here that he names the great apes previously described in early editions, reporting on forests filled with baboons, monkeys, and apes as well as two other kinds of "monsters," *pongo* and *engeco*, both now believed to be references to gorillas and chimpanzees.

Battell uses Bantu terms for the creatures, signaling perhaps that they are unlike others encountered before (in either classical or contemporary sources). The etymology of these terms is complex but both seem to refer to native terms for chimpanzees, terms that loosely translate as "mock human."⁴³ Battell's view is framed by Purchas's overall project, a work dedicated to amassing an expansive, Christian compendium of world religion. It is likely that Purchas heavily edited Battell's text in order to emphasis a theme of pilgrimage; Battell himself was likely illiterate, reporting his tale to Purchas and his son (who transcribed it).⁴⁴ Indeed, early editions of *Purchas His Pilgrim* only mention Battell by name (usually in the context of reporting about Africa as an exotic and wild space, including tales of animals, witches, cannibalism, and reports of non-binary gender expression, especially among African religious leaders); his "strange account" appeared in full in the 1625 edition.

Battell's "strange adventures" offer a rare, first-person perspective of sixteenth-century Portuguese expansion into Senegambia, but there are no other accounts or papers that corroborate his account (besides those published by Purchas), making it impossible for historians to verify his claims, both about African animals and habitats and about the Jaga people. What is clear is the literary ways in which the text is oriented towards Purchas's Christian worldview. Likewise, editorial expansions in each subsequent edition suggest that we can only classify the text as fiction. As scholar Jared Staller points out, the narrative emphasizes Purchas's Reformation agenda in the text as a whole; and his description of African human rituals are clearly biased by Purchas's Calvinist worldview.[45] But Battell's report of Jaga (Imbangala) warrior culture is one of few primary sources available to historians of sixteenth-century Africa; likewise, his details about African animals, including elephants, hippos, rhinos, and zebra, offer a glimpse of these species in wild habitats that are now encroached by humans. For this reason, postcolonial scholars note that it may be useful to read Battell's account "against" itself for historical clues about African native cultures prior to European colonialism even as we recognize the text's participation within that history.[46] Chimpanzees, as monsters and as "great" apes, are part of both strategies.

Describing the "provinces of Bongo, Calongo, Mayombe, and Maikesocke," Battell notes that there are many people who live near the river, and that the woods nearby are filled with "baboons, monkeys, apes and parrots, that it will feare any man to trauile in them alone," and there are "two kinds of monsters, which are common in these woods, and very dangerous."[47] These creatures are called *pongo* and *engeco* by native tribes, and they differ in size; *pongo* is "more like a Giant in stature, then [sic] a man," with hollow eyes and long brows; the engeco, "a strange kind of Monster," is a lesser kind.[48] *Pongo*, he notes, "are never taken alive, because they are so strong, that ten men cannot hold one of them, but yet they take many of the yong ones with poisoned Arrowes."[49]

Battell's account may be the first, but it describes what would soon become common practice, especially as European interest in these creatures increased. Poaching infants poses great violence to simian adults; even today it is estimated that ten adult chimpanzees are killed in order to successfully capture an infant alive. Battell's account seems to corroborate this, or at the very least provide clues to how the first infant chimpanzees were captured and transported to Europe to be put on display in aristocratic menageries.

The first record of a chimpanzee displayed alive in Europe is described in Nicolaas Tulp's *Observationum Medicarum* (1641). Tulp, a Dutch scientist and anatomist (memorably captured in Rembrandt's *The Anatomy Lesson of Dr. Nicolaes Tulp*) describes the creature at the very end of a short essay on medical anomalies (both human and animal). Though most of the figures and reports in the volume were the result of direct study, Tulp's discussion of the chimpanzee was not. He drew instead on reports about the creature (including tales of bestiality reported to him by Samuel Blommaert, a Dutch merchant and director of the Dutch West Indies Company who traveled to Borneo in the first two decades of the sixteenth century, and who was later Tulp's neighbor in Amsterdam) and on his own observations of a creature on display in the 1630s in the menagerie of The Hague.

The animal was on display as part of the private collection of Frederick Henry, the Prince of Orange. It had been given as a gift to the Prince by Dutch traders working in Angola. The menagerie of The Hague was among Europe's finest, displaying rare creatures from around the world all collected during Dutch corporate, colonial expansion. The chimpanzee was young and female; though there are no records to document this, it presumably lived a short life. (A nineteenth-century source reports that it lived in the menagerie for four years before dying of a cold; other nineteenth-century sources contradict this, reporting instead four separate gifts of similar animals to the Prince).

In his *Observations*, Tulp reports that the creature was as tall as a human child of three years old and as big as a child of six, with ears that resembled a human; it was bald, with wiry hair on the back of its head, and its face, he argued, counterfeited human form: its nostrils bent inwards "like a wrinkled and toothless old woman," but otherwise it resembled humans so much in form that they were like "two eggs in a basket."[50] He does not name the creature as a chimpanzee; rather he labels his chapter *Satyrus Indicus* (Indian Satyr), connecting the African creature he observed first hand to second-hand reports of Asian "satyrs," including Jacob de Bondt's 1658 account of a Malaysian "satyr," known as an "orang utan," a "wonderful monster with a human face, so human-kind not only in groaning but also in wetting the face with weeping." Tulp's image cites Bondt's in its form and he explicitly labeled it *Homo sylvestris "orang-outang"* emphasizing that the creature was linked to a host of histories about human and animal forest dwellers in classical accounts ("Homo sylvestris"), travel narratives, and native Malay accounts ("orang-outang"). That Bondt's tale of Asian orangutans is heavily influenced by Jobson's account of African chimpanzees (particularly accounts of their capacity and refusal to speak) only complicates the histories of these animals.[51]

Tulp's many names for the creature signal that premodern categories were conflicted: presumed to be a chimpanzee, reported as an orangutan, satyr, and *Homo sylvestris* (and translated into English as baboon), it is unclear exactly what kind of animal is being described even as the text aims to provide ever more specific and scientific detail. Yet its other names hint at different etymologies. "Chimpanzee," like "orangutan," reflects other histories: both are native terms for the creatures. Chimpanzee as a term first appeared in Portuguese in the eighteenth century, as a Europeanized way of repeating ci-mpenzi, a Bantu language spoken by the Kongo and Ndundu people.[52] Likewise, the Malay term "orang utan" emphasizes that the animals are humanoid forest dwellers.

Renaissance Afterlives

The history charted above does not provide any clarity on the questions facing the court; rather, it demonstrates the deep roots for our fascination with and anxiety about our resemblance to chimpanzees. If the history of habeas relief troubles the concept of fundamental rights for natural persons, then the history of Renaissance chimpanzees equally troubles our scientific categories of species difference. Patrick Lavery's right to "own" Tommy as property and Tommy's right to be recognized as a creature worthy of rights are at direct odds, but as I have tried to show here, such a paradox hardly matters when we have defined the species as *Pan*: property or person, human or animal. Tommy is both now, because of how we have defined the species.

In seeking to expand legal personhood to include animals, the Nonhuman Rights Project was specific in their choice of species of plaintiff. Tommy himself was not: his status as the first animal client to petition for such a writ was happenstance. Steven Wise and the Nonhuman Rights Project filed twelve such motions in different New York county courts. They were prepared to file more, but the animals died in captivity before they could do so.

This, too, fits a pattern. Chimpanzees born in the wild can live well into their seventies, though few do. Poaching, disease, and habitat loss have greatly impacted chimpanzee populations in the wild, especially since 1950.[53] These human impacts have resulted in an 80 percent decline in the western African chimpanzee, a subspecies residing in both the tropical lowland forests of Liberia and Côte d'Ivoire, as well as the woodland savannas in Guinea, Guinea-Bissau, Senegal, and Mali. (Chimpanzees were in Benin, Burkina Faso, and Togo but are now extinct there.)[54]

The mortality rate is even higher for chimpanzees in captivity; most die in their early teens. This, too, is a pattern that reaches back to the Renaissance: "Old" Jack of the Paris Garden, mentioned in at least three Renaissance plays (and described by a character in *Syr Gyles Goosecappe* as "the great baboone, that was to be seene in Southwark") was an ape, whose baiting provided part of the entertainments at early modern London's most famous bear-baiting arena.[55] The plays that mention him do so to denigrate human characters, mostly gallants, either for their "aping" of "Italianate" fashion, pulling faces, or traveling in "troops."[56] But almost all also mention his age, which suggests that he was renowned for his survival in such a violent entertainment industry. It is likely that no other "baboon" (a Renaissance term for a trained, captive ape rather than for a specific species) lived very long.[57] Likewise, the archives of "monkey" hill in nineteenth-century London's zoo are filled with overwhelming deaths of simians in captivity, both monkeys and apes. Most arrived and died within the same month due to disease and poor nutrition, so much so that caretakers remark upon the grim aspect of labor. Tommy's survival, like those of his historical predecessors, speaks mostly to human neglect.

The Nonhuman Rights Project sought to change this; indeed, Steven Wise's book, *Rattling the Cage*, has been deemed to be an "animal magna carta" by Jane Goodall, connecting legal history, animal history, and rights-based arguments of liberty in explicit ways. In the end, the court ruled that Tommy was property, preferring a system of welfare protections rather than rights-based liberation. As Gary Francione has argued, our court systems are designed to protect property rights and wealth; under such a system, "animals almost never prevail."[58]

As Judge Fahey summarized in his judgment, the law is an inadequate vehicle to decide the ethical dilemmas surrounding the restraint of these creatures. Animals, especially simians who mirror our human capacities in "genetic, cognitive, evolutionary, and taxonomic" ways, do not fit neatly on either end of a legal continuum of rights constructed through modern jurisprudence, with personhood on one end and property on the other. Fahey writes: "While it may be arguable that a chimpanzee is not a 'person,' there is no doubt that it is not merely a thing."[59] Semantics, Judge Fahey suggests, fail to capture the issues at stake. Yet he, too, relies on "definitional" categories: noting that a writ of habeas corpus does not rely on one being recognized as a "person" in order to protect unlawful imprisonment, Fahey argued instead that the central question at hand was not "whether a chimpanzee has the same rights and duties as a human being, but instead whether he or she has the right to liberty protected by habeas corpus."[60] Shifting the question out of the legal domain and into ethics, Fahey sought to move the discussion away from questions about verisimilitude and an expansive legal personhood towards a concept of an individual, one who is not human but nonetheless is like humans in deserving recognition and respect.

I end with perhaps the least interesting aspect of the proceedings in order to frame the philosophical quandaries at the heart of this case: semantics. To think of this as a problem of semantics allows us to ask questions about oblique histories, histories that matter tremendously but that cannot be acknowledged in the law. How do we speak about animals, especially those that we privilege as being most "like" us? How does that recognition of verisimilitude operate within legal discourse? And what does it reveal about the continuum of rights our courts have constructed? Our nonhuman legal proxies are valid if they are aligned with "our" interests; Tommy and his history reminds us to question the antecedents that define those interests.

It is perhaps not surprising that the next client the Nonhuman Rights Project took after Tommy's appeal was denied was an elephant. As Steven Wise now argues, "apes are so close to us that it makes some people uncomfortable."[61]

Notes

1. See Amanda Tyler, "A Second Magna Carta Act: The English Habeas Corpus Act and the Statutory Origins of Habeas Privilege," *Federal Courts, Practice & Procedure, Notre Dame Law Review* 91 (2015–16): 1949–96, 1954.
2. Nonhuman Rights Project, on behalf of Tommy v. Lavery, et al. (162358/2015), <https://www.nonhumanrights.org/content/uploads/Fulton-Cty-hearing-re.-Tommy-12-2-13.pdf> (last accessed May 7, 2019).
3. Nonhuman Rights Project, Inc., on Behalf of Tommy v. Patrick C. Lavery, &c., et al. Nonhuman Rights Project, Inc., on Behalf of Kiko, v. Carmen Presti et al. (May 2018), Motion No. 2018-268. New York State Court of Appeals. Fahey, concurring opinion, <http://www.nycourts.gov/ctapps/Decisions/2018/May18/M2018-268opn18-Decision.pdf> (last accessed April 24, 2019).
4. Nonhuman Rights Project, on behalf of Tommy v. Lavery, et al. (162358/2015).
5. Steven Wise, *Rattling the Cage: Toward Legal Rights for Animals* (New York: Perseus Publishing, 2000), 2.

6. Charles Siebert, "Should a chimp be able to sue its owner?," *New York Times Magazine*, April 23, 2014, <https://www.nytimes.com/2014/04/27/magazine/the-rights-of-man-and-beast.html> (last accessed April 24, 2019).

7. Ben Ashford, "Missing feared DEAD," *Daily Mail*, August 7, 2016, <http://www.dailymail.co.uk/news/article-3629770/Chimpanzee-center-legal-rights-battle-star-new-documentary-struggle-missing-feared-dead.html> (last accessed April 24, 2019).

8. Nonhuman Rights Project, on behalf of Tommy v. Lavery, et al. (162358/2015).

9. Nonhuman Rights Project, on behalf of Tommy v. Lavery, et al. (162358/2015).

10. See Amanda Tyler, *Habeas Corpus in Wartime* (Oxford: Oxford University Press, 2017), 11.

11. John Locke, *Two Treatises of Government* (London, 1690), sig. Aa4 v, p. 360, sig. Aa3 v, p. 359.

12. Locke, *Two Treatises*, sig. Aa4 v, p. 360, sig. Aa3 v, p. 359.

13. Since the time of the hearing, an Argentine court has recognized Cecilia, a chimpanzee, and Sandra, an orangutan, as "Nonhuman legal persons," though the judge clarified that she was recognizing "species" rights, not civil rights as recognized in the Civil Code. See Gabriel Samuels, "Chimpanzees have rights, says Argentine judge as she orders Cecilia be released from zoo," *Independent*, November 2016, <https://www.independent.co.uk/news/world/americas/argentina-judge-says-chimpanzee-poor-conditions-has-rights-and-should-be-freed-from-zoo-a7402606.html> (last accessed April 24, 2019).

14. See Thomas Hobbes, *Leviathan*, introduction by K. Minogue (London: Dent, 1987), 83–4, cited in Jeanne Gaakeer, "'*Sua cuique persona*?' A Note on the Fiction of Legal Personhood and Reflection on Interdisciplinary Consequences," *Law and Literature* (2016), <https://doi.org/10.1080/1535685X.2016.1232920> (last accessed April 24, 2019).

15. See Cary Wolfe, *Animal Rites: American Culture, the Discourse of Species and Posthumanist Theory* (Chicago: University of Chicago Press, 2003), 74.

16. See Tyler, *Habeas Corpus in Wartime*, 15.

17. Nonhuman Rights Project, on behalf of Tommy v. Lavery, et al. (162358/2015).

18. Jane Goodall, *Through a Window: My Thirty Years with the Chimpanzees of Gombe* (Boston: Houghton Mifflin, 2000), 246.

19. The term "anthropolitical" has been coined by Ana Zentella as an area of linguistics that "sees through the language smokescreen that obscures ideological, structural, and policial impediments to equity." See Ana Celia Zentella, *Growing Up Bilingual: Puerto Rican Children in New York* (Malden, MA: Blackwell, 1997).

20. One could perhaps also argue this is true in other intellectual histories. See, for instance, Emiko Ohnuki-Tierney, *The Monkey as Mirror: Symbolic*

Transformations in Japanese History and Ritual (Princeton, NJ: Princeton University Press, 1989).

21. Affidavits were filed on chimpanzee capacity for communication (Aff. Davis), learning and social cognition (Aff. Anderson), tool-use and cognition (Aff. Boesch), emotional perception, gestural communication (Aff. Fugate and Aff. Savage-Rumbaugh), personality structure and psychological well-being (Aff. Anderson), intelligence (Aff. Jensvold), and memory (Aff. King) as well as their physiological and anatomical resemblance to humans (Aff. McGrew), even more so than to other simians (Aff. Matsuzawa), the relationship between chimpanzee brain volume and human ancestors (Aff. Osvath). All of these affidavits are available on the Nonhuman Rights Project's website at <https://www.Nonhumanrights.org/client-tommy/> (last accessed April 24, 2019).

22. See also Judith Peraino, *Listening to Sirens: Musical Technologies of Queer Identity from Homer to Hedwig* (Berkeley: University of California Press, 2006), 23.

23. Georgia Brown, "Defining Nature Through Monstrosity," in *Early Modern Ecostudies: From the Florentine Codex to Shakespeare*, ed. Ivo Kamps, Karen Raber, and Thomas Hallock (Basingstoke: Palgrave Macmillan, 2008), 55–76.

24. John van Wyhe and Peter Kjaergaard, "Going the Whole Orang: Darwi, Wallace, and the Natural History of Orangutans," *Studies in History and Philosophy of Biomedical Sciences* (June 2015): 53–63, 54.

25. The former is from German naturalist Johan Blumenbach's *De Generis Humani varietate native liber* (1776); the latter, from the tenth edition of Linnaeus's *Systema Naturæ* (1758).

26. Christina Skott, "Linnaeus and the Troglodyte: Early European Encounters with the Malay World and the Natural History of Man," *Indonesia and the Malay World* 42.123 (2014): 141–69, 143.

27. John Pickrell, "Chimps Belong on Human Branch of Family Tree, Study Says," *National Geographic*, May 20, 2003, <https://www.national-geographic.com/science/2003/05/chimps-belong-on-human-branch-of-family-tree-study-says/> (last accessed April 24, 2019).

28. Katherine Pollard, "What Makes Us Human?," *Scientific American* 300.5 (2009): 44–9.

29. See Skott, "Linnaeus and the Troglodyte," 144.

30. Stephen Batman's translation of Anglicus Bartholomaeus mentions troglodytes in the section "of Amazonia," reflecting one example of how medieval knowledge shaped Renaissance cartography. See Bartholomaeus, *De Proprietatibus Rerum* (London, 1582), sig. Ooiiiiv, p. 214.

31. "A Brief History of Chimpanzees," *Nature* 437 (2005): 48–9. (Herodotus also mentions Libyan accounts of *cynocephali*, or "dog-headed men," who lived to the east, an account that shaped the history of another species of simians: baboons.)

32. See Surekha Davies, *Renaissance Ethnography and the Invention of the Human* (Cambridge: Cambridge University Press, 2016), 35.

33. See Paul E. H. Hair, "Material on Africa (Other than the Mediterranean and Red Sea Lands) and on the Atlantic Islands, in the Publications of Samuel Purchas, 1613–1626," *History in Africa* 13 (1986), 117–59, 125.
34. Paul E. H. Hair, *Africa Encountered: European Contacts and Evidence, 1450–1700* (London: Routledge, 1996), 295.
35. Richard Jobson, *The Golden Trade, or, A Discovery of the River Gambra* (London, 1623), sig. T5 v, p. 152.
36. Jobson, *Golden Trade*, sig. V r, p. 153.
37. Jobson, *Golden Trade*, sig. V r, p. 153.
38. Samuel Purchas, *Purchas His Pilgrimage* (1613), sig. Ss v, p. 466.
39. Purchas, *Purchas His Pilgrimage* (1613), sig. Ss v, p. 466.
40. For more on the reception history of Battell's narrative within Jaga historiography, see Jared Staller, "Rivalry and Reformation Politics: Reflections on Andrew Battell's Jaga Materials Printed by Samuel Purchas from 1613 to 1625," *History in Africa* 43 (2016), 7–28.
41. Purchas, *Purchas His Pilgrimage* (1613), Sig. Eee r, p. 581.
42. Battell reports on ritualized infanticide, conscription of enemy adolescent children, and cannibalism.
43. Gísli Pálsson, "Life at the Border: Nim Chimpsky et al.," in *Anthropology and Nature*, ed. Kirsten Hastrup (London: Routledge, 2013), 166–84, 168.
44. See Staller, "Rivalry and Reformation Politics," 15.
45. Staller, "Rivalry and Reformation Politics," 15.
46. See David Wheat, *Atlantic Africa and the Spanish Caribbean, 1570–1640* (Chapel Hill: University of North Carolina Press, 2016), 96.
47. Samuel Purchas, *Purchas His Pilgrim* (1625), sig. Mmmmm 4 v, p. 982.
48. Purchas, *Purchas His Pilgrim* (1625), sig. Mmmmm 4 r–v, pp. 981–2.
49. Purchas, *Purchas His Pilgrim* (1625), sig. Mmmmm 4 v.
50. Purchas, *Purchas His Pilgrim* (1625), sig. Mmmmm 4 v.
51. See Laura Brown, *Homeless Dogs and Melancholy Apes: Humans and Other Animals in the Modern Literary Imaginary* (Ithaca, NY: Cornell University Press, 2010), 33.
52. Jeanne Fahnstock, *Rhetorical Style: The Uses of Language in Persuasion* (Oxford: Oxford University Press, 2011), 37.
53. E. V. Lonsdorf, D. Travis, A. E. Pussey, and J. Goodall, "Using Retrospective Health Data from the Gombe Chimpanzee Study to Inform Future Monitoring Efforts," *American Journal of Primatology* 68.9 (2006): 897–908.
54. Hjalmar S. Kühl, Tenekwetche Sop, Elizabeth A. Williamson, Roger Mundry, David Brugière, Genevieve Campbell, Heather Cohen, Emmanuel Danquah, Laura Ginn, Ilka Herbinger, Sorrel Jones, Jessica Junker, Rebecca Kormos, Celestin Y. Kouakou, Paul K. N'Goran, Emma Normand, Kathryn Shutt-Phillips, Alexander Tickle, Elleni Vendras, Adam Welsh, Erin G. Wessling, and Christophe Boesch, "The Critically

Endangered Western Chimpanzee Declines by 80%," *American Journal of Primatology* (2017), <https://doi-org.proxygw.wrlc.org/10.1002/ajp.22681> (last accessed April 24, 2019).

55. *Sir Gyles Goosecappe, Knight* (London, 1606), sig. A2r.
56. See John Marston, *The Scourge of Villanie: Three books of Satyres* (London, 1598), sig. Hv.
57. See W. Strunk, Jr. "The Elizabethan Showman's Ape," *Modern Language Notes* 32 (1917): 215–21. See also Holly Dugan, "'To Bark with Judgement': Playing Baboon in Early Modern London," *Shakespeare Studies* 41 (2013): 77–93.
58. Gary L. Francione, *Animals, Property, and the Law* (Philadelphia: Temple University Press, 1995), 107.
59. Fahey, concurring opinion.
60. Fahey, concurring opinion.
61. Karin Brulliard, "Thee elephants in Connecticut just got a lawyer," *The Washington Post*, November 14, 2007, <https://www.washingtonpost.com/news/animalia/wp/2017/11/14/three-elephants-in-connecticut-just-got-a-lawyer/?utm_term=.5979f995ff30> (last accessed April 24, 2019).

Chapter 7

Race, Personhood, and the Human in *The Tempest*

Amanda Bailey

For cultural theorist Sylvia Wynter, *The Tempest* is one of the foundational texts of "Western Europe's dazzling rise to global hegemony."[1] Over the past thirty years, interpretations of Shakespeare's play have been framed by discussions of conquest, dispossession, white settlement, slavery, and indigeneity.[2] Readings of *The Tempest* as a colonialist text map European accounts of New World contact, as well as narratives of Old World encounters—including those between England and Ireland—onto the play's power relations.[3] Analyses of the play's complicity in the dehumanization of non-Anglo peoples invoke the principles of universal human rights as the basis of reparative readings. What remains unexamined, however, are the presuppositions informing liberal humanism. In accordance with the tenets of universally applicable natural law, personhood was understood as pinioned to the human body, which, in turn, entitled its owner to a host of rights ranging from property to life. As scholars have shown, the notion that humanness entailed basic rights was "one of the constitutive elements of the colonial matrix of power."[4] Wynter's oeuvre explores the evolution of the idea of racial difference and shows that this idea, even in its incipient stages, was framed by the proposition that there existed various genres of the human.[5] As Wynter stresses, the most significant—and overlooked—outgrowth of Europe's early territorial expansion was renewed attention to the question: what is a human?

As Wynter explains, while medieval thought conceived of the human as primarily Christian, early modern thought recast the human in secular terms, ascribing to him rationality, self-interestedness, and self-possession. The seventeenth century marked an epistemic shift in the universal ideal of the human, which became the terrain on which

Western Europe erected the idea of the human-as-man.[6] Insofar as the humanity of the law's subject was recognized by the idiom of personhood, the human became synonymous with *homo politicus*, the political subject of the state.[7] In the early phases of European global expansion, the human-as-man, Wynter argues, served as the measuring stick against which all other forms of being were rated. Consequentially, those not regarded as fully human were assigned an inferior schedule of rights and liberties.[8] The conception of human-as-man was legitimated by systems of knowledge that valued only one "genre of the human," which was buttressed by "physiological and narrative matters that systematically excide[d] the world's most marginalized."[9]

In the pages that follow, I approach *The Tempest* as a text that wrestles with the question of what is the human. More particularly, I consider the ways blackness in *The Tempest* serves as an experimental site for a new category of personhood imposed upon those barred from becoming subjects of the law but subjected to the law. My approach reveals that this play attempts to provide an imaginary solution to the impasse between, on the one hand, the overlay of the human and the person, expressed by the idea of the human-as-man, and, on the other hand, the need to account for indigenous peoples who because of their phenotype, genealogy, or culture stood at the precipice of legal recognition. Indeed, the most significant contribution of *The Tempest* to the history of colonialism may be its elaboration of the ways the legal category of personhood stretched to accommodate genres of the human. Striving to retain the human as the prima facie site upon which personhood is erected, Shakespeare's play explores the power of personification in the colonial context. This context generated new and urgent questions about whether those perceived as quasi- or subhuman could be made accountable, even as they were systematically denied ownership of property and self. Thus *The Tempest* advances the wedding of equality and exclusion that would come to drive global capitalism as the play demonstrates that in the colonial context, the designation of personhood always entailed what Saidiya Hartman describes as a careful calculation of interest and injury.[10] By staging the potential and the limits of a legal imaginary that recognized only humans as entitled to personhood, *The Tempest* also acknowledges genres of the human that fell outside of the Anglo-European, white, humanist model of human-as-man.

*

The Tempest is framed by the question of the human, which arises at the onset and is fundamental to Prospero's status as a discoverer of *terra nullius* rather than a conqueror of an already inhabited realm. He reassures Ariel, and the audience, that when he first arrived, the island was uninhabited except for Caliban's North African mother. In referring to Sycorax, Prospero explains:

> This blue-eyed hag was hither brought with child,
> And here was left by th'sailors.
>
> . . .
>
> Then was this island—
> Save for the son that she did litter here,
> A freckled whelp, hag-born—not honoured with
> A human shape.[11]

In accordance with the logic of this origin story, the expected child upon birth turns out to be something other than human.[12] The word "litter," used here as a verb, animates a meaning reserved in the period for descriptions of animals in the act of bringing forth young.[13] In this instance, Sycorax is depicted as birthing a "whelp," or a wild animal, or what in modern parlance might described as a "cub."[14] The word "whelp," which animalizes Caliban, is also the word for an offspring so monstrous it exceeds the parameters of even the animal.[15] Importantly, Caliban does not represent the dehumanized subject who as result of having been disenfranchised is reduced to animality. Rather his ontology marks the parameters of the human species. Not quite a *Homo sapiens*, Caliban is permitted life but is ineligible for rights.[16]

As Prospero emphasizes, this "whelp" assumed "a human shape" (1.2.286). Prospero subsequently uses the word "shape" in commanding Ariel to put on the "shape" or the disguise of a sea-nymph (1.2.306). In this respect Caliban, not unlike Ariel, assumes humanness as a disguise or costume.[17] The similarities between Ariel and Caliban end there. While Ariel is coerced into serving Prospero, his labor is secured by means of consensual agreement. Ariel acknowledges his indebtedness to Prospero, who has rescued him from imprisonment, and Ariel's sense of obligation qualifies him for personhood as conceptualized within early modern legal and political thought.[18] Those who enjoyed personhood in early modern England were recognized by common law as capable of rational self-governance and thus entitled to the freedom to exercise the consensual apparatus necessary for participation in civil society. In this way, personhood was yoked to the notion of human rights, a concept that evolved from those Roman jurists who regarded natural rights as the central component of natural law. Natural law, in turn, presumed a universal humankind, since the community of humanity was conceived of as prior to the nation.[19] Accordingly, as de facto members of the universal human community, all humans held rights that since the Middle Ages were regarded as *dominium*, that is, as a form of property.[20]

While the seventeenth century marked the period during which the category of the human would become circumscribed by ideas about physiognomic difference, in this same period the category of the person enjoyed a certain degree of elasticity. The person was not co-extensive with the human since to be human was neither necessary nor sufficient for personhood. For instance, corporations could be recognized as persons and achieve civil standing. Because the "person" was a fiction of law, the term could be applied to a range of entities that did not qualify for citizenship or even subjectivity. Insofar as personhood allowed for the recognition of those who existed outside of political life, personhood performed an indispensable duty in accommodating shifting relations of power—particularly in regard to England's contact with global others—by allowing those considered abject, servile, irrational, and dangerous to become answerable to the law.

Ariel's tasks are delineated by his "charge" (1.2.239), the scope of which is defined by "articles" of agreement between himself and Prospero (1.2.195). The term "charge" is synonymous with "liability," and the word signals Ariel and Prospero's mutual responsibilities.[21] Ariel does not hesitate to call out Prospero on potential breach of contract, and he regularly reminds Prospero that he too is obligated to perform his promise. Insofar as Ariel is endowed with the qualities of a personhood, understood as the designation of the consensual subject, he shows himself capable of assuming responsibility for his actions and is eligible for entitlement. For this reason, Ariel conceives of freedom as a possession to which he has rights; he lobbies for "*my* liberty" (1.2.247, emphasis mine). Ownership is both affirmation and compensation for his willingness to honor the vehicle of contract.

Caliban, however, identified by Miranda as an exemplar of a "vile race" (1.2.361), is barred from contractual arrangements.[22] His is an existence marked by exposure to unrelenting arbitrary and capricious violence. Julia Reinhard Lupton, who reads *The Tempest* through the lens of the politico-theological category of the creaturely, regards the legal threshold and subjective possibility of personhood secured through covenant as held in potential for Caliban. For Lupton, Caliban exemplifies what Giorgio Agamben calls "bare life," that is, "pure vitality denuded of its symbolic significance and political capacity and then sequestered within the domain of civilization as its disavowed core."²³ As part of Creation, Caliban cannot be excluded from the common lot of humanity since he is always already enfolded within it, even as its "chaotic exception."²⁴ Caliban's humanity certainly "remains a question rather than a given in the play," yet this character is made legible through an ontology shot through with ideas about the human species as racialized.²⁵ As Wynter stresses, circa 1600, any prenational universalist scheme was premised on the notion that certain creatures would never qualify for the gift of grace or become eligible for proprietary benefits.

While Caliban does indeed reside in the zone of indistinction between beast and man, arguably, existing before or outside of the law, he serves as an exemplar of bare life only when abstracted from the colonial context that occasions his very existence in the first place. "Slave" is the word that is used to designate his being, and the term is ascribed to him five times in immediate succession upon his first appearance (1.2.311, 1.2.316, 1.2.324, 1.2.348, 1.2.355). Insofar as Caliban is denied "genealogy, cultural memory, social distinction, name, and native language," that is, all that constitutes the human, this character indexes Shakespeare's awareness of enslaved Africans in England, as well as his familiarity with an emergent discourse in English culture that naturalized the enslavement of black-skinned people.²⁶ As early as the period of the crusades, followed by Europe's Eastern and Western expansion, black-skinned peoples were characterized as "not far removed from apes, as man made degenerate by sin."²⁷ By the time of Shakespeare's play, English discourse was replete with stereotypes of Africans as "embodiments of evil, blackened by sin, driven by lust, and hungry for murder and revenge."²⁸ This prejudice stemmed from roots in biblical tradition, in which the sons of Ham were cursed with blackness and condemned to slavery. Thus, from its inception, the notion of blackness as somatic/physiological effectively plotted non-white bodies on a matrix of ontological distinction. In the seventeenth century, the explanatory model that legitimated the expropriation and internment of Native Americans and the enslavement of Africans was informed by natural law. The partial humanity of the Other was recognized only insofar as it served as an experimental site for the conception of the human-as-man, a conception that revealed the lineaments of a political humanism underwriting so-called universal humanism.

The non-white subject who can never transcend the racialized body complicates Agamben's idea of the *homo sacer* who marks the threshold between inside and outside of the political. As Alexander

Weheliye argues, by seeking recourse to the notion of "an indivisible biological substance anterior to racialization," the discourse of bare life misconstrues how ideas of race shaped the very idea of the human.[29] Moreover, the racialized body could not be the object of the sovereign decision since it was, as Orlando Patterson has shown, always-already socially dead.[30] So long as social death served as a substitute for literal death, the black body was an anomaly at once alive and dead. Neither self-owning nor an owner of other subjects or objects, Caliban cannot be recognized in the proprietary terms underwriting a notion of humanness linked to personhood. Rather he is himself a fungible form of property. We are reminded frequently of Caliban's exchange-value. Caliban is identified as a "strange fish" for which the English would "give a piece of silver" (2.2.28), "a present for any emperor" (2.2.28–9), and as a "thing" (5.1.267) that "money [may] buy" (5.1.268). As a vendible, "plain fish," that is "no doubt marketable" (5.1.269), this character demonstrates that "if the sovereign decision on the state of exception captures bare life in order to exclude it," then the biopolitics of slavery confirms "the profitable inclusion of socially dead beings."[31]

If we understand the project of Shakespeare's play as safeguarding the category of the human by distinguishing it from social death and alienable property, we can see how the play works to ensure that the human remains linked to political and juridical notions of enfranchisement and belonging. For this reason, Shakespeare brackets off the ontological problem of Caliban by the reduction of this character to a set of attitudes, behaviors, and pathologies that through the generic aspects of comic form place him at a remove from the play's more serious concerns about the interactions of human nature with legal processes, state-building, and geopolitics. But insofar as the borders of the human are defined by the not-quite- and nonhuman, blackness persists as an experimental site for personhood's capacities. The King of Tunis, referred to only in absentia, offers another touchstone for the question of what is the human. Tunis represents the limit concept that troubles the fundamental categories of personhood and the human, and he is permitted what Orlando Patterson describes as liminal incorporation.[32] The sovereign decision on the state of exception in this instance is replaced by the institutionalized containment of a permanent anomaly that confounds the difference between life and death, as well as the separation of destruction and profit. As a quasi-human, Tunis marks an aporia in the crucial distinction between person and property and points the way toward a novel form of "living property" that violates humanist notions of the proprietary subject.[33]

Scholars have discussed *The Tempest*'s "cultural double vision," whereby the New World is refracted through the Old World. The association the play makes between Tunis and Carthage provides a hinge between England's imagined imperial past and desired colonial future.[34] More particularly, at the time of Shakespeare's play, North Africa was recognized as the main arena over which the Iberian and Ottoman empires vied for political and commercial control. The coastal city of Tunis marked the crucial boundary point between Italy and Africa. Whoever controlled Tunis, dominated the flow of goods between the Western and Eastern Mediterranean.[35] Through a palimpsest of Algiers, Tunis, Bermuda, Carthage, and Virginia, *The Tempest* simultaneously charts contemporaneous site-specific non-European places as spaces of otherness and references classical sources in its categorization of non-Europeans. The conflation of Old and New Worlds allows the play to oscillate between residual and emergent ideas of property in person.

The King of Tunis, ideally, will facilitate the movement of goods between Italy and Africa, including the traffic in African slaves. Yet, he himself is not an exchangeable commodity. He confronts the Europeans with the problem of his coeval status as monarch and African, an admixture that the play attempts to resolve by mapping the king's two bodies onto the slave's two bodies. The king's two bodies provided a template for contractual personification since the sacred, immaterial body of the king outlived the natural body, and in this way guaranteed the continuity and indivisibility of the regime. This formulation fortified the idea of the sovereign as a "*persona mixta*" whereby the king's authority was premised on the unique distinction of being at once a biological and personified entity.[36] Just as the medieval doctrine of kingship recognized the sovereign as having both a mortal, natural body and a corporate body immune to corruption and finitude, as Stephen Best reminds us, the slave had two bodies. One was biological and the other functioned as a form of alienable property. In order for the marriage between Claribel and the King of Tunis to have meaning, Tunis must be capable of promise and reciprocity. Alonso regards him as indebted to Naples, and by extension Milan, as Italy has offered its daughter in exchange for a profitable trade route. The King of Tunis is animated by European contract law, even though as an African he remains what Stephen Best describes as property personified.

The provisional nature of Tunis's humanity is suggested by the court party's response to the union, as all unanimously register the wedding in a funeral key and imagine the marriage as presaging a loss analogous to the destruction of property and life wrought by the storm at sea. We are first introduced to the shipwrecked party through an extended discussion of the catastrophe that shapes the first half of the tragicomedy—not the tempest but rather the decision of Alonso, the King of Naples, to marry his "*fair*," meaning light skinned, daughter Claribel to the African king (2.1.70, emphasis mine). Alonso castigates himself:

> Would I had never married my daughter there! [Tunis]
> For, coming thence, my son is lost; and, in my
> Rate, she too, who is so far from Italy removed.
> I ne'er again shall see her. (2.1.107–11)

Alonso's advisors in their catastrophic thinking dilate the scope and scale of Alonso's decision to marry Claribel to an African by suggesting that its effects ripple back to Italy. Sebastian emphasizes, "Sir, you may thank yourself for this great loss, that would not bless our Europe with your daughter, but rather loose her to an African" (2.1.123–5). He continues, "We have lost your son, I fear, forever: Milan and Naples have mo' widows in them of this business' making than we bring men to comfort them: The fault's your own" (2.1.127–31). There is general consensus that Alonso has ignored sage council, represented by the kneeling and importuning of his advisors (2.1.128), as well as the noticeable suffering of his daughter, who in marrying Tunis weighed "loathness and obedience" (2.1.130).

   In an effort to comfort Alonso, the king's advisor Gonzalo imagines their unfortunate circumstance as an opportunity; he envisions the island as a *tabula rasa* that may afford a return to a Golden Age. Gonzalo's idealized commonwealth is distinguished by "no kind of traffic," and no marriage, formal education, property ownership, or "contract [or] succession" (2.1.147–51). While Gonzalo's evocation of Montaigne's "Of Cannibals" is regarded as confirmation of this character's naïveté, at this moment the play allows for the bold admission that global commercial dominance, property ownership, contractualism, and succession are the drivers of imperial ambition, which is best expressed by marital alliance rather than outright conquest. At the center of Gonzalo's description is a paean to "all things in common nature" (2.1.158), a selective collective that ensures that nature's abundance is represented not only by quantity, its plentitude, but also by quality, every entity that benefits from nature's abundance is a being "of it[s] own kind" (2.1.163). The utopian order retains the "king on't" (2.1.145), even as the "name of magistrate" (2.1.149) is unnecessary, since the state of nature reveals a community of humans who are already de facto subjects of the law.

Gonzalo's speech is based on the Aristotelian presumption of the prepolitical state of man, which affirms that man is always already a sociopolitical being, at once a human and a person.[37] Insofar as society did not exist for those who remained in a nonpolitical state of nature, the social contract was premised on the transition from natural man to civil man or *homo politicus*. As civil society was seen as founded on the consent of equals, only man enjoyed the apparatus of consent. Through the exercise of agency, man realized himself as a self-owning, rights-bearing entity. Gonzalo reminds his listeners that in his commonwealth, he "would with such perfection govern" (2.1.167), since the law of nature organizes the physical and organic world in accordance with graduated degrees of perfection, the epitome of which is human-as-man. Rather than a digression, Gonzalo's speech shores up Alonso's decision to marry his daughter to an African, as this idealized vision confirms that the social contract codifies an already existing morality, such that "[w]hat is right and wrong, just and unjust, in society will largely be determined by what is right and wrong, just and unjust, in the state of nature."[38] Thus letters, or humanistic learning, traffic, property ownership, martial alliance, and contractual arrangements are all a working out of the state of nature, ensuring that Claribel as Queen of Tunis will retain her humanity, and presumably her "fairness," allowing her to function as an extension of European rule and factotum of Italian power.

Yet from the vantage point of the more cynical Antonio and Sebastian, Claribel's presence in Tunis has displaced the Italian polis, and the union potentially imperils the integrity of the European body politic. Most alarmingly, assuming the death of Ferdinand, the presumptive heir of Naples and Milan would be the progeny of Claribel and Tunis. As Marjorie Raley stresses, because the Tunisian marriage has shifted the masculine center of power away from Naples to Tunis, "Tunis has gained more than Europe in the deal."[39] Gonzalo's reference to the "Widow Dido" (2.1.75), and his conflation of Tunis and Carthage whereby he announces "This Tunis, sir, was Carthage" (2.1.82), are the antecedents to his utopian vision. Historical tragedy, imagined via the apparition of Dido, vexes the seemingly inexorable dictates of natural law and focuses our attention on the liminal status of the African king. The connection between Carthage and Africa, as critics have noted, predated Virgil. According to ancient myth, the widow Dido selects suicide over the consummation of her enforced marriage to an African.[40] The overlay of Dido and Claribel suggests to members of the court party, as well as to the audience, that even if nature is oriented toward perfection, history allows for human agency. Claribel may follow in the footsteps of her predecessor and choose death over consummation with Tunis. As much is confirmed by Alonso who speaks not of nuptial celebrations or the promise of an heir, but of his son and daughter being both "lost" to him forever (2.1.110–12).

The anxiety surrounding the pairing of Claribel and Tunis spills over into the next scene, which follows on the heels of Alonso's musing "what strange fish hath made his meal on thee?" (2.1.113). The "thee" refers here to Alonso's son Ferdinand, in particular, but also to Alonso's heirs in aggregate: Ferdinand, Claribel, as well as the unborn progeny of Claribel and Tunis. Alonso's imagined "strange fish" is material-ized in the form of Caliban, who upon being discovered by Trinculo is described as a "strange fish" (2.2.27). In the early seventeenth century, "fish" was the word used to describe a promiscuous woman or female prostitute.[41] A "strange fish," Caliban is coded as exotic and erotically serviceable insofar as his sexuality can potentially be oriented, as in the case of Tunis, toward advancing European hegemony. However, Caliban's expressed desire to "people" the island with "Calibans" (1.2.352–3) registers an extra-legal procreative agenda that can be understood only as depravity, arguably all the more so since he pro-poses the unorthodox commingling of "people," that is humans, and Calibans. Caliban offers to "fish for" Stefano (2.2.153), and insofar as he is Stefano's fishmonger, the term in the early modern period for a pimp, he is associated again with an unlicensed erotic activity when he urges Stefano to "deeply consider" (3.2.3.93) Miranda, who "will become [Stefano's] bed . . . And bring forth brave brood" (3.2.99–100).

The "strange fish" also conjures the King of Tunis, a figure who con-flates the quasi- or nonhumanness of Caliban and the *persona mixta* of King Alonso, whom Ariel describes to Ferdinand as transformed by "a sea-change" into a thing "rich and strange," now residing "full fathom five" on the ocean floor (1.2.400–5). Here Ariel's song depicts the dismembered sovereign body, a violation of the humanist presump-tion of the bounded self, made into a "strange" and potentially a fun-gible form of property in its dispersed condition. A monstrous hybrid of human remnants and exotic materials, such as pearl and coral that yield great profit, this vision of the transmuted self speaks to European fears of the degenerative effects of non-European climates on European bodily integrity. As Monique Allewaert stresses, the transformation of the human body "was a key anxiety" expressed by Anglo-Europeans writing about the American colonies.[42] The figure of the "strange fish" points to the ways that in the colonial context the personified sovereign could devolve into the property personified.

Finally, the strange fish that destroys the heir evokes the figure of Medea, the dark-skinned queen who kills her children and who hovers on the edge of this play's psyche. As critics have noted, Medea's incantation by which she raises the dead in Book 7 of Ovid's *Metamorphoses* inflects Prospero's renunciation speech whereby in adjuring his "rough" or violent magic (5.1.49), he reflects on having "bedimmed / the noontide sun," opened "graves" and "waked their sleepers" (5.1.41–50). As Jonathan Hayes explains, Medea offered a prism through which the early modern English viewed dark-skinned people across the globe.[43] For instance, in George Sandys's accounts of his extensive travels throughout Egypt and the Middle East in the early 1600s, Sandys claimed to have seen Ovid's Medea everywhere he went.[44] In the act of renouncing his "potent art" (5.1.50) and burying his books, Prospero curiously resurrects the royal African Other, and by association Claribel's marriage at Carthage/Tunis. The threat to the Virgilian project persists so long as Claribel remains exiled on the very coast from which Aeneas fled in order to found a new political order that would come to serve as the seat of Western European civilization.[45]

The King of Tunis returns at the play's end with Gonzalo's summary of the play's tragicomic arc such that "in one voyage / Did Claribel her husband find at Tunis, / And Ferdinand her brother found a wife / Where he himself was lost / . . . and all of us ourselves, / When no man was his own" (5.1.212–16). As John Kunat emphasizes,

> Claribel had not been mentioned since the second act when Sebastian had cited her marriage as an example of Alonso's disregarding counsel. The reintroduction of her name here . . . signals a return of the repressed by which the unassimilated African marriage reasserts its right to legitimacy.[46]

If indeed the project of the play is to wrestle with the challenges of incorporating the African king, Gonzalo's recap reassures his listeners that all are restored self-propriety. Every European man may reclaim himself as his own property rather than the property of another. Yet, even if in the final analysis each European man is "his own," the lingering prospect of creolization represents a loose end that potentially unravels the tidy closure the play promises. The play accounts for this by activating the magic of personification beyond the instrument of legal personhood.

Throughout the play, Prospero deploys spectacle as a medium by which to transmute coercion into consent. He mobilizes "direful spectacle" (1.2.26) at the play's opening to "touch" the "virtue of compassion" (1.2.26–7) in Miranda, who "suffers" with those she sees suffering (1.2.5–6). Meta- and intra-theatricality in *The Tempest* have been discussed in relation to the play's interest in the court masque, the early modern form of court dramaturgy by which the monarch asserted his authority. We can consider Prospero's use to the masque form in the colonial context as a precursor of early nineteenth-century dramatic enactments scripted by abolitionists who aimed to unleash indignation through the phantasmal vehicle of identification that would unsettle and disturb viewers. By highlighting the crimes committed by those who had been cruel to their slaves, the theatrics of shock and awe aimed to rouse the conscience of slave owners. Prospero too relies on spectacle to rehearse injustices and rouse the sensibilities of members of the court party complicit in his banishment. Prospero creates a shared experience of horror in the harpy masque, which is an example of pleasure "ensnared in a web of domination, accumulation, abjection, resignation, and possibility."[47] In this respect, magic and theater—and magic as theater— function like the legal process of personification, a means by which to rehumanize those who are guilty of treachery by animating their accountability through the manufacture of fictitious personae.

Prospero's wedding masque reactivates the concerns raised by the court party in their discussion of Alonso's decision to marry Claribel to an African. In an extended interlude, the myth of Proserpine provides a vehicle for a return to the theme of disappearing daughters. Alluding to Proserpine's abduction by the "dusky," or dark-skinned, Dis (4.1.89), the god of the underworld, the masque invokes the genre of the pastoral in its representation of this interracial pairing as part of the natural order. The cost of the enforced union is acknowledged by the grief of Proserpine's mother Ceres. The role of Ceres is performed by Ariel, and this role-play allows the service contract to underwrite the celebration of the marital contract, allowing the masque, like the play as a whole, to implicitly conflate serviceability and sexuality, and in this way condone the realization of imperial ambition through marital alliance. Through repeated references to contractual bonds, which form the chorus, stanzas emphasizing the bounty of the natural world link its plentitude to the introduction of the legal mechanism of contract. Nature's abundance is elided with real wealth, as labor and expropriation are repressed, and Miranda and Ferdinand are ensured "honour" and "riches" (4.1.107). They are similarly assured that "scarcity and want shall shun [them]" (4.1.116) so long as they hold off from consummating their relationship until "a contract of true love" is ratified (4.1.133).

The masque is described by Ferdinand as "harmonious charmingly" (4.1.118), and its mollifying effects derive from its ability to mystify the antagonism between Proserpine and Dis by representing the union as fundamental to the "long continuance and increasing / . . . / Earth's increase and foison plenty, / Barns and garners never empty" (4.1.107–11). The analogy between Claribel and Tunis and Proserpine and Dis allows for colonial expansion conceived in a general way as planting to assume the particular project of inseminating European women with the aim of producing heirs who can serve as extensions of European authority. Miranda's procreative potential is an especially valuable commodity, and she is described by her father as Ferdinand's "compensation" (4.1.2), an "acquisition, worthily purchased" (4.1.14–15), and later as his (Ferdinand's) "own" (4.1.33). Yet the Old World strategy of extending empire through dynastic marriage took on new contours in a New World context since such alliances introduced a threat to the racial integrity of European hegemony through creolization. As intermarriage forged new identities that had no equivalent in the Anglo tradition, multiracial heirs strained the idea of human-as-man. In the initial stages of colonial expansion, "property's personification" offered a means of granting non-Western quasi-humans the burden of personhood without the entitlements of self-ownership.[48]

I have been arguing that the egalitarian principles of contract, premised on the proto-Enlightenment ideal of man as rational and self-possessed, needed to be reconciled with the expropriation, dispossession, and subjection of human beings across the globe. Critics who have discussed *The Tempest* in light of early modern social contract theory emphasize service as the dominant institution and prevailing condition of life in the period.[49] However, the privileging of service as the predominant framework for social relations in *The Tempest* does not account for early seventeenth-century England's economic and ideological investment in a thriving global slave trade. As recent scholarship has shown, the English Crown was not late to the trade in African slaves relative to the Iberians. England was actively involved in the Mediterranean slave trade throughout the fifteenth century, and there are records of African slaves living in London throughout the sixteenth century.[50] Thus the principles that guide this play may be less informed by the established social contract and more aptly captured by the emergent "racial contract," which linked humanness to personhood while granting the status of humanness selectively.[51] The terms of the racial contract restricted "egalitarianism to equality among equals."[52] Those who were ontologically excluded from the category of the human proved to be essential to the establishment of the human-as-man.[53]

The discussion of the human that opens *The Tempest* returns at the play's end when Ariel impresses upon Prospero the suffering of the court party. Ariel hopes to move Prospero by comparing his own nonhuman status with Prospero's humanness, which may be affirmed by his capacity for compassion. "If you now beheld them your affections / Would become tender . . . / Mine would, sir, were I human" (5.1.16–19). By recognizing that the members of the court party are repentant, Prospero assures Ariel, "And mine [affections] shall [become tender]," since I am "one of their kind" and thus "kindlier moved than thou art" (5.1.24). Here Prospero affirms rationality, empathy, and morality as fundamental human attributes. Even the unnaturally treacherous Antonio and Sebastian are in the end brought back into the fold of the human as they show themselves capable of culpability. They, in turn, are juxtaposed to the "strange thing" (5.1.292) whose sole value is to make or create "a man" on the island or back in Europe (2.2.28–9). Caliban has made Prospero the "man," as confirmed by Caliban's resolution to "swear[ ] [himself]" to Stefano (2.2.144) and "get a new man!" (2.2.176). In accordance with the terms of the racial contract, the restoration of Antonio and Sebastian to the status of human is predicated on Caliban's inability to experience remorse and take responsibility for his actions.

If the King of Tunis confounds the tenets of the proprietary subject, then Caliban provides its ground. "Drawing on the medieval legacy of the Wild Man, and giving this color," the subhuman, as political theorist Charles Mills stresses, established "a particular somatotype as the norm" and affirmed that any deviation from this norm "*unfits* one for full personhood and full membership in the polity."[54] Identified by Prospero at the play's opening as "*my* slave" (1.2.311, emphasis mine), Caliban is denied recognition by the law even after having been discovered at the play's end of inciting sedition. Prospero's public acknowledgment of ownership of Caliban, "this thing of darkness, I acknowledge mine" (5.1.77–8), is not a new development but a continuation of the denial of Caliban's humanness. Owing nothing and having ownership over nothing, Caliban remains a cipher in the eyes of the law. Indeed, his primary function is to affirm the humanness of the Europeans, and his myopia toward his own liability is refracted by Sebastian's and Antonio's awakening to their own respective consciences. By accepting responsibility for Prospero's banishment from Milan, the aristocrats are rehabilitated by the same structure of accountability that effects Caliban's subjugation.

What subject status and recognition of humanity is available to those not endowed with personhood? Can *The Tempest* acknowledge the human independent of personhood—that is, with a status neither bequeathed nor revoked by juridical authority? What genres of the human exist in the play beyond the world of the human-as-man? While *The Tempest*'s singular achievement may be the staging of the elasticity of contract and its affective capacities, the play does gesture toward what remains outside the formulation of the human as synonymous with person-in-property. Relations that escape capture by the racial contract, if only momentarily, show fissures in the play's humanist discourse of the subject as it strains to conceal relational possibilities that push against a view of the human as grounded in personhood-as-ownership. What remains outside the formulation of the human as synonymous with person-in-property is the flesh. The play is ultimately unable to magically accommodate the flesh via the fantastic figuration of personhood.

I return to the "fish"iness of Caliban, which affirms his status at the interstice of the human and nonhuman. Both Caliban, who regards himself as his "own king" (1.1.342), and the King of Tunis in different ways unsettle the "declensions of personhood" that uphold the racialization of property in the play.[55] As I have suggested, the "strange fish" is a synecdoche for the quasi-human, at once a racialized natural body and a personified form of fungible property. The word "fish" and the word "flesh" share a homophonic relation. By considering Caliban as "strange flesh," that is, as part-human/part-fish, or as partial in his human-fleshedness, we can explore how this character confronts us with the conundrum of the flesh as that which is temporally and conceptually "*antecedent* to the body."[56] Insofar as the flesh is the surplus of the law's claim on the body, Caliban's corporality is the "vestibular gash" in the "armor of Man."[57] As Alexander Weheliye argues, since flesh may function as "simultaneously a tool of dehumanization and relational vestibule to alternate ways of being that do not possess the luxury of eliding phenomenology with biology," the flesh is neither an aberration nor wholly excluded.[58] While not at the center of being, flesh is of it, and as such the flesh is "the cornerstone and potential ruin of the world of man."[59] Caliban as "strange flesh" attests to the enduring potential of racial difference that cannot be accommodated by personhood.

Caliban's flesh is intrusive. Pushed "even to the roaring" (4.1.193), racked with cramps and pinches it "roars" (1.2.372). Ariel's clarion call "Hark, they roar!"(4.1.259) reminds Prospero of the propulsive force of the resistance. Caliban's flesh, like the mutinous party he commandeers, is connected to the roarers at the play's opening. The physical waves and the mutinous crew alike reject subjugation to King Alonso and refuse submission to the law. The roarers introduce the possibility of "newly created" creatures, like those that Antonio "new formed" and mobilized (1.2.83–4) to effect Prospero's banishment from Milan. By staging the analogy of the tempest-tossed ship of state, which as David Norbrook reminds us held wide appeal for early seventeenth-century political thinkers, Shakespeare offers an alternative to the idea of the body politic as naturalized by social contract.[60] If on land, sovereignty resides in the decision over who lives and who dies, on the ship, as on the island, we are presented with a permanent state of emergency. Here decisions are executed in the absence of any legal framework. Authority is not accountable to the nation state or any institution empowered by the monarch or his supranational networks. Yet, unlike the island, where the state of exception forms the core of the sovereign decision-making of Prospero who exercises authority over the lives and bodies of the colonized and enslaved, onboard the ship new and potentially insurrectionary elements may arise.

The play establishes at the opening that the "roarers" care not for the "name of king" (1.1.15–16), who himself is placed in a situation where the social order is suspended. The word "roarers" connotes misrule, generally, and the rebellion associated with "riotous people" (1.1.n.5) or the resistant multitude, specifically. Even the king's councilor is unable to "command" the elements (1.1.19), which include the seditious crew. In the face of their own impotency, Antonio and Sebastian attempt to maintain their status as humans by classifying the insubordinate Boatswain as a "dog" (1.1.37) and a "cur" (1.1.39). Even after we learn that the roarers are the product of manufactured chaos, as in the case of Caliban, Stephen, and Trinculo's plot to overthrow Prospero, at such moments of controlled chaos, the play nonetheless acknowledges the contingent potential of that which resides in the gap between subjection to monarchal authority and the efficacy of personification. The roarers could at any moment assume any shape, perhaps that of the "treacherous army" levied by Antonio to extirpate Prospero from Milan (1.2.128). The roarers, like the flesh, are in excess of the social order, as indicated by the fact that in this play the punishment for treason can never be staged. The Boatswain's insurgency is revisited at the play's end, when he along with the ship's crew is brought back on stage. Gonzalo comments, "I prophesied if a gallows were on land this fellow could not drown" (5.1.220–1). At this moment, the Boatswain is "newly created" (1.2.81), transformed from a "dog" back into a "fellow" as he is recognized as eligible for punishment and thus subjected to the law. Yet his hanging is deferred indefinitely.

Investigations of the human have gained prominence in Shakespeare Studies, exemplified, for instance, by the "bio" turn characterizing eco-criticism, animal studies, and posthumanism. Scholars have urged us to think beyond the divide between humans and nonhumans and to consider the agentic capacities of animals, vegetables, and even minerals. Sylvia Wynter's project, which serves as the inspiration for this chapter, urges us to push beyond a universalist, liberal conception of the human, and in so doing, consider what lies outside of the epistemologies that institute and reproduce the human-as-man. As my analysis of *The Tempest* has shown, critical approaches to the play have yet to fully engage how indenture and enslavement were premised on the ontological problem of what is the human. The racialized body, which could not be accounted for by the discourse of universal human rights, served as a referent of emerging forms of dominium and domination that in turn revealed that inclusion did not entail freedom. Because non-white persons were rendered legally and politically accountable, even as they were not regarded as fully human, we can only comprehend the full scope of *The Tempest*'s investment in a colonial imaginary by attending to the play's interest in the genres of the human.

Notes

1. Sylvia Wynter, "Afterword: Beyond Miranda's Meanings: Un/Silencing the 'Demonic Ground' of Caliban's 'Woman,'" in *Out of the Kumbla: Caribbean Women and Literature*, ed. Carole Boyce Davis and Elaine Savory Fido (Trenton, NJ: Africa World Press, 1990), 355–72, 358.
2. Scholars have explored Shakespeare's familiarity with narratives of England's early attempts at settlement in Jamestown, the colonial politics of England's engagement with Ireland, and England's involvement in the Mediterranean slave trade. See Paul Brown, "'This thing of darkness I acknowledge mine': *The Tempest* and the Discourse of Colonialism," in *Political Shakespeare: New Essays in Cultural Materialism*, ed. Jonathan Dollimore and Alan Sinfield (Manchester: Manchester University Press, 1985), 48–71; Francis Barker and Peter Hulme, "'Nymphs and reapers heavily vanish': The Discursive Con-Texts of *The Tempest*," in *Alternative Shakespeares*, ed. John Drakakis (New York: Methuen, 1985), 191–205; Stephen Greenblatt, *Shakespearean Negotiations: The Circulation of Social Energy in Renaissance England* (Berkeley: University of

California Press, 1988), 129–63; Deborah Willis, "Shakespeare's *Tempest* and the Discourse of Colonialism," *Studies in English Literature, 1500–1900* 29.2 (1989): 277–89; John Gilles, *Shakespeare and the Geography of Difference* (Cambridge: Cambridge University Press, 1994); Barbara Fuchs, "Conquering Islands: Contextualizing *The Tempest*," *Shakespeare Quarterly* 48 (1997): 45–62.

3. Such readings presume that *The Tempest* validates a Eurocentric conception of normalcy, and in so doing, advances the ideological underpinnings of European domination of non-European others.

4. Walter Mignolo, "Citizenship, Knowledge, and the Limits of Humanity," *American Literary History* 18.2 (Summer 2006): 312–31, 312.

5. Sylvia Wynter, "Unsettling the Coloniality of Being/Power/Truth/Freedom: Towards the Human, After Man, its Overrepresentation—An Argument," *The New Centennial Review* 3.3 (Fall 2003): 257–337, 288. Wynter's project is to track the conceptual terms by which the ontological understanding of the human is constituted. Her use of the word "genre" points us toward the ideological hegemonies that underpin ideas such as the human-as-man, the quasi- or not-quite human, and the subhuman. Each genre of the human is imprinted by particular historical, material, and cultural investments. For Wynter, circa 1600, only the European, white, rational, and self-possessed man was regarded as fully human. See Sylvia Wynter and David Scott, "The Re-enchantment of Humanism: An Interview with Sylvia Wynter," *Small Axe* 8 (September 2000): 119–207; Katherine McKittrick, ed., *Sylvia Wynter: On Being Human as Praxis* (Durham, NC: Duke University Press, 2015).

6. Mignolo discusses sixteenth-century debates about the humanity of various indigenous peoples in light of predominant religious, scientific, and cultural presumptions about the lack of the humanity of African slaves, as well as Jews, Moors, Ottomans, and Russians. Mignolo, "Citizenship, Knowledge," 322.

7. Wynter writes, "nowhere is this mutation of ethics [from religious ethic as defined by universalist Christian perspective replaced by the reason of state ethic grounded in civic humanist values] seen more clearly than in two plays written in the first decades of the seventeenth century [*The Tempest* and the Spanish play *The New World Discovered by Christopher Columbus*]." Wynter, "Unsettling Coloniality of Being," 289. She goes onto explain that while the human had been defined by the evangelical mission of the Church, in the late sixteenth century, the imperializing mission of the state offered an alternative definition of the human, one that justified territorial expansion and conquest. As a corollary, enslavement was no longer regarded as the legacy of original sin but became tied to the irrational aspects of human nature. One could be a slave to one's passions; the rational human, i.e. human-as-man, subdued his private interests in order to adhere to the laws of the state, i.e. to the common good (289).

8. Charles W. Mills, *The Racial Contract* (Ithaca, NY: Cornell University Press, 1997), 56.
9. Sylvia Wynter and Katherine McKittrick, "Unparalleled Catastrophe for Our Species? Or, to Give Humanness a Different Future: Conversations," in McKittrick, ed., *Sylvia Wynter: On Being Human as Praxis*, 9–90, 9.
10. Personhood under slavery was inescapably bound to violence as "the law constituted the subject as a muted pained body or a trespasser to be punished." Saidiya Hartman, *Scenes of Subjection: Terror, Slavery, and Self-Making in Nineteenth-Century America* (New York: Oxford University Press, 1997), 84.
11. William Shakespeare, *The Tempest*, *The Norton Shakespeare*, 2nd edn., ed. Stephen Greenblatt, Walter Cohen, Jean E. Howard, and Katharine Eisaman Maus (New York: W. W. Norton, 2008), 1.2.271–86. All further references to the play are to this edition and will appear in the body of the text.
12. Julia Reinhard Lupton approaches *The Tempest* through the lens of political theology and posits that: "if we want to find a new universalism in the play (as I believe, urgently, we must), we will do so not by simply reasserting that 'Caliban is human' but rather by saying that 'all humans are creatures,' that all humans constitute an exception to their own humanity, whether understood in general or particular terms." Julia Reinhard Lupton, "Creature Caliban," *Shakespeare Quarterly* 51 (2000): 1–23, 21.
13. "litter, *v.*," def. I.7.a. *OED Online* (Oxford: Oxford University Press, May 2019), <http://www.oed.com/view/Entry/109238> (last accessed May 31, 2019).
14. "whelp, *n.*," def. II.2.a. *OED Online* (Oxford: Oxford University Press, May 2019), <http://www.oed.com/view/Entry/228186> (last accessed May 31, 2019).
15. "whelp, *n.*," def. III.3.a. *OED Online* (Oxford: Oxford University Press, May 2019), <http://www.oed.com/view/Entry/228186> (last accessed May 31, 2019).
16. Vaughan and Vaughan discuss Caliban in the context of both early modern source materials and the history of performance. See A. T. Vaughan and V. Mason Vaughan, *Shakespeare's Caliban: A Cultural History* (Cambridge: Cambridge University Press, 1991).
17. One is reminded here of Richard Jobson's defense in his *The Golden Trade, or, A Discovery of the River Gambra* (London, 1623) that Englishmen did not buy or sell "any that had our own *shapes*" (emphasis mine). Qtd. in Emily C. Bartels, "*Othello* and Africa: Postcolonialism Reconsidered," *The William and Mary Quarterly*, 3rd Series, 54.1 (January 1997): 45–64, 60.
18. In Roman law, "person" was the term for any juridical entity recognized by law. On the legal and philosophical formulation of the person, see William Blackstone, *Commentaries on the Laws of England, 1765–79*,

15th edn. (London: T. Cadell and W. Davides, 1765); C. B. Macpherson, *The Political Theory of Possessive Individualism* (New York: Oxford University Press, 1962); Samuel von Pufendorf, *Political Writings of Samuel Pufendorf* (New York: Oxford University Press, 1994); Stephen Best, *The Fugitive's Properties: Law and the Poetics of Possession* (Chicago: University of Chicago Press, 2004). Lupton argues for the potential of the category of the "minor" for political reform that allows for the elasticity of personhood in *The Tempest*. For Lupton, Caliban, before the arrival of Prospero, is "a person in process," that is "neither fully adult nor fully child." Julia Reinhard Lupton, "The Minority of Caliban," in *Thinking with Shakespeare: Essays on Politics and Life* (Chicago: University of Chicago Press, 2011), 187–219, 201, 203.

19. Fifteenth-century jurists speak of "the law of nature and nations," since the law of nations was seen as a working out of natural law. Thus, in theory, the law of nations applied equally to all. Anthony Pagden, "Human Rights, Natural Rights and Europe's Imperial Legacy," *Political Theory* (April 2003) 31.2: 171–99, 175.

20. Pagden, "Human Rights," 175. As M. J. Radin emphasizes, "to achieve proper self-development—to be a *person*—an individual needs some control over resources in the external environment. The necessary assurances of control take the form of property rights." M. J. Radin, *Reinterpreting Property* (Chicago: University of Chicago Press, 1993), 35.

21. Sidia Fiorato, "Ariel and Caliban as Law-Conscious Servants Longing for Legal Personhood," in *Liminal Discourses: Subliminal Tensions in Law and Literature*, ed. Daniela Carpi and Jeanne Gaakeer (Berlin: De Gruyter, 2013), 113–29, 114–15.

22. In the early modern period, the word "race" could signify difference in lineage, clan, as well as species.

23. Lupton, "Creature Caliban," 2.

24. Lupton, "Creature Caliban," 3.

25. Lupton, "Creature Caliban," 13.

26. Ewa Plonowska Ziarek, "Barelife on Strike: The Biopolitics of Race and Gender," *South Atlantic Quarterly* 107.1 (Winter 2008): 89–105, 95. See also Mark Rifkin, "Indigenizing Agamben: Rethinking Sovereignty in Light of the 'Peculiar' Status of Native Peoples," *Cultural Critique* 73 (Fall 2009): 88–124; Emily Weissbourd, "'Those in Their Possession': Race, Slavery, and Queen Elizabeth's 'Edicts of Expulsion,'" *The Huntington Library Quarterly* 78.1 (Spring 2015): 1–19.

27. Wynter, "Unsettling Coloniality of Being," 302.

28. Bartels, "*Othello* and Africa," 53.

29. Alexander G. Weheliye, *Habeas Viscus: Racializing Assemblages, Biopolitics, and Black Feminist Theories of the Human* (Durham, NC: Duke University Press, 2014), 4.

30. On social death, see Orlando Patterson, *Slavery and Social Death: A Comparative Study*, 2nd edn. (Cambridge, MA: Harvard University Press, 2018), 38–45.

31. Ziarek, "Barelife on Strike," 96.
32. On liminal incorporation, see Patterson, *Slavery and Social Death*, 45–51.
33. Best, *Fugitive's Property*, 2.
34. Jerry Brotton has characterized the play as staging the "*geopolitical bifurcation* between the Old World and the New." *The Tempest* elaborates historically specific political and commercial relations in, and imperial ambitions towards, East and West alike. Jerry Brotton, "'This Tunis, sir, was Carthage': Contesting Colonialism in *The Tempest*," in *Post-Colonial Shakespeares*, ed. Ania Loomba and Martin Orkin (New York: Routledge, 1998), 23–42, 37.
35. Brotton, "'This Tunis, sir, was Carthage,'" 33–4. The role of Africa and Africans, as critics have acknowledged, is crucial to an understanding of this play's racial politics. See Marjorie Raley, "Claribel's Husband," in *Race, Ethnicity, and Power in the Renaissance*, ed. Joyce Green MacDonald (Madison, NJ: Fairleigh Dickinson University Press, 1997), 95–119; John Kunat, "'Play me false': Rape, Race, and Conquest in *The Tempest*," *Shakespeare Quarterly* 65.3, 307–27, 311. On North Africa as a commercial hub in the period, particularly in regard to the traffic in slaves, see Weissbourd, "Race, Slavery, and 'Edicts,'" 14.
36. Best, *Fugitive's Property*, 5.
37. On the late Elizabethan Aristotelian revival, see Charles Schmitt, *Aristotle and the Renaissance* (Cambridge, MA: Harvard University Press, 1983).
38. Mills, *Racial Contract*, 15.
39. Raley, "Claribel's Husband," 110.
40. Raley, "Claribel's Husband," notes that in Tertullian's and Servius's accounts, Dido commits suicide to avoid consummating her marriage to an African king. See also Stephen Orgel, ed. *The Tempest: The Oxford Shakespeare* (Oxford: Oxford University Press, 2008).
41. Raley, "Claribel's Husband," 113.
42. Particular concerns were about the effects of tropical heat and humidity on the Anglo-constitution. Monique Allewaert, *Ariel's Ecology: Plantations, Personhood, and Colonialism in the American Tropics* (Minneapolis: University of Minnesota Press, 2013), 2.
43. Jonathan Hayes, *Humanist as Traveler*, qtd. in Ernest B. Gilman, "Sycorax's 'Thing,'" in *Solon and Thespis: Law and Theater in the English Renaissance*, ed. Dennis Kezar (Notre Dame, IN: University of Notre Dame Press, 2007), 99–123, 119.
44. See Gilman, "Sycorax's 'Thing,'" 116. Herodotus cites from personal observation that the Colchians of his day (484 BC–424 BC) were "black-skinned" and had "wooly" hair. *The History of Herodotus*, trans. George Rawlison, qtd. in William P. McDonald, "The Blackness of Medea," *College Language Association Journal* 19.1 (September 1975): 20–7, 23n.5.

45. On the Virgilian parallels in *The Tempest*, see Jan Kott, "*The Aeneid* and *The Tempest*," *Arion: A Journal of Humanities and the Classics* 3.4 (1976): 424–51; John Pitcher, "A Theatre of the Future: *The Aeneid* and *The Tempest*," *Essays in Criticism* 34.3 (July 1984): 193–215.
46. Kunat, "'Play me false,'" 326.
47. Hartman, *Scenes of Subjection*, 49.
48. Best, *Fugitive's Property*, 37. Self-possession did not "liberate the former slave from his or her bonds but rather sought to replace the whip with the compulsory contract." Hartman, *Scenes of Subjection*, 6.
49. Sidia Fiorato, for instance, writes: "The social 'place' of every individual was substantially determined by their relation to a more powerful master, thus forming an unbroken chain of hierarchy of service that stretched from the lowliest peasant to the monarch (who owed service to God). It was an expression of the social contract which applied to everyone, to the point that it was almost impossible to conceive of a properly human existence outside a master–servant relationship." Fiorato, "Ariel and Caliban as Law-Conscious," 113.
50. François Laroque, "Italy vs. Africa: Shakespeare's Topographies of Desire in *Othello*, *Antony and Cleopatra*, and *The Tempest*," *Shakespeare Studies* 47 (2009): 1–16, 12n.40. See also Imtiaz Habib, *Black Lives in the English Archives, 1500–1677* (London: Ashgate, 2008); Gustav Ungerer, *The Mediterranean Apprenticeship of British Slavery* (Madrid: Editorial Verbum, 2008). The independent voyages of Sir John Hawkins in the early sixteenth century are no longer considered the initial moment of British involvement in the slave trade. Ungerer establishes that the English trafficked in African slaves throughout the early half of the fifteenth century as English merchants based in Andalusia participated in the Iberian slave trade.
51. Mills, *Racial Contract*, 63. On the rise of the contract form in the late sixteenth century, see Victoria Kahn, *Wayward Contracts: The Crisis of Political Obligation in England, 1640–1674* (Princeton, NJ: Princeton University Press, 2004).
52. Mills, *Racial Contract*, 56.
53. Mills writes: "White supremacy is the unnamed political system that has made the modern world what it is today. You will not find this term in introductory, or even advanced, texts in political theory. . . . But though it covers more than two thousand years of Western political thought and runs the ostensible gamut of political systems, there will be no mention of the basic political system that has shaped the world for the past several hundred years." Mills, *Racial Contract*, 1.
54. Mills, *Racial Contract*, 54 (original emphasis).
55. Best, *Fugitive's Property*, 85.
56. Weheliye, *Habeas Viscus*, 39 (emphasis mine).
57. Weheliye, *Habeas Viscus*, 39.
58. Weheliye, *Habeas Viscus*, 44.
59. Weheliye, *Habeas Viscus*, 44.

60. David Norbrook, "'What cares these roarers for the name of king?':
Language and Utopia in *The Tempest*," in *The Politics of Tragicomedy:
Shakespeare and After*, ed. Gordon McMullan and Jonathan Hope
(London: Routledge, 1992), 21–54, 33.

Part III

Processes of Personhood: Eating, Lusting, Mapping

Liquid *Macbeth*
David B. Goldstein

Liquidity

As artists and directors have intuitively known for centuries, the banquet in Act 3 of *Macbeth*—the one rudely interrupted by the ghost of
Banquo taking possession of the tyrant's chair—is never about food.
It is always about drink (Figure 8.1). Rarely, if ever, is eating fore-
grounded in the scene. When food appears on the banquet table, as it
did in Jack O'Brien's production of the play at Lincoln Center in 2014
(Figure 8.2), it is conspicuously left untouched. In Robert Richmond's
recent production of Davenant's Restoration *Macbeth* (a version in
which the banquet scene is barely altered) at the Folger Shakespeare
Library, the sole physical marker of the fact that there was a banquet
happening at all was a single cup, manipulated threateningly throughout the scene. A nineteenth-century prompt book of the play prepared
for Mary Warner, who played Lady Macbeth for a production directed
by Samuel Phelps, illustrates clearly the centrality of drink and the
irrelevance of food to so many productions of the play. Despite a carefully drawn diagram of the banquet scene including two tables, both
set "with various eatables Wine &c" (Figure 8.3), subsequent hand-
written stage directions refer only to filling goblets with wine, and
none whatsoever to any stage business involving eating.[1] Perhaps most
arrestingly, the camera in *Throne of Blood*, Akira Kurosawa's film
adaptation of the play, surveys a row of pristine bowls of uneaten rice,
while the Macbeth character throws back saucer after saucer of sake.[2]

This single-minded focus on drink stands in contrast to numerous Shakespearean banquets, both onstage and off: for instance, the
banquet in *Titus Andronicus*, in which eating is essential to the plot;
As You Like It, whose al fresco picnic scene commonly has Jaques
taking a bite out of an apple; *Timon of Athens*, whose first banquet
must include food for the subsequent banquet of lukewarm water

and stones to make any dramatic sense; and the feast that precedes *Hamlet*, in which "The funeral baked meats / Did coldly furnish forth the marriage tables."[3] This is all the more remarkable because the banquet scene in *Macbeth*, which takes up Act 3, scene 4, is replete with references to food and eating. Lady Macbeth welcomes the thanes with an expansive meditation on the relationship between hospitality and meals that simultaneously functions as a scold to Macbeth, who has been at the side of the stage conversing with the first murderer: "To feed were best at home; / From thence, the sauce to meat is ceremony: / Meeting were bare without it."[4] "To feed," meaning to eat merely, alone like an animal, is best conducted at home. The point of a formal banquet is to eat in company, to activate the commensal pleasures and risks of the table. When Macbeth sees the ghost of Banquo and begins to act erratically, Lady Macbeth notes the slippage by telling the thanes to do exactly what she has just told Macbeth *not* to do: "Feed, and regard him not" (3.4.55). As the banquet unravels, its risks overtaxing its pleasures, Lady Macbeth suddenly longs for a domestic commensality she can control rather than a public one she cannot.

The subtleties of these lines about eating are often lost in stage productions, however, because the eating itself is lost. A more influential line upon artists and directors, by far, occurs during Macbeth's attempt to regain control of his emotions and the meal, just before the second appearance of the ghost:

> Come, love and health to all,
> Then I'll sit down. Give me some wine, fill full.
> I drink to th' general joy o' the whole table,
> And to our dear friend Banquo, whom we miss.
> Would he were here!   *Enter Ghost.*
>   To all, and him we thirst,
> And all to all. (3.4.85–90)

The multiple ironies of the moment are irresistible. Macbeth wishing love to the thanes he is happy to tyrannize, health to remind us of those he has killed, joy in the midst of horror; and his final invocation to Banquo, whose ghost Macbeth has just seen and who thirsts in hell for revenge just as Macbeth thirsts for the oblivion of drink—make for great theater. All of these dramatic threads are cathected into Macbeth's wine goblet, which never lies far from him in artistic depictions of this scene. It is always still dangling from his hand in disbelief, or forgotten on the table, or dashed incredulously to the floor (Figure 8.4). The wine goblet stands in for a host, so to speak, of thematic interactions in the play: the violation of hospitality inherent in Macbeth's assassination of the king under his own roof; the mockery made of commensality first by Macbeth's killing of his dear friend and banquet-partner, Banquo, and then by Banquo's appearance at Macbeth's banquet; a parody of Eucharistic binding; and a collapse of the merrymaking that alcohol presages and encourages in displays of camaraderie and power. Macbeth's wine also establishes a link with the blood that rhetorically and theatrically spills out from its characters (Figures 8.5 and 8.6). The wine goblet locates itself at the intersection of *Macbeth*'s various dramatic axes.

At the heart of this ubiquitous stage business is a broad and complex matrix of associations. *Macbeth* is more than a play in which a wineglass helpfully stands in for an array of thematic concerns. It is a play that fundamentally concerns and enacts a problematic of liquidity, in which an obsessive catalog of fluids—water, milk, wine, poison, blood—pools into an understanding of human nature at once permeable and transformative. When the weird sisters, in the play's unforgettable opening lines, ask when they three will meet again, the choices—"In thunder, lightning, or in rain?"—are not merely atmospheric (1.1.2). The association of evil with water, and more generally with fluid indeterminacy and unfixity, remains consistent throughout the play, and indicates what I call a metaphorics of ingredience that is one of *Macbeth*'s master topoi, along with those well-studied topoi of sight and time. *Macbeth* is a drinking tragedy, one that turns the most convivial of acts into an emblem of moral, social, categorical, and environmental collapse. More interesting, it is a play about the failure of subjects and objects to remain in their proper respective philosophical and material spheres, thus calling into question whether subjects and objects have ever really behaved properly at all.

The question of how Shakespeare approaches subjects and objects—or, put another way, how he considers personhood and whatever is opposed to it—has a long history, dating back most obviously to the 1996 publication of the edited volume *Subject and Object in Renaissance Culture*.[5] In revisiting the question, I draw in part from ecologists and object theorists, especially of Actor-Network Theory and New Materialism, who, among the various object-oriented theorists at work today, have in common an interest in the fluid boundary between actors, actions, and those acted upon. Graham Harman, in outlining his "Axioms of Immaterialism" to counter the central tenets, as he sees them, of New Materialist philosophers such as Jane Bennett and Karen Barad, insists that for him, "Everything is split up according to definite boundaries and cut-off points rather than along continuous gradients," and further, "Substances/nouns have priority over actions/verbs."[6] *Macbeth*, I will argue, adopts the opposite view. In this play, anchored firmly in an early modern understanding of what Gail Kern Paster and others call "the ecology of the passions," little is defined securely by definite boundaries, and the operational movement of the action is gradient-like.[7] Not only do substances/nouns *not* have priority over actions/verbs, but in fact substances acquire verb-like characters, or inhabit roles which are simultaneously subject and verb. Further, *Macbeth* uses liquidity and ingredience as markers for continuities among human and nonhuman actors, noting and making visible the various articulations among bodies and the actions that connect them, while challenging the sense that those bodies are distinct from each other in a firmly measurable, material sense. As Karen Barad says of quantum mechanics (and while I hesitate to draw conclusions about literary forms from her work, perhaps the association will be helpful), "'measurements' are causal intra-actions."[8] The ways in which *Macbeth* measures the quantities (ingredients) of persons and objects are contingent upon the interactions among those persons and objects. If we are to assign a philosophical perspective to this play, or at least to my reading of it, it will be opposed to object-oriented ontology, and in sympathy with Jane Bennett when she writes that

> perhaps there is no need to choose between objects or their relations. . . . One would then understand "objects" to be those swirls of matter, energy, and incipience that hold themselves together long enough to vie with the strivings of other objects, including the indeterminate momentum of the throbbing whole.[9]

The term Shakespeare uses in *Macbeth* to express this phenomenon of the contingency of objects is "ingredience."

Ingredience

To return, or swirl, to and through the play: in the midst of his first soliloquy, oscillating between the poles of gentility and violence, Macbeth worries that the judgment he metes out on Duncan's life will return to pronounce him guilty. "This even-handed justice," he frets, "Commends th'ingredience of our poisoned chalice / To our own lips" (1.7.10–12). He who commits the toxic act of murdering one's guest and king, Macbeth reasons, may inevitably find himself victim of that self-same toxin.

The choice of the word "ingredience" to describe the alimentary action of that chalice is a fascinating one. The word is somewhat rare in the period, showing up perhaps a hundred times over the hundred-year span 1550–1650.[10] It carries a trio of related meanings: either the ingredient or ingredients of a compound, or the action by which those ingredients enter the compound, or the compound's interaction with its consumer. This makes sense, since the singular "ingredient" also meant "that which goes into," and still does. Robert Cawdry, in his 1609 dictionary of difficult and etymologically foreign English words, considers ingredience synonymous with "ingress," defining it laconically as "entrance in."[11] Another such dictionary, the 1616 *English Expositor*, defines it as "A going in: or that which goeth into the making of a thing."[12] The term also appears in numerous printed recipes, especially in the sixteenth century, as a synonym for "ingredient" or "ingredients," often for medicines of one sort or another. In all cases, the term hovers close to its etymological root, in-gradi, to step or go in. In the first decades of the seventeenth century, the term appears largely in recipe books, ecclesiastical debates, and scientific and medical manuals, with a scattering of sightings in poems and two occurrences in Holinshed's *Chronicles*. It appears nowhere in drama before turning up in a James Shirley play in 1640,[13] with two notable exceptions: Shakespeare, who uses it three times, once in *Othello* and twice in *Macbeth*; and Middleton, who deploys it in *A Chaste Maid in Cheapside*.[14] That the second use of "ingredience" in *Macbeth* appears in a passage possibly written by Middleton indicates that both playwrights, alone among their contemporaries, had it on the brain, although whether Middleton might have been influenced in his choice by Shakespeare will remain an open question.

Its use in *Othello* occurs in a speech by Cassio in the 1622 Quarto. Having been tricked by Iago into drunkenly fighting Montano, thereby losing Othello's trust, Cassio howls, "Euery vnordinate cup is vnblest, and the ingredience is a diuell."[15] Every drink in excess, in other words, is by definition damned, and holds the devil within it. In this context, to modern ears, the primary definition of ingredience appears to be "ingredient": "what's inside an alcoholic beverage is the devil." This seems to be the Folio's understanding as well, since in that text, and therefore by most subsequent editors, the word is changed to "ingredient." But there is no reason why the primary definition cannot be "ingress," and in fact such a reading resolves the awkward disagreement in number between the singular ingredient and the plurality of the compound. Every drink that enters the mouth brings the devil with it. The ingress of drinking is devilry. The term works to describe *both* the substance of alcohol and its imbibing. Ingredience here refers to object as well as action. The same is true of the corresponding passage in *Macbeth*. Justice turns the ingredients of poison back upon the poisoner, and in so doing poison enters the poisoner's mouth. The ingredients produce an ingredience: the object demands an action.

In both instances, the term brings together the same set of valences: poison (for Cassio, the literal poison of alcohol in the form of addiction and loss of control, and for Macbeth, the metaphorical poison of deceit), drinking, and theology (for Cassio, all unnecessary strong drink is damned, leaving only the necessary and blessed wine of communion; for Macbeth, the ecclesiastical terms "commend" and "chalice" equally suggest Eucharistic ritual and practice). There is something about ingredience for Shakespeare that insists not only upon linking object and action, but linking them in a context charged with material and spiritual risk. And not just for Shakespeare. Many early modern writers cited a passage in Martin Gregory's emphatically Catholic gloss to 11 Corinthians 24 in the Douay-Rheims Bible concerning the Last Supper. Defending Romish practice against Protestant memorialism, Gregory urges readers to remember that "There is a difference betvvixt the making of a medecine or the substance and ingredience of it, and the taking of it."[16] In other words, the ingredients of the Eucharistic bread may be earthly, but that does not mean the experience of ingesting it cannot be divine. Here ingredience means "that which goes into a substance," but its appearance at this moment suggests that the issue is precisely ingredience itself. There is a difference between ingredients and ingredience, and in that difference lies *the* difference—between remembering God and consuming God, between bread and the communal transformation of that bread.

Ingredience thus condenses into one term a broad concern with acts of eating, drinking, and ingestion, both for Shakespeare and for the Renaissance in general. In Shakespeare's plays, acts of material consumption reflect upon spiritual and ethical behaviors and concerns, and food and drink are always flowing from object into action, or showing how object and action are in fact part of a continuum of what we are likely to call *drama* and which Shakespeare called *play*, the acting out of embodied figures in concert and interaction with objects, both physical and imagined. (This borderline between physical and imagined object is under constant pressure in Macbeth, where kitchen knives become hallucinated daggers, which become real ones.)

Although we in literary studies now think of ingredience as an archaic term, it is alive and well among geographers and phenomenologists, who use it to describe precisely the sort of phenomenon that *enters* the self, complicating the distinction between object and action—or, relatedly, between exterior and interior. The geographer Edward Casey, for example, writes:

> The relationship between self and place is not just one of reciprocal influence . . . but also, more radically, of constitutive coingredience: each is essential to the being of the other. In effect, there is *no place without self and no self without place.*[17]

This "constitutive coingredience" signifies among phenomenologists the same sort of notion, I think, as does historian Timothy Reiss's idea of pre- and early modern circles, those "existential spheres to which the person enlaced in them was in a reactive relation," or Gail Kern Paster's humorally inflected ecology of the passions, in which subjectivity is "regularly breached and penetrated by its phenomenological environment."[18] In Shakespeare's lexicon, as in Casey's, ingredience stands as a central term for the ecological inter-essence of subject, object, and world. Ingredience becomes that which both constitutes a thing—a potion, a drink, a medicine, a food—and denotes the entering into the body of that thing, which thereby convokes the co-inhabitation of thing and body. In a play greatly concerned with how an ingredient becomes an ingredience, it seems appropriate that this unusual term plays such an important linguistic role.

It is also a short step from Shakespeare's ingredience to the New Materialist approaches to matter that I mentioned earlier, and specifically to Bruno Latour's concept of an "actant," a liminal phenomenon that is "neither an object nor a subject but an 'intervener.'"[19] To speak of actants instead of actors, writes Latour, is to describe "associations of humans and nonhumans in a state of uncertainty."[20] We need not accept the object-oriented theories that the concept of the actant has influenced in order to identify that Shakespeare has a vested interest in the mediated and mediating space among actors, objects, and audiences.[21] In *Macbeth* he explores this state of uncertainty in a more focused way than perhaps in any other of his plays, and "ingredience" is a useful signpost to mark this exploration.

Ingredience is also a helpful way of conceiving the tension and relation between what food studies calls the culinary and the commensal, or between food imagined as an object and eating as enveloped in human and nonhuman interactions. The culinary tends to indicate the what of eating—the constellation of ingredients on our plate. This structure immediately directs us outward, of course, to the relations that produce those ingredients and that therefore connect the human body to the soil from which those ingredients are derived, and to all those humans and animals that had a role in, or gave their lives for, the resulting comestible as it arrives at our mouths. The commensal suggests a different set of relationships: those of the table, of the ways humans give meaning to food and to their social structures and environments, as well as the relationships between humans and the nonhuman "messmates" (to use Donna Haraway's term) with which we share the experience of eating, and whom we eat, and who consume us.[22] If an ingredient forms the chief building block of the culinary, then ingredience describes the action whereby the culinary crosses into the commensal, activating the processual multiplicity of human table-relations. Ingredients are the objects of cuisine, but thinking about ingredients in motion, in a state of entrance and transformation, helps us conceive schematically of the movements of eating across time and through as well as into communities of eaters. Put another way, food *is* its ingredients, but its *meaning* is determined by the action of eating or drinking. As an object, stripped of relationality, it is meaningless. Only in relation and under the sign of activity does food itself activate and begin to generate and shed meaning on its environmental journey, its tying together the apparent binaries of human and nonhuman, interior and exterior.

The second instance of ingredience in *Macbeth* (whether scripted by Shakespeare or Middleton) appears at the end of the list of the ingredients in the witches' cauldron:

> Finger of birth-strangled babe
> Ditch-delivered by a drab,
> Make the gruel thick and slab.
> Add thereto a tiger's chawdron,
> For th'ingredience of our cauldron. (4.1.30–5)

Here as well as in the other instances, the term marks the moment where object slides into action, actant into act. An enumeration of ingredients culminates in the suggestion that all these ingredients will make possible a specific ingredience, an efficacy. This transformation is dramatized by the immediately subsequent entrance of Hecate, whose ensuing chant extends the list of ingredients while beginning to imagine the cauldron as a commensal space:

O, well done. I commend your pains,
And everyone shall share i'th' gains.
And now about the cauldron sing,
Like elves and fairies in a ring,
Enchanting all that you put in. (4.1.39–43)

The specific components of the potion require a kind of communal activation through enchantment, resulting in a promised collective reward, a "sharing in the gains." Of course, the witches are not eaters but parodic cooks, as Diane Purkiss has noted.[23] Their focus is the potion's effect not on themselves but on Macbeth, whose own ingredience into the scene happens shortly. The potion enters Macbeth through openings other than the mouth, namely through sight—"Call 'em, let me see 'em" (4.1.62)—and hearing—"Had I three ears, I'd hear thee" (4.1.77). Yet in a typical early modern confusion, it is immaterial how the potion's materiality enters Macbeth. All bodily openings are consumptive openings, and all give access to the roiling interior of the self. The apparitions, internalized by Macbeth, continue his subjective transformations.

But such a reading, which still holds to a distinction between subjects and objects—between persons and the objects that enter them—is yet insufficient. What takes place in this scene is rather a co-ingredience of potion and person, whereby it becomes hard to tell—to rephrase a chestnut of criticism on the play—whether the witches transform Macbeth, or whether their presence acts as a catalyst for an already ongoing transformation. The notion of ingredience helps us pose a somewhat unusual answer to that debate: Macbeth, the witches, and the cauldron that the witches use to call up visions that are equally phantasmal, real, and figments of Macbeth's fears and desires, are all contingent objects, "swirls of matter, energy, and incipience that hold themselves together long enough to vie with the strivings of other objects." If objectivity, as Barad argues, is "about being accountable and responsible to what is real,"[24] then in Macbeth's interaction with the witches in this scene we witness a kind of contestation about how to define both objectivity and the objects upon which those measurements are based. The objects that emerge from the cauldron are inseparable in their reality from their effects upon both Macbeth's and the viewers' minds. Macbeth's attempts to define and locate them throughout the scene, like his verbal description and interpretation of each apparition as it emerges, illustrate the dramatic process by which images become objects which become mental projections which become behaviors which produce performances which produce new images and objects. What you eat is what you are, as much because what you eat transforms you as because you chose to eat it in the first place.

To say that the scene "illustrates" this process of co-transformation is also insufficient. Rather, the apparitions, by prefiguring how the play will end, *enact* the process by which actor, narrative, and dramatic action transform each other. The apparitions all duly reappear in dramatic form later in the play. The first, the armed head, turns out to be Macbeth's own, converted into gruesome onstage presence by Macduff in the final scene. The second, the bloody child, conjures the offstage loss of the Macduffs' children. And the third, a crowned child with a tree in his hand, images the way in which Birnam Wood will move across the stage in the actors' hands. One could simply describe these elements of the scene as dramatic foreshadowing, which of course it is. But to summarize the apparitions as literary devices is to obscure, or indeed shadow, the deeper and concisely material ways in which fore*shadowing* and pre*figurement* work in this play. The device, in other words, is not merely a literary or even a theatrical one. It is also philosophical and ecological, showing how actions emerge from objects, thereby uncovering the swirl that unites them as contiguous forms of possible matter.

How the term ingredience worked its way into *Macbeth* at all will necessarily remain a matter of speculation. But strikingly it occurs in one of Shakespeare's possible sources for discussions of witchcraft in early modern England: Lambert Daneau's *Dialogue of Witches*, probably translated by Thomas Twyne and discussed by Reginald Scot. Twyne uses "ingredience" in an ambiguous way: mostly as a synonym for the plural ingredients, but with a secondary sense of entrance. In a passage about how Satan supplies his witches with poisons, Daneau and Twyne write, "So that the meanes whereby Sorcerers doe intoxicate, are partly manifest and starke poisons, whose ingredience, as they terme them, are deadly and mortiferous, and condemned by the learned Phisitions, for thinges that kil presently."[25] The primary meaning here seems to be the particular poisonous elements of a compound. But since "poisons" is plural, it is hard to tell whether it is the *substance* or *actions* of these poisons that is deadly and condemnable. Since the passage continues to discuss the poisons' action rather than their contents, ingredience in retrospect takes on a more active connotation. Indeed, some poisons can, according to Daneau, infect a human invisibly, without ingestion, by means of "holding a certen roote within their teeth which Satan deliuereth vnto them, which they chawe, & so doo kill and destroy men with only talking with them."[26] The passage thus echoes both how the potion acts on Macbeth, and how the witches have done so all along—by intoxicating through speech and sight. It also echoes Banquo's initial reaction to the witches' prophecy in Act 1, scene 3: "have we eaten on the insane root / That takes reason prisoner?" (1.3.85–6). Whether or not the passage influenced Shakespeare directly, its concerns about the radical and diffuse means of ingesting poison, and about the subtle transformations from objects into corporal processes, permeate the play.

Hospitality

Swirling back to the initial use of the term ingredience, Macbeth's first soliloquy constitutes a curious speech act, a weaving through of space and time rather than a standing outside it. Most Shakespearean soliloquies occur in a kind of suspended animation—while the speaking functions dramatically, the time of the speaking does not.[27] Macbeth, however, cannot find a quiet space in his own play in which to think. "If it were done, when 'tis done, then 'twere well / It were done quickly" (1.7.1–2), he tells us hastily. But we can hear the clock ticking behind him, can feel the meal taking place from which he has absented himself. In fact, Shakespeare has given us that palpable feeling of interruption through the unprecedented use of a dumbshow immediately prior to the soliloquy, by having "*a Sewer and divers Servants with dishes and service*" (1.7.sd) troop across the stage with music and torches.[28] The decision to stage the procession to the banquet, but redact the banquet itself, can exert a material force in performance—the pressure of the banquet is felt invisibly, while Macbeth unravels his anguished monologue about the violation of hospitality inside a time cramped by the demands of that very hospitality. It is a concise illustration of how hospitality in the play both extends its riches and forecloses the possibility of enjoying them—it provokes the performance of hospitality, but takes away the desire. As Lisa Hopkins points out, the interruption that ends the soliloquy, Lady Macbeth's abrupt reminder that Macbeth is forsaking his hosting duties, foreshadows the ways in which the appearance of Banquo at the banquet of Act 3 will produce in Macbeth another, more public violation of hospitality.[29] The ingredience of this poisoned chalice is commended to the later banquet, and to the eyes of the audience.

Much has been written about the fact that *Macbeth*, with its banquet placed at the structural center of the play, flanked by an offstage banquet in Act 1 and a boiling cauldron in Act 4, is indeed one of the great Shakespearean tragedies of eating and hospitality.[30] Drinking in the play, as we have seen, is about much more than liquid in its objective form—it is about liquid as an actionable phenomenon, one which, like hospitality, is always in relational movement. For Julia Reinhard Lupton, "Hospitality is a sequence of sociosymbolic actions that links the world of objects and the provisional persons who tend them . . . to dramatic action."[31] Hospitality and consuming food and drink are among the chief processes that form ligatures among objects, actions, and persons. The staging of Macbeth's soliloquy in an insistently temporal dramatic situation underlines the fact that ruminations about ingredients presage the entering in of those ingredients into physical and social realities. Macbeth challenges us to think about the relationship between drink and hospitality as one not of fixed referents—the host combines ingredients of which the guest partakes—but rather of "provisional persons," gestures, currents, ingrediences. The guest enters the house; food and drink enter the guest; complex exchanges occur along a porous gradient shaped by multiple forces, physical and temporal.

If we may imagine locating both drinking and hospitality as between action and object, so too for poison. We tend to think of poison as a substance, but it is also a movement. A poison is not poison until it enters a body and its drama of sociality. In William Blake's "The Poison Tree," poison grows from and through passionate engagement: "I was angry with my foe: / I told it not, my wrath did grow."[32] Poison in the poem is nominally an object—a tree that "bore an apple bright"—but it is the actions of the poem—the speaker's tending and watering, and the foe's violation of hospitality conventions by stealing into the speaker's garden to take it for himself—that create the poison as situation: "And my foe beheld it shine, / And he knew that it was mine."[33] A similar phenomenon is at work in the witches' enumeration of ingredients in *Macbeth*'s cauldron scenes: most of what goes into the cauldron, such as "lizard's leg and howlet's wing" (4.1.17), is poisonous less because of its chemical makeup than because of associations with poisonous activity, most notably in the case of poisonous humans like Jews, Turks, and Tartars. It is not the ingredient but the entrance in—entrance into criminality, and entrance of that criminality into another's hospitable body—that creates poison as poisonous. Thus poison in *Macbeth* is not precisely the opposite of hospitality, but rather its radical extension: it shares the same fluid dramatic structure as hospitality, moving along its gradience but in the opposite direction, dissolving bonds and breaking communal relationships. Poisoning can take place in the absence of eating or drinking, but not in the absence of welcoming, as in Macbeth's too-easy entrance into the witches' perverted hospitality—"Open locks, whoever knocks" (4.1.46). In order to undo its own dramatic ethics, poisonous hospitality must first beckon the guest—Macbeth, Banquo, ourselves.

The witches, as we have seen and as scholars have pointed out, are associated overwhelmingly with water, and secondarily with watery air. Their first scene starts in rain and ends in "the fog and filthy air" (1.1.13). In their next scene they relate the strange tale of the sailor's wife who denied chestnuts to one of the sisters, in an echo of the charges frequently leveled at witches in early modern Europe,[34] and in a parody of the broken commensality that will follow when the Macbeths assassinate their king in a violation of what the anthropologist Tan Chee-Beng calls "hospitality commensality."[35] Less well understood is why the witches' revenge takes place on the sea, where "in a sieve I'll thither sail" (1.3.8). The First Witch threatens to "drain [the husband] dry as hay" (1.3.18), transferring the liquid that makes up most of our bodies to herself, accruing female power while reducing male potency.[36] In a Galenic sense, the witch threatens to use a medicinal tactic—purgation—against itself by letting out liquid until the man becomes empty, just as Macbeth calls Banquo "marrowless" (3.4.92) when he sees him at the feast. Macbeth himself of course suffers from the opposite problem, at least at first—he is "too full o' th' milk of human kindness" (1.5.17) to do the deed from which humanity shrinks. The witches announce themselves both as a principle of liquidity and as an existential threat to the fluid balance of others. They are actants, entities who are able to make trial of another's internal equilibrium as well as emblems of the trial itself. It is fitting that their climactic scene involves a giant soup pot out of which human heads emerge. If they begin the play by threatening to draw forth liquid from a man, they end by drawing forth men from liquid—spirits who cause immediate internal effects in the man who views them.

The witches' principle of fluidity seeps into the surrounding drama. In Act 1 scene 2, sandwiched between the first two witches' scenes, Malcolm asks his Captain about the battle between Macbeth and Macdonwald. The Captain responds, "Doubtful it stood, / As two spent swimmers, that do cling together, / And choke their art" (1.2.7–9). The image of swimmers clutched in each other's arms, drowning or saving each other in their exhaustion, emblematizes fluidity in multiple ways—in its watery locale, its dissolution of boundaries between fighting and rescuing, and its homoerotic echoes of two male bodies entwined in sport and war. The violent birth imagery that follows—Macdonwald courting Fortune "like a rebel's whore" (1.2.15), only to suffer a reverse Caesarean section when Macbeth "carve[s] out his passage" (1.2.19) to him, splitting Macdonwald open with his bloody sword—only emphasizes the discomfiting intensity of the initial simile. It is not simply that Macdonwald's and Macbeth's fates are inseparably intertwined. It is that Macbeth is the actant of Macdonwald's fluid transformation from dominating male lover to violated mother. Macbeth acts in this metaphor as lover, doctor, and deathbringer, as well as the instrument of all those subjects. He is already starting to embrace the role toward which the weird sisters will encourage him. Likewise, after he and Banquo encounter the witches for the first time, they both register the destabilizing liquidity the sisters embody. Banquo muses, "The earth has bubbles, as the water has, / And these are of them" (1.3.79–80). The earth has bubbles? This is stated as a true fact, as if one always knew one would find bubbles in the earth, everybody knows that can happen. The *OED* cites this passage as evidence for the definition of bubble as either "a thin membrane of liquid enclosing a volume of air or another gas" or "a gas-filled cavity formed in a substance," again underscoring the way in which the image challenges us to think about how the supposedly solid earth can act like water under the right circumstances.[37] Regardless of whether such a phenomenon appears in Lucretius or Pliny, here it does indeed communicate a straightforward knowledge both of the witches' kinship with fluidity, and of the almost casual ease with which they can locate the fluid within the apparently solid.

We might be tempted simply to mark fluidity as a feature of all the play's language and imagery, regardless of character or situation. But this is not the case. The language starts with the witches and eddies quickly into the speech of Macbeth and even more palpably of his wife, who invokes fluid famously both in her opening soliloquy, where she begs evil spirits to exchange her milk for gall, and in her closing one, where she cannot manage to wash her hands because Duncan "had so much blood in him" (5.1.40). It is worth pausing here over the fact that in her initial scene, Lady Macbeth uses "spirits" in two different senses. In the first, she wishes to "pour my spirits in thine ear" (1.5.26), thus fantasizing that she can use speech as a liquid that will flow directly into Macbeth's brain, uncomfortably like the poison that Claudius uses to kill the elder Hamlet. In the second, she calls:

> Come you spirits
> That tend on mortal thoughts, unsex me here,
> And fill me from the crown to the toe, top-full
> Of direst cruelty. Make thick my blood,
> Stop up th' access and passage to remorse,
> That no compunctious visitings of nature
> Shake my fell purpose, nor keep peace between
> Th' effect and it. (1.5.40–7)

The meaning of "spirits" as an alcoholic or medicinal liquid flows into its denotation as a group of demonic or magical beings, and then back again, since the spirits of the second usage become precisely the actants that Lady Macbeth imagined her own speech effecting in her husband's body (and therefore akin to the apparitions the witches call forth from their cauldron). The spirits imaginatively stop up her passages with their own spirits, filling her with their liquid emotions. Lady Macbeth further emphasizes the strange region between actor, actant, and acted with the twisting end of her sentence, in which it is not at all clear what "the effect" and "it" refer to. Is "the effect" the effect of cruelty, that is, murder, with "it" referring to remorse? In that case, the line means something like "let no natural urges mediate between murder and remorse." But "the effect" may also refer to the physical stopping up of Lady Macbeth's body, while "it" may modify "fell purpose," and so on. It is less important what the terms refer to than that they effect the undermining of any stable understanding of who acts, with what instrument, and upon whom. Lady Macbeth, who will act upon Macbeth in precisely the way she wishes to be overtaken, is both the cause, the effect, and the "it." Lady Macbeth, like the witches, here becomes a principle of ingredience itself, distributed among the play's causes, objects, transformations, and effects.

If Macbeth and Lady Macbeth embrace, or are infected by, the witches' mode of fluid ingredience, other characters in the play steadfastly resist it, most notably Duncan and Banquo. Duncan's few short scenes are full of agricultural language and devoid of maritime or medical references. Upon greeting Macbeth after the battle, he tells him, "I have begun to plant thee, and will labor / To make thee full of growing" (1.4.28–9). Banquo, though conspicuously not Macbeth, responds, "There if I grow / The harvest is your own" (1.4.32–3). When Duncan and Banquo approach Macbeth's castle, they discuss the sweet and delicate summer air, the secure construction of the castle, and the martlet that lives in its crannies:

> This guest of summer,
> The temple-haunting martlet, does approve,
> By his loved mansionry, that the heaven's breath
> Smells wooingly here. No jutty, frieze,
> Buttress, nor coin of vantage, but this bird
> Hath made his pendant bed, and procreant cradle:
> Where they must breed and haunt, I have observed
> The air is delicate. (1.6.3–10)

It is not that Duncan and Banquo fail to conceive of metamorphosis. It is that their model for change emanates, paradoxically, from solidity, and in turn from the persistence of secure categories. If the martlet makes every "jutty and frieze" her nest, that does not prevent those jutties from continuing to function as architecture. Things are what they are. A martlet is a martlet and a castle is a castle, and both are treated as reliable metaphors for hospitality and domesticity.[38] This is the world of Duncan's imagination. It is no wonder that he finds it impossible to predict what is about to happen to him.

The problem of ingredience comes to infect the play with increasing anxiety about the boundaries between actors and objects. These culminate in a scene in which the terror of mutability infects even the solidity of landscape: Birnam Wood removes to Dunsinane. The spectacle of a forest moving across the land is a queasy one, and suggests a liquidity of solid matter that one neither expects nor enjoys. In John Woods's pastoral view of the scene (Figure 8.7), the moving woods themselves are almost overtaken by the marshy water that frames and reflects them, and by the swooping clouds above. But this dramatic moment in the play is complicated by the fact that the terror of mutability is not ours, but Macbeth's. For the audience, the usual feeling is less one of terror than (at least in an effective production) of excitement, of a hastening toward an end devoutly to be wished. And we are fully aware that the moving forest is a cheap parlor trick whose dubious strategic importance is outweighed by its fulfillment of Macbeth's prophecy. For Macbeth, however, the effect is metamorphic and destabilizing. It precipitates an existential crisis: "I 'gin to be aweary of the sun" (5.5.48). Rather than drive Macbeth up to the light, the experience causes him to retreat further into the liquid shadows: "Blow wind, come wrack" (5.5.50), as if he wanted nothing but to be on the heath again, perhaps side by side with King Lear, bellowing at chaos-causing sisters. He holds his metaphorical goblet of wine aloft until the end.

As critics, we generally laud fluidity as an ethical and interpre-
tive good. We reject fixity, entrapment, categorization; we champion
metamorphosis and change. We are fascinated by the liminal, the
threshold, the space between. It is not at all clear to me that Shakespeare felt the same way. Of course Macbeth is not Shakespeare, as
the difference between the audience's and the protagonist's reaction
to Birnam Wood usefully illustrates. Yet the scene works because we
know it is not real mutability, but rather a reinstantiation of the fixity
in which Duncan and Banquo believed. The play ends with the solid
triumphant and the liquid in retreat, and that is obviously meant to
be a good thing. No one wants to live in Macbeth's Scotland. No one
wants to hold oneself open to the possibility that the entrance of a
foreign body into the self can expose the self's inherent foreignness.
We do not tend to think of ourselves as ingrediences, both actors and
actants, vectors of change and permeability. The solid earth makes
for a secure, measured existence. But it makes for bad drama. Drama
is itself both an instance and a principle of ingredience. It is the actors
and the act, the thing and its effect. We take its gall and thrill when
it turns to milk within us.

Figure 8.1 Auguste Delvaux (1786–1836), printmaker. Macbeth, *3, aufz. 4, scene*
(19th c). ART File S528m1 no.43 (size XS). Used by permission of the Folger
Shakespeare Library.

Figure 8.2 Ethan Hawke and Anne-Marie Duff, *Macbeth*, dir. Jack O'Brien, 2014. Photo by T. Charles Erickson.

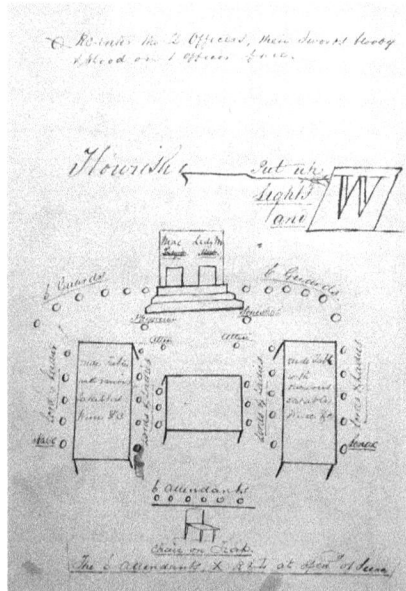

Figure 8.3 Diagram of Act 3, Scene 4 from a *Macbeth* prompt book for Mary Warner, 19th c. PROMPT Mac. 41. Used by permission of the Folger Shakespeare Library. Photo by David B. Goldstein.

THE BANQUET SCENE IN "MACBETH".

Figure 8.4 Charles William Sharpe (1818–99), printmaker. *The Banquet Scene in* Macbeth (19th c). ART File S528m1 no.104 copy 1 (size S). Used by permission of the Folger Shakespeare Library.

Figure 8.5 Patrick Stewart as Macbeth in the Chichester Festival Theatre production *Macbeth* during BAM Spring Series, 2008. Courtesy BAM Hamm Archives. Photo by Richard Termine.

Figure 8.6 Kate Fleetwood as Lady Macbeth in the Chichester Festival Theatre production *Macbeth* during BAM Spring Series, 2008. Courtesy BAM Hamm Archives. Photo by Richard Termine.

DUNSINANE AND BIRNAM WOOD.

The tyrant: people on both sides do fight.
The noble thanes do bravely in the war.
The day almost professes yours.
And little to do.

Figure 8.7 John Woods (active 1830–49), printmaker. *Dunsinane and Birnam Wood . . .* Macbeth, *act 5, scene 7.* ART File S528m1 no.104 copy 1 (size S). Used by permission of the Folger Shakespeare Library.

Notes

Thanks to Liz Pentland, for her careful and ever-patient eye; to Gail Kern Paster, for her generous reading of an earlier draft; to Matthew Casaca and Kristen Smith, for their tireless help with research; to the undergraduate and graduate students at York University whose classroom responses to *Macbeth* have helped shape my own (including Gurpreet Banwait, whose essay on corruption and decay in the play was especially influential); and to the generous and incisive audiences at the conferences and colloquia where I first presented portions of this chapter, including the Sixteenth Century Society Conference, the World Shakespeare Congress, the Renaissance Society of America, and the Early Modern Colloquium at Northwestern University. Thanks to York University, the Social Sciences and Humanities Research Council of Canada, and the Folger Shakespeare Library for providing funding and time for the research for and dissemination of these ideas.

1. William Shakespeare, *Macbeth*, from vol. IV of *Works*, ed. Alexander Chalmers, 1809. Promptbook prepared for M. Warner. Folger PROMPT Mac. 41.
2. I thank David Posner for alerting me to this reference.
3. William Shakespeare, *Hamlet*, ed. A. R. Braunmuller (New York: Penguin, 2001), 1.2.180–1. Counter-examples include the banquet at the end of *Taming of the Shrew*, which mentions no food, but in a play in which the main character is subjected to food deprivation, this is perhaps not surprising.
4. William Shakespeare, *Macbeth*, ed. Sandra Clark and Pamela Mason (London: Bloomsbury, 2015), 3.4.33–5. All further references to the play are to this edition and will appear in the body of the text.
5. Margreta de Grazia, Maureen Quilligan, and Peter Stallybrass, eds., *Subject and Object in Renaissance Culture* (New York: Cambridge University Press, 1996).
6. Graham Harman, *Immaterialism* (Malden, MA: Polity Press, 2016), 15.
7. See, for example, Gail Kern Paster, "Becoming the Landscape: The Ecology of the Passions in the Legend of Temperance," in *Environment and Embodiment in Early Modern England*, ed. Mary Floyd-Wilson and Garrett Sullivan (London: Palgrave Macmillan, 2007), 137–52.
8. Karen Barad, *Meeting the Universe Halfway: Quantum Physics and the Entanglement of Matter and Meaning* (Durham, NC: Duke University Press, 2007), 340.
9. Jane Bennett, "Systems and Things: A Response to Graham Harman and Timothy Morton," *New Literary History* 43:2 (2012): 227.
10. I arrived at this figure by using the word as an EEBO keyword search term.
11. Robert Cawdry, *A Table Alphabeticall Contayning and Teaching the True Writing and Vnderstanding of Hard Vsuall English Wordes, Borrowed from the Hebrew, Greeke, Latine, or French &c.: With the Interpretation*

Thereof by Plaine English Words, Gathered for the Benefit and Help of All Vnskilfull Persons: Whereby They May the More Easily and Better Vnderstand Many Hard English Words, Which They Shall Heare or Read in Scriptures, Sermons, or Elsewhere, and Also Be Made Able to vse the Same Aptly Themselues / Set Foorth by R.C.; and Newly Corrected, and Much Inlarged by T.C. (London, 1609), E8v.

12. J. B., *An English Expositor: Teaching the In[ter]pretation of the Hardest Words Vsed in Our Language. With Sundry Explications, Descriptions, and Discourses* (London, 1616), I4r.

13. James Shirley, *The Coronation: A Comedy* (London, 1640).

14. Thomas Middleton, *A Chaste Maid in Cheapside* (London, 1625), 64. In that usage, "ingredience" is a synonym for "ingredients," and is modernized thus in contemporary editions.

15. William Shakespeare, *The tragœdy of Othello, the Moore of Venice, As it hath beene diuerse times acted at the Globe, and at the Black-Friers, by his Maiesties Seruants* (London, 1622), p. 37; 2.3 in modern editions.

16. *The Nevv Testament of Iesus Christ, translated faithfully into English, out of the authentical Latin, according to the best corrected copies of the same, diligently conferred vvith the Greeke and other editions in diuers languages; vvith arguments of bookes and chapters, annotations, and other necessarie helpes, for the better vnderstanding of the text, and specially for the discouerie of the corruptions of diuers late translations, and for cleering the controuersies in religion, of these daies: in the English College of Rhemes*, ed. Martin Gregory (Reims, 1582), p. 452.

17. Edward S. Casey, "Between Geography and Philosophy: What Does it Mean to Be in the Place-World?," *Annals of the Association of American Geographers* 91.4 (December 2001): 684 (original emphasis).

18. Qtd. in David B. Goldstein, *Eating and Ethics in Shakespeare's England* (Cambridge and New York: Cambridge University Press, 2013), 10.

19. Jane Bennett, *Vibrant Matter: A Political Ecology of Things* (Durham, NC: Duke University Press, 2010), 9.

20. Bruno Latour, *Politics of Nature: How to Bring the Sciences into Democracy* (Cambridge, MA: Harvard University Press, 2004), 75.

21. But cf. Gail Kern Paster's discussion of how sprits and gall function as "actants" in Lady Macbeth's first monologue, and elsewhere in Shakespeare. Gail Kern Paster, "Bodies without Borders in *Lear* and *Macbeth*," in *Shakespeare in Our Time: A Shakespeare Association of America Collection*, ed. Dympna Callaghan and Suzanne Gossett (London and New York: Bloomsbury, 2016), 183.

22. Donna Jeanne Haraway, *When Species Meet* (Minneapolis and London: University of Minnesota Press, 2008), 4.

23. Diane Purkiss, *The Witch in History: Early Modern and Twentieth-Century Representations* (London and New York: Routledge, 1996), 212. See also Wendy Wall, *Staging Domesticity: Household Work and*

English Identity in Early Modern Drama (Cambridge and New York: Cambridge University Press, 2002), 199–200.

24. Barad, *Meeting the Universe Halfway*, 340.
25. Lambert Daneau, *A Dialogue of Witches, in Foretime Named Lot-Tellers, and Novv Commonly Called Sorcerers VVherein Is Declared Breefely and Effectually, Vvhat Soueuer May Be Required, Touching That Argument. A Treatise Very Profitable . . . and Right Necessary for Iudges to Vnderstande, Which Sit Vpon Lyfe and Death. Written in Latin by Lambertus Danaeus. And Now Translated into English*, trans. Thomas Twyne (London, 1575), F8r.
26. Daneau, *Dialogue of Witches*, F8r.
27. Hamlet's first soliloquy, "O that this too too sullied flesh would melt," takes place in an island of time, between the King and Queen's exit and Horatio's entrance. The time Hamlet spends on the bare stage with us does not disturb the time the other characters inhabit; rather, the play holds its breath and waits to recommence. When Iago turns to the audience and tells us, "Thus do I ever make my fool my purse," he too stops the time of the play, as if he were stepping out of a frame and then back into it.
28. On the unprecedented nature of the stage direction, see Lisa Hopkins, "Household Words: *Macbeth* and the Failure of Spectacle," *Shakespeare Survey* 50 (1997): 105.
29. Hopkins, "Household Words," 106.
30. See David B. Goldstein and Julia Reinhard Lupton, eds., *Shakespeare and Hospitality: Ethics, Politics, and Exchange* (London and New York: Routledge, 2016), 1–2.
31. Julia Reinhard Lupton, "Macbeth's Martlets: Shakespearean Phenomenologies of Hospitality," *Criticism* 54.3 (Summer 2012): 367.
32. William Blake, *The Complete Poetry and Prose of William Blake*, ed. David V. Erdman, Newly Revised Edition (New York: Doubleday, 1988), 28.
33. Blake, *Complete Poetry and Prose*, 28.
34. Purkiss, *Witch in History*, 209–10.
35. Tan Chee-Beng, "Commensality and the Organization of Social Relations," in *Commensality: From Everyday Food to Feast*, ed. Susanne Kerner, Cynthia Chou, and Morten Warmind (London: Bloomsbury, 2015), 15.
36. Cf. Purkiss, *Witch in History*, 210.
37. "Bubble, *n. and adj.*," *OED Online* (Oxford: Oxford University Press, December 2018), <http://www.oed.com//Entry/24071?rskey=NENK41&result=1&isAdvanced=false> (last accessed May 31, 2019).
38. Lupton, "Macbeth's Martlets," *passim*.

Chapter 9

Things in Action: Shakespeare's Sonnet 129, *Macbeth*, and Levinas on Shame

John Michael Archer

"Th'expense of spirit in a waste of shame," Shakespeare writes in sonnet 129, "Is lust in action" (129.1–2).[1] When we read Shakespeare's sonnet 129 alongside Emmanuel Levinas's linkage of shame with justice, we begin to comprehend the neglected role that legal terms and forensic rhetoric play in the poem, even though such historical and taxonomic matters were certainly far from Levinas's thought. Shame is a condition of human being before a primordial justice that the community's laws and customs have framed out. The sphere of morality, as Walter Benjamin maintained, is defined by law and by justice in its juridical sense.[2] Levinas's treatment of shame comes from a section of *Totality and Infinity* entitled "Truth and Justice." Here we read that to welcome the Other and question one's freedom is to acknowledge one's own injustice. "We therefore are also radically opposed to Heidegger who subordinates the relation with the Other to ontology," Levinas avows, "rather than seeing in justice and injustice a primordial access to the Other beyond all ontology."[3] At a later stage, he adds: "The existent qua existent is produced only in morality."[4] For Levinas, ultimately it is ethics as the relation of self and Other, not morality as legalistic code, that constitutes justice, however, to begin with, and in a sense before existents or beings have been constituted—including the legal persons of accused and accuser and the laws, also existents, that summon them. But justice notoriously devolves into the patriarchal family's struggle with eroticism in *Totality and Infinity*, cast entirely from a man's viewpoint. Shame is attached to the erotic by Levinas only so that it may suffer expulsion from the ethical encounter as its bad or wasted potential, trailing misogynous language in its wake. Similar claims have been made of Shakespeare as sonneteer and tragedian, although I am not sure they stick. By reading sonnet 129 together with, or near to, *Totality and Infinity* and a few other works by Levinas, I would propose that law and judgment are at stake in a poem about erotic unfulfillment. It is this proposition that drives my interpretation back toward legal-historical instantiations of justice in Shakespeare's time. Legal personhood, bound up with concepts like right, property, and the proper, becomes visible through the scrim of sexual personhood in sonnet 129, albeit from a masculine and aristocratic perspective that limits justice and sexuality alike. My "near reading," which is often also a close reading as well as a historical one, begins with a section on forensic rhetoric and the legal concept "thing in action," both of which define a juridical taxonomy the poem shares. The second section turns to Levinas's well-known use of another text by Shakespeare, *Macbeth*, in *Totality and Infinity* and elsewhere in his corpus. I shall resume my near reading of sonnet 129 with particular reference to Levinas's understanding of shame in his very early work *On Escape*, adhering to *Macbeth* while taking up the traditional question of the 1609 *Sonnets* as a sort of drama or sequence.

I

From the start of Shakespeare's sonnet 129, the poet-speaker adopts the stance of a Ciceronian orator before an unnamed court, defining his charge against lust, as if to win a conviction. It is unclear what the crime is. "Th'expense of spirit in a waste of shame" refers primarily to the "lust" of the next line, of course, and annotators have lent it a range of specific sexual connotations (129.1–2). The phrase could also assimilate lust to a kind of homicide, however—not manslaughter, for there are no extenuating circumstances behind this shameful waste of life. As a passive state, lust

> Is perjured, murd'rous, bloody, full of blame,
> Savage, extreme, rude, cruel, not to trust. (129.3–4)

It is homicidal indeed, then, but perjured first of all, that is, either subject to swear falsely or the subject of false witness itself (129.3). Unsatisfied lust contains murderous and cruel thoughts, falsifying men's hopes. Until enacted, it dissimulates according to the implicit social contract it holds to, not in spirit (although it holds spirit in, unexpended), but only according to the letter of what "the world well knows" (129.13). Lust's legalistic surface masks violence, concealing the power of a sovereign self that combines Georges Bataille's sovereignty of personal extremity with Carl Schmitt's sovereign state of juridical exception.[5]

Unacted lust induces an evacuation of subjectivity in opening the possibility of false witness. That is, the sovereign self or person is paradoxically unstable and corrupt in its perjured self-concealment because of the operations of language.[6] It is also uncertain what or who is being witnessed falsely. The sonnet's expense or waste of spirit could refer to solitary masturbation, a lustful activity. Yet until the mid-sixteenth century, at least, a "lust" could also be a source of pleasure—an object or a person.[7] Could we conceive "lust in action" as an object as well as an action, that is, as a chattel or piece of property, or even a person made into a kind of chattel: the obscure man or woman in question, blamefully withholding, or is it giving, bodily intimacy? Lust does seem to shift from the passion of the pursuer to the object of pursuit, who is "Past reason hunted, and no sooner had, / Past reason hated as a swallowed bait" (129.6–7). So, savagery, cruelty, and untrustworthiness may also characterize the figure lusted after, for she or he is retrospectively full of blame in the poem as well. Like masculine lust, this figure can be thought to be

> Mad in pursuit, and in possession so,
> Had, having, and in quest to have, extreme,
> A bliss in proof, and proved, a very woe. (129.9–11)

The word "extreme" is repeated from the opening list of charges. Lust blends pursuer and pursued, removing them ecstatically to the same "outside" space, to follow the Latin etymology.

It also has consequences for temporality. As Bradin Cormack puts it in an analysis of sonnet 129's conclusion, "sex presents itself as the liminal act that, disappearing into the threshold of the present, opens onto the times of future and past and thereby organizes those effectively unreal times into Time."[8] The moment of "bliss," sex in action, restructures time as a state of extremity, exception, and indifferentiation during its every instantiation. In traditional philosophical terms, a "state" is a *hexis*, or a "having." Yet the sexual act is strangely elided within the clause "Had, having, and in quest to have," which inverts the temporal order of the chase. The order is reinstated again in the following verse, which proves the object of the hunt "a very woe," and thus finally a "woman" in truth (for the pun, see *Troilus and Cressida* 2.2.111).

    The idiom "in possession" casts light upon the curious phrase "lust in action" in the sonnet's opening lines, which bear repeating:

> Th'expense of spirit in a waste of shame
> Is lust in action; and till action, lust
> Is perjured, murd'rous, bloody, full of blame, . . . (129.1–3)

Action may mean the sexual act itself, but it also connotes "legal suit" (there is merciless punning on this basis early in *Henry IV*, Part 2, for instance: *2 Henry IV*, 2.1.1–10). According to a popular legal dictionary reprinted throughout the early modern period, a "thing in action," from the Law French term *chose in action*,

> is when a man hath cause, or may bring an action for some dutie due to him, as an action of debt upon an obligation, . . . trespasse of goods taken away, beating, or such like, and because that they are things whereof a man is not possessed, but for recovery of them is driven to his action, they are called things in action.[9]

A "thing in action" was distinct from property "in possession," which was also termed "chattels." The expressions *chose* (or thing) *in action* and *chose in possession* were regularly paired in legal discourse. Because goods were no longer in the possession of the person who had a claim to hold them, or damages had been incurred but not paid, they could be considered "in action," which imparted the capacity to recover personal damages in court. If the analogy holds, Shakespeare's "lust in action," like a *chose in action*, puzzlingly remains "in action" even though it is depicted in a state of suspense "till action": in legalistic jargon, to be "in action" is not to be active, but to impart the capacity to start a legal action or suit. According to this (admittedly technical and secondary) level of reading, to be "in action" and waiting "till action" refer to the same condition, then. To read along legal lines is to supplement and partly displace the way the opening of the sonnet is usually interpreted. From the common law perspective, Shakespeare does not commence with a dichotomy between actual lust devolving into shame on the one hand, and the state of angry expectation that precedes the actualization of lust and shame on the other; instead, something close to the latter condition is meant from the start. "Th'expense of spirit in a waste of shame" is not, or not only, the effective depletion of either vital energy or semen, but rather the exercise of what Stephen Booth terms "non-physical" or "mental energy" in his list of possible explications of the line.[10] Several times in the

Sonnets, Shakespeare associates "spirit" with something like imagination, and specifically with the poetic imagination: "Was it his spirit, by spirits taught to write," that has silenced him, the poet wonders of his literary rival (86.5; and see 80.2, 108.2)? In other words, one can read "lust in action" as inactive except in a non-physical or intangible way—as spiritual, in other words, although in a profane sense. It only leads to a misuse of shame, an affective state better suited to acts than intents where law is concerned (compare *Measure for Measure* 5.1.371, 5.1.450–4).

The terms *chose in action* and thing in action are still used today to refer to the right to sue in a court of law, to recover a debt, or money for damages, for instance. In a specialized sense, shares in a company and financial instruments are also regarded as things in action because they are intangible in a way analogous to property that is not in possession. This reflects a remarkable historical reversal whereby things in action, once almost impossible to grant, assign, or transfer under common law, have become properties that may be traded.

The taxonomy of things in action encodes a reciprocal relation between process and materiality. The second volume of William Blackstone's *Commentaries on the Laws of England*, titled "Of the Rights of Things," charts the process of reversal in how the term *chose in action* was used. Although an eighteenth-century work, Blackstone's magisterial treatise retrospectively clarifies earlier explanations of the common law like those found in Rastell; even its errors are instructive. According to his nineteenth-century American expositor William Gardiner Hammond,

> Blackstone never treats a chose in action as a mere right or title to choses in possession, or to other property, as it is so frequently regarded now. It is to him distinctly a kind of property, not of right to property. This is implied in his entire treatment of the subject, beginning with the first statement of the distinction in chapter 25.[11]

A look at that passage suggests that Hammond may have been too absolute about a shifting set of terms:

> Property, in chattels personal, may be either in *possession*; which is where a man hath not only the right to enjoy, but hath the actual enjoyment of, the thing: or else it is in *action*; where a man hath only a bare right, without any occupation or enjoyment.[12]

The definition of *chose in action* follows some pages later, when Blackstone returns to

> property in *action*, or such where a man hath not the occupation, but merely a bare right to occupy the thing in question; the possession whereof may however be recovered by a suit or action at law: from whence the thing so recoverable is called a thing, or *chose, in action*.[13]

Is a "bare right" a piece of property, that is, a material *thing*? By the eighteenth century, it was, at least, not *nothing*; bareness confers a kind of minimal thingness to the right. The right is bare of the "actual enjoyment" of something, all the same. Here, Blackstone casts light back upon another aspect of the legal language of sonnet 129, where lust is "Enjoyed no sooner but despised straight" (129.5). The matrix or frame that holds together rights, property, and enjoyment as both possession and pleasure is personhood. Between the legal fictions of things in action and things in possession, however, personhood is limned in its barest or least form: an outline of spectral possibility tracing itself on the bodily world yet faintly "despised," or looked down upon (*despecere*), in the process.

Shakespeare's line reflects some accidental light forward upon Blackstone as well. If the jurist does not concern himself with the emotional consequences of recovery at law, he nevertheless cannot escape the paradoxical condensation of legal temporality:

> If a man promises, or covenants with me, to do any act, and fails in it, whereby I suffer damages, the recompense for this damage is a *chose* in action: for though a right to some recompense vests in me, at the time of the damage done, yet what and how large such recompense shall be, can only be ascertained by verdict.[14]

At the very moment of failure, a right to recompense "vests," or imparts an absolute entitlement of enjoyment, in the plaintiff (or "in me," as if to emphasize the interpersonal force of the example). What kind of thing could this suddenly-appearing entity possibly be? A *chose in action* is an uncertain thing whose nature and size can only be determined later, by a court of law. "By the rules of the antient common law," however, as Blackstone soon recalls, "there could be no future property, to take place in expectancy, created in personal goods and chattels," as opposed to land.[15] We may deduce that a *chose in action* must be a kind of personal property in the present, then, although a strangely vacant kind. Despite Blackstone's continued talk of rights and of possession in recovery, Hammond proves correct in his basic assertion that a thing in action was treated as property by the jurist. It was something that could be given by the law, as Blackstone states:

> the law gives an action of some sort or other to the party injured in case of non-performance; to compel the wrong-doer to do justice to the party with whom he has contracted, and, on failure of performing the identical thing he engaged to do, to render a satisfaction equivalent to the damage sustained. But while the thing, or its equivalent, remains in suspense, and the injured party has only the right and not the occupation, it is called a *chose* in action; being a thing rather in *potentia* than in *esse*: though the owner may have as absolute a property in and be as well entitled to, such things in action, as to things in possession.[16]

So one may have an absolute property in a thing in action, just as with a possession, in the intangible present, even though this present is the past of a future verdict on the exact scope of the thing. In the meantime, the *chose in action* "remains in suspense," a probable recollection of a rare early modern synonym, *chose en suspense*.[17] Blackstone's language, though striving for Enlightenment clarity, is itself almost as slippery as a poet's: what is, or are, "the identical thing," "the thing, or its equivalent" that remains, or remain, suspended? Which is it? A *chose in action*, "being a thing rather in *potentia* than in *esse*," has being, then, but only as a possibility. Could the owner remain satisfied, though in suspense, with his property in a thing in action, if he is as entitled to it as he would be to an actual (that is, not *in* action) thing? And could he then give it away or sell it?

Blackstone's stress on contract in the passage is also of note. Earlier, he insists "that all property in action depends entirely upon contracts, either express or implied," and later, that "a contract *executory* [for future implementation] conveys only a *chose* in action."[18] Perhaps Shakespeare's poet-speaker in sonnet 129 might not only be viewed as a Ciceronian prosecutor in a felony case, but also as a lawyer in a civil trial pertaining to a broken contract over something between different parties of some sort. Who are the two persons involved? Are there two persons involved?

As Charles Sweet pointed out, however, Blackstone erred in restricting things in action to "personal" or moveable property: "the most important kind of choses in action in former days were choses in action real," that is, pertaining to land.[19] For this reason, we must be careful with explanations of thing in action like the following:

> This right to bring an action whether of contract or of tort was strictly personal. Only the person who had the right could sue on it; only the person liable could be sued. Neither the benefit nor the burden could be transferred to a third person.[20]

Clearly, "personal" in this instance means restricted to a particular individual, or "in privity," to use the period's own language.[21] Before the eighteenth century, the right to sue could not be granted, assigned, or transferred to others at common law. The restriction was, in fact, a feudal hold-over relating to land transactions, which were "personal" in the ordinary-language sense, or between individuals, even though "real" or matters of realty. There was a long-standing fear that allowing third parties to take over "a *chose* in action real" and initiate a law suit for fees would enable profiteering from land disputes. An Act of 1540 had decried the "buying of titles and pretenced rights of persons not being in possession, whereupon great perjury hath ensued, and much in quietness, oppression, vexation, troubles, wrongs and disinheritance."[22] So, until action, lust "Is perjured, murd'rous, bloody, full of blame, / Savage, extreme, rude, cruel, not to trust" (129.3–4). Even if its illegitimate assignment to other agents is prohibited, a thing in action, as a kind of standing to initiate a law suit or wage law, contains within itself the prospect of litigiousness and the potential, at least, for corruption and the violence it spawns. Its outcome was "not to trust." According to S. J. Bailey, common law sought to block transfers of things in action for land and chattels because they were "too personal" in the everyday sense, then, and also to the extent they were "uncertain" for reasons that have been mentioned.[23] Even the king cannot transfer things in action as rights to sue for land or damages, because at common law "there is no donation of an uncertain thing."[24] For Shakespeare, by an extension of this type of legal mentality, the self too might be so sovereign as to become shut off from the other, paradoxically in its own desire for it. Uncertainty and the personal "in privity"—for the poet, these are also ways of understanding the temporality and locality of human feelings. Among such feelings are lust and shame.

As an early modern person, one had a *chose in action* concerning a piece of land or a trespass or a debt whether one decided to implement it or not. A thing did not become "in action" or active only upon the start of a law suit; a thing in action simply constituted a cause, a kind of right, for someone to wage law in the first place or choose not to. It may be for this reason that a 1651 selection from Brooke's *La Graunde Abridgement* mistakenly renders *chose in action* as "Choice in action."[25] "Th'expense of spirit in a waste of shame / Is lust in action," and thus "Mad in pursuit, and in possession so" (129.1–2, 129.9). As with *chose in action*, "lust in action" is paradoxical: both are at once always in potential and perpetually enacted, passive and active, if not yet accomplished, and unstable in consequence if accomplished.

Lust in action, as has been remarked, connotes masturbation as much as sex with a partner, and the likely pun on "waste" as "waist" points to the lustful person's own midriff as the repository of "spirit" as ejaculate. The phrase "and till action" is also a pun, mixing action as mere activity along with legal suit, and the following verses expand upon the circumstance of performed yet paradoxically suspended lust in the present rather than suggesting a still earlier emotional stage. How else could lust be perjured and murderous already, before entering the sphere of action in the ordinary sense, not to mention the jurisdiction of justice and injustice, of trust and perjury? By the eighteenth century, as we have seen, a *chose in action* was for Blackstone arguably a thing and thus a form of property in itself, and not just a title or a right to property. Again, however, as a thing, it bestowed, in itself, a right to compensation in place of the thing that was lost. Yet, as Hammond explains, in its original conception "a thing in action was, so to speak, the complement, the shadow of the thing in possession, and it was a thing *in action*, because the very purpose of an action was to make of it a thing in possession, to the proper owner."[26] In the early seventeenth century, then, a thing in action must still in many cases have allowed for something like a right in property simply to become property in possession, rather than enabling monetary recovery for a property violation. The legal concept blended some absent thing to be recovered, compensation for it or for some other loss that incurred damages (such as loss of bodily health), *and* the right to initiate an action at law in such cases. In Shakespeare's loose legal usage, "lust in action" *can* "prove" to be lust "in possession," in possession of the object of lust itself, all too readily and shamefully. And yet, "Before," lawful enjoyment of lust is only "a joy proposed; behind, a dream" (129.12, punctuation modified). The legalistic recovery of lust by lust, already an erotic game of shadows, is doomed to dissatisfaction. An improper waste of potential, it can never seize the present, in an endless rehearsal of the linear, commonplace concept of time.

II

According to Levinas in *Totality and Infinity*, "Before the *cogito* existence dreams itself, as though it remained foreign to itself"; on the other hand, enjoyment "is made of the memory of its thirst."[27] So one might rephrase Shakespeare's final definition of lust or its object in this way: "Before, a dream proposed; behind, a joy." Levinas's entire strategy could in fact be seen as a reversal of Shakespeare's poem and perhaps of the entire 1609 cycle of sonnets. That the twentieth-century philosopher is addressing Shakespeare's *Sonnets* in *Totality and Infinity* is of course a daring and unprovable contention. Levinas's references to several of Shakespeare's plays are well known, however, and he remained engaged with *Macbeth* in particular throughout his career, as Jeremy Tambling has shown in an incisive discussion to which I am indebted.[28] There are several explicit if scattered references to the tragedy in *Totality and Infinity*: what follows regards these citations with especial care, in contradistinction to a trend which downplays Levinas's later readings of *Macbeth* in favor of his earlier, more concerted engagements with it.[29] Macbeth is a type of the will, or the type of a willful person, in *Totality and Infinity*; in separating himself from the Other and from morality as the carapace of ethics, he also confirms the Other in spite of himself. Levinas writes in a central passage:

> The suicide to which it [the will] resolves itself in order to escape servitude is inseparable from the pain of "losing," whereas this death should have shown the absurdity of every game. Macbeth wishes for the destruction of the world in his defeat and his death ("and wish th'estate o'th'world were now undone")—or more profoundly still, he wishes that the nothingness of death be a void as total as that which would have reigned had the world never been created.[30]

Such personal nullity is a sort of illusion that cannot overcome the terrible endurance of existence. This is an essentially philosophical rather than an expository reading of a moment in Shakespeare's play (that is, it may be true, although it is probably "not accurate"). Let me quote the passage at somewhat greater length than the philosopher does:

> I pull in resolution, and begin
> To doubt th'equivocation of the fiend
> That lies like truth. . . . .
> I gin to be a-weary of the sun,

> And wish th'estate o'th'world were now undone.
> Ring the alarum-bell! Blow wind, come wrack,
> At least we'll die with harness on our back. (*Macbeth* 5.5.41–3,
> 5.5.48–51)

A certain Macbeth may indeed crave an escape from being, as Andrew Cutrofello observes in an illuminating reading that blends several Levinasian texts that meditate upon the tragedy.[31] Yet having proclaimed the devaluation of the world, in Levinas's ironic view, Macbeth actually confirms its value in willing the total loss of the world along with his own death. Rather, he might simply have abandoned the world, endorsing the absurdity of life as the idiot's tale he has also just stated it to be. Instead of "signifying nothing" (5.5.28), the world is *made* to signify his own defeat. Even as it becomes "wrack" or waste, I would add, the world is also rendered paradoxically useful by Macbeth according to a restricted economy that makes ruin the sign of conquest, even the self-conquest of a supposedly valiant sacrifice for a lost cause. In *Time and the Other*, a text from 1948, Levinas had already coupled Macbeth and the nullification of suicide through the warrior's repeated urge to fight against impossible odds.[32]

In an earlier section of *Totality and Infinity* which he subtitles "The Love of Life," Levinas directly casts Macbeth as a suicide who cries out against the failure of suicide itself: taking one's own life, a single life, cannot solve the wider problems of existence or transvalue the world which survives you. Macbeth's enjoyment in life is too strong, for he remains attached to the earth's values, "riveted to being," and refuses true escape from being despite his death-wish.[33] There is an indeterminate erotics of power, an enjoyment in Macbeth's fantasy of an undone world, that finds correlatives in the *Sonnets*.

In a rhetorical analysis, Jackson G. Barry has noticed the link between the condensed temporality of lust in sonnet 129 itself, especially its tenth line, and the doings and undoings of *Macbeth*.[34] Sonnets 109 and 112 offer variations on the idea of a murder-suicide pact of ontological intensity. The latter, crux-filled poem tells the beloved:

> You are my all-the-world, and I must strive
> To know my shames and praises from your tongue;
> None else to me, nor I to none, alive. (112.5–7)

Shames in this poem are hardly different from praises. Each type of speech proceeds intimately from the tongue of the beloved, who constitutes "my All the world" in the Quarto text.[35] "World" means social world or even global population, it seems, as in the tragedy. Life itself is circumscribed within the feedback mechanism, the totality, of the relationship. The couplet's notorious difficulty brings the claustrophobia of the sonnet to an extreme conclusion. The Quarto reads:

> You are so strongly in my purpose bred,
> That all the world besides me thinks y'are dead. (112.13–14)[36]

The final line is often emended, Macbeth-like, to: "That all the world besides, me thinks, are dead."[37] However it should be rendered, the verse must complete in some sense the seventh line's ominous monopolization of life by the lovers. The second-person plural in Macbeth's own conclusion, "At least we'll die with harness on our back," may be a royal we, but it bears the traces of a couple or an erotic community that takes prospective pleasure in total negation of some sort. The couplet of sonnet 109 had already prepared for such a consummation: "nothing this wide universe I call, / Save thou, my rose; in it thou art my all" (109.113–14).

The figure of a defiant Macbeth confronting the world and death remained a compelling emblem for Levinas. At the start of *Otherwise than Being*, his second major work, he calls for the transcendence of the very concept of "being" in philosophy. The "otherwise" he imagines is not the same as dying, however. If that were true, then being would remain the dominant term after all, for, as in *Totality and Infinity*, a solitary death still allows the continuation of being as the factual and barren plane of existence assumed by much ontology. There is a deceptive alternative:

> My death is insignificant—unless I drag into my death the totality of being, as Macbeth wished, at the hour of his last combat. But then mortal being, or life, would be insignificant and ridiculous even in the "irony with regard to oneself" to which it could in fact be likened.[38]

Tambling, who quotes the first sentence, feels that such insignificance echoes "in the emptiness of the play's last scene."[39] Yet Shakespeare was not a romantic or self-defeating ironist for Levinas, and this is in fact the reason that the playwright stands apart from his destructive tyrant. Macbeth's desire to take the whole of being with him, in the form of mortal life, would really leave "being" intact as the mere negation "non-being," the bare stage upon which the finite totality of human experience is immolated—a ridiculous, if frightening, pretense. As in the hyperbolic profession of love that ends sonnet 112, all the world survives to think the death of all-the-world, after all. As

Otherwise than Being proceeds, it refashions the erotic language of love and life into a new philosophical lexicon in which, for instance, the term "presence," associated with being, is replaced with "proximity," an embodied, skin-to-skin closeness that is "non-erotic" in vocation yet initially charged with libido.[40]

The reference to *Macbeth* at the very beginning of *Otherwise than Being* suggests that Levinas thought of Shakespeare's play as a link between his middle and later thought. Let us return to the earlier text. There are several indirect engagements with the tragedy toward the conclusion of *Totality and Infinity* that provide for Levinas to take up where he left off, particularly in the elicitation and quelling of eroticism. First, I will consider an early reference to *Macbeth* in a section where being still very much presides over the world. The passage begins with Descartes, a foundational thinker in *Totality and Infinity*. Levinas recalls the passage from the first of the *Meditations* about the "evil genius" or supernatural intelligence that may have set up the world as an array of illusions in order to ensnare the solitary thinker. "This possibility is constitutive of *apparition* as such,"[41] when the Other takes the form for us of the malicious spirit Descartes posits in the course of his experiment in radical doubt. Awareness of pure appearance raises another specter, a linguistic not a visual one this time, the specter of equivocation. Levinasian equivocation does not take place between the narrow meanings of words but between speech itself and incoherence, laughter, and finally silence. Equivocation is further imagined as a form of mockery that destroys language by driving it back upon a merely factual notion of truth, in a paradoxical literalism:

> The spectacle of the silent world of facts is bewitched: every phenomenon masks. . . . It is the situation created by those derisive beings communicating across a labyrinth of innuendos which Shakespeare and Goethe have appear in their scenes of sorcerers where speech is antilanguage.[42]

The equivocation of the fiend that lies like truth and the apparitions that convey it to Macbeth are on Levinas's mind. Witchcraft and conjuring must be a throwback to Shakespeare's world, for they do not appear in the *Meditations* passage.[43]

Levinas also has the apparitions and equivocations of *Macbeth* before his gaze in his treatment of eroticism late in *Totality and Infinity*, in which sexuality and sexual difference finally impinge upon his arguments about need, desire, and enjoyment. The tenderness of a male caress, which he calls "the tender," reaches for what does not yet exist and becomes a "no man's land" or wasteland between being and not-yet-being. This weightless and equivocal non-being is named "femininity" and "the Beloved."[44] Now it is female nudity, not equivocation in language, that inverts signification into double- and non-meaning and finally into speechless exhibition. Levinas is thinking of the visual arts. But first, and through the partly-visual medium of theater, I would suggest, we discover "the very lasciviousness of erotic nudity—the laughter that deflagrates in Shakespearean witches' sessions full of innuendos, of all possibility of speech."[45] This is the no-man's-land of the Scottish heath, with its hailings and apparitions. To recur once more to an earlier work, *Existence and Existents* from 1947, we find a similar meditation on "Spectres, ghosts, sorceresses" which clearly informs the passage in *Totality and Infinity*.[46] This early and relatively lengthy citation of *Macbeth* has been much discussed, but mostly to resolve the supernatural feminine into the figure of Banquo's ghost amid the witches as a figure for a "there is" (*il y a*) that persists through death, a key Levinasian concept.[47] Lady Macbeth may be as important as Banquo in the later text, however, even though she makes an appearance in neither work, early or mid-career. She is perhaps recalled in Levinas's reintroduction of two other key concepts in *Totality and Infinity*, the prohibition on killing and the face-to-face encounter: "The principle 'you shall not commit murder,' the very signifyingness of the face, seems contrary to the mystery which *Eros* profanes, and which is announced in the femininity of the tender." The face-to-face encounter should be the first access to the infinite or the Other, but the feminine intercepts the face and offers a temptation to total negation in the erotic.[48] A viewing of Roman Polanski's still striking film of *Macbeth* makes these dark chords reverberate with the playtext, formally and intellectually. Yet Levinas's own montage-like and scattered allusions to the play are uncanny in themselves. Their character is part and parcel of his quite traditional take on sexuality and the feminine, which is prejudicial in itself and also ignores same-gender male and female desire, at least in the erotic relation.[49] Nietzsche's *Gay Science* is an unexpected intertext:

> "Is it true that God is present everywhere?" a little girl asked her mother; "I think that's indecent"—a hint for philosophers! One should have more respect for the bashfulness with which nature has hidden behind riddles and iridescent uncertainties. Perhaps truth is a woman who has reasons for not letting us see her reasons? Perhaps her name is—to speak Greek—*Baubo*?[50]

In Levinas, Nietzsche's truth, already ambiguous, becomes completely feminine and thus deficient in his masculine view because of its very facticity. It is placed outside the truth of the Other.

Baubo, the cultic old woman who selectively reveals herself to Nietzsche throughout *The Gay Science*, helps explain why Levinas reads Shakespeare's witches as lewd feminine revealers and concealers. He repeatedly links women to obscenity, darkness, incoherence, and incompletion. For the man, the Other's "face" is engulfed by the naked display of the female body; woman, not heterosexual eroticism, is held accountable by the philosopher. "It is necessary that the face have been apperceived for nudity to be able to acquire the non-signifyingness of the lustful," he writes. "The feminine face joins this clarity and this shadow." The face is not just the countenance, for it can present as the whole body or any of its parts, as "a hand or the curve of a shoulder"—and as presumably a waist, too, a waist of shame.[51] Again, the feminine face subverts facial expression into "indecency, already close on the equivocal," which Levinas associates with what he calls "voluptuosity." In tenderness, the masculine comes to enjoy its suffering like a courtly lover or Petrarchan sonneteer. The voluptuous sensation overtakes the category of desire for the Other. For Levinas, desire is not based on lack and its supposed fulfillment. "This is why voluptuosity is not only impatient, but is impatience itself, . . . for it goes without going to an end." Voluptuosity does not depend on the ordinary understanding of need, for then it would come to an end with the possession of the object.[52] Insofar as lust is suspended in action without possession in sonnet 129 it resembles the endless tenderness, and also the Shakespearean tendering, the fruitless reaching, of the love-poetry tradition that the poem channels. "I found (or thought I found) you did exceed / The barren tender of a poet's debt," as the lover states elsewhere (83.3–4). Unlike Petrarch's sonnet cycle and its heirs, the later *Sonnets* depict, not endless pursuit of the remote Beloved, but the aftermath, sometimes anxious and sordid, of the Beloved's capture within an ongoing voluptuosity.

The independence of voluptuous feeling from need can be traced to an early essay of Levinas from the mid-1930s, the manifesto-like *On Escape*, in which he develops a few other terms and ideas that appear later in his work as well. All human beings are "riveted" to their existence by affect, as Macbeth will later be in *Totality and Infinity*. Nevertheless, they feel a need to escape, not a kind of being, but being itself. We do not desire escape to a particular destination, either, not even death as non-being—but simply to "get out" of being.[53] Much later, in *Otherwise than Being*, Levinas will renew

his critique of ontology by completely repudiating being as a philosophical category, with Macbeth's fate as a sort of prologue. In the
early text, the parallel to Martin Heidegger's ontological distinction between object-oriented "fear" and open-ended "anxiety" is
still clear.[54] As with anxiety, to confront need is to begin to realize
how one exists in the world. Yet for Levinas, already, need is not an
ontological mood that disrupts philosophy's reflective or intentional
consciousness, the "I," but a condition of "oneself," a sensory and
affective subjectivity bound up with the body. Need is derived from
self-perception and related to a series of intimate, embodied affects,
among which shame is prominent. Negative feelings like shame nevertheless provoke the need to escape, not one's body, but through
one's body in some indeterminate way. Escape is the need to break
free from "the fact that the I [*moi*] is oneself [*soi-même*]."[55] Giorgio
Agamben has provided an influential discussion of Levinas's concept
of shame in *On Escape*, although he hastily identifies the affective self
with "physiological life" pure and simple.[56] In fact, life in Levinas's
early text serves only as the remote substratum of the auto-affection
or self-intimacy he is most concerned with. For Levinas, then, shame
arises from the impossibility of escape from "oneself" as an embodied subject, an impossibility that also testifies to its need. It is indeed
often linked to the body in its nakedness before others. But shame
for Levinas is not a biological event any more than it is a social
or moral judgment; "its deepest manifestations are an eminently
personal matter,"[57] he observes. We might recall lust as a thing in
action, its own object. Levinas states:

> What appears in shame is thus precisely the fact of being riveted to oneself,
> the radical impossibility of fleeing oneself to hide from oneself, the unal-
> terably binding presence of "I" to "oneself" [*du moi à soi-même*]. . . . It
> is therefore our intimacy, our presence to ourselves, that is shameful. It
> reveals not nothingness but rather the totality of our existence.[58]

"Nothingness" pertains to the common understanding of need as pri-
vation. In *On Escape*, Levinas formulates an alternate theory of need
which is also found in *Totality and Infinity*. Need is tied to being, but
not as a nothingness within it; instead, being for us is a continuous,
embodied presence of which need is the sign. There is an implicit
parallel, I would add, to Aristotle's position on potentiality in his
encounter with the Megarian school in Book IX of the *Metaphysics*.
In a course from 1931, Heidegger provided a foundational discussion
of the *having* of potential, as an answer to earlier Greek thinking

about potential's erasure *in action* or enactment, that has directed much recent philosophical understanding of the passage.[59] Both the Megarians and Aristotle think having and acting in terms of presence. Aristotle, however, believes that the capability for someone to perform an action does not disappear when the person is not performing the action, as the Megarians had claimed. The person still has the potential to perform the action.[60] For Levinas, need is like potential. So, "the satisfaction of a need does not destroy it."[61] Consumption and release are both followed by disappointment. The cycle of need, however, is evidence of continuity through embodiment in general rather than an encounter with nothingness in the renewed absence of the desired object. The affect Levinas calls "malaise" thus persists as "a kind of dead weight in the depths of our being."[62] Yet pleasure, too, another of the embodied feelings he addresses, shows how "need expresses the presence of our being and not its deficiency."[63] Heidegger, incidentally, turns to Aristotle's *De Anima* amidst his reading of *Metaphysics* IX to show how *having* means, not possessing, but holding oneself in relation to that which is striven for, the *orekton*, as an origin rather than an object: "Only this needing, this wanting, leads to a producing," that is, to *poiesis*.[64] It is in this way that he sets up being as presence as the context for Aristotle's encounter with the Megarians. In reaction to Heidegger, the later Levinas might have substituted bodily "proximity" for the presence he still evoked in *On Escape* and abandoned being as a philosophical concern altogether. Like voluptuosity in *Totality and Infinity*, pleasure in *On Escape* seemingly goes on without the thought of finitude that being evokes. Pleasure is "affectivity" itself, and as suggested by Aristotle, whom Levinas does belatedly cite at this point, it is extraneous to actualization, as a kind of continuous potentiality that tends toward the self's departure from being rather than being's end.[65] Yet "it is an escape that fails," for "on a strictly affective level, pleasure is disappointment and deceit."[66] How do pleasure and voluptuosity compare with the lust of sonnet 129?

Let us restart our reading of the sonnet through Levinas's ideas about malaise, pleasure, and shame in *On Escape*, which look forward to the engagement with Shakespearean *poiesis* in *Totality and Infinity*. "Th'expense of spirit in a waste of shame / Is lust in action," and "till action" lust is indeed deceitful or "perjured," in Shakespeare's legal idiom, and "not to trust" (129.1–4). In the midst of pleasure, Levinas writes, "The [human] being feels its substance somehow draining from it; it grows lighter, as if drunk, and disperses."[67] Expending its spirit or substance, our being enacts a lust

that perdures before, during, and after action despite the momen-
tary dissemination and lightening that its release effects. The word
expense, from the Latin root *pendere*, which means both "to weigh"
and "to measure out," conveys the dead weight within our being that
need continually signifies. Levinas's evident belief in being as continuous presence through bodily experience would seem to counter the
sonnet's inability to grasp the present moment. "But it is precisely the
instant that is split up in pleasure," the philosopher admits. "It loses
its solidity and its consistency, and each of its parts is enriched with
new potentialities." Despite the multiplication of potential within
action itself, frustration follows as linear time resumes: "The instant
is not recaptured until the moment when pleasure is broken, after the
supreme break, when the [human] being believed in complete ecstasy
but was completely disappointed, and is entirely disappointed and
ashamed to find himself again existing."[68] Levinas's subsequent analysis of such shame realizes the "waste of shame," the vain condition
of being, in which the poet despises what was enjoyed in possession
but has now proved to be an extreme sorrow. "The being who has
gorged himself falls back into the agonizing disappointment of his
shameful intimacy," his embodied, embarrassing self-presence, "for
he finds himself anew after the vanity of his pleasure."[69] Gorging,
like drunkenness, paradoxically mixes consumption within the initial association of pleasure with draining away in Levinas's text, and
so in Shakespeare, too, the sonnet's opening expense of spirit may be
traced to lust as "a swallowed bait, / On purpose laid to make the
taker mad" (129.7–8). As an example of shame, Levinas describes
how "The whistle that Charlie Chaplin swallows in *City Lights* trig-
gers the scandal of the brutal presence of his being."[70] A humiliating
sibilance betrays the tramp's existence, first of all to himself, despite
the tattered bourgeois costume with which he has encased his body.
Expen*s*e, *s*pirit, wa*s*te, *s*hame, lu*s*t—do these words not also express
a whistling sound in enunciation? Mere coincidence may bar such a
comparison, and yet the fleshly intimacy of swallowing and respira-
tion does have something primal about it commonly knowable to
Shakespeare as to Chaplin and Levinas. We are dealing both with
tradition and phenomenal experience, after all:

> All this the world well knows, yet none knows well
> To shun the heaven that leads men to this hell. (129.13–14)

"To shun" is Shakespeare's word for "to escape" or "to evade,"
although the verb's didacticism restores the moralism Levinas would

purge from shame. The moral stance is in line with the sonnet's speechifying pretext, but it is undermined in turn by "the heaven," however ironized, which exerts such a common allure. What kind of heaven would lead men to hell? Is there anything redemptive, after all, in such an earthly paradise?

In sonnet 129, Shakespeare collapses need and satisfaction, potential and possession, and in doing so, well before Descartes, he implies the phantom of an evil genius who "lays snares for my credulity."[71] Lust, or the lusted after, is

> Enjoyed no sooner but despised straight;
> Past reason hunted, and no sooner had,
> Past reason hated as a swallowed bait,
> On purpose laid to make the taker mad. (129.5–8)

Laid by whom, or what? The heaven of the sonnet's final line? It is as if some entity has ensnared the lover within irreversible linear temporality, where passing beyond reason merges hunting and hating after the fact. The quarry is apprehended as a poison only upon being consumed, a rapid relay marked by the rhyme of "swallowed bait" with "straight." In possession, a thing in action reveals that to take possession, to be a taker, is really to be made something in turn by the object, to be made mad. Forensic oratory has given way to mock-sermonizing, suggesting a distorted Calvinist theology by which the lustful person is purposely entrapped rather than left to fallen depravity. Once more we stumble upon *Macbeth*. "Were such things here," Banquo marvels of the witches, "Or have we eaten of the insane root / That takes the reason prisoner?" (1.3.83–5). "And oftentimes," he adds,

> to win us to our harm
> The instruments of darkness tell us truths,
> Win us with honest trifles, to betray's
> In deepest consequence. (1.3.123–6)

When Descartes experimentally replaces a good God with an all-powerful trickster in his opening Meditation, shapes, colors, and all external things suddenly become uncertain, the trumpery of dreams.[72] In sonnet 129, the past is a dream, the future "a joy proposed," and the present a "having" without duration, a possession that destabilizes the person in madness. In *Macbeth* as in *Hamlet*, and despite some controversy, the philosophical crosscurrents between Shakespeare and Descartes exert their pull.[73] With the unsettling concepts of alienated purpose, baiting, and insanity we land upon the waste territory at the shoreline of a first philosophy that will ultimately place the autarchy of the self into question.

Sonnet 129 concerns certainty and uncertainty, justice and injustice, as well as erotic success and failure. Shakespeare does not offer an alternative to lust in action, or to lust in possession either, then. For instance, there is no indication of procreation as guarantor of property, even unwanted procreation; there is only a waste of shame. This is in line with the movement of Shakespeare's sonnet cycle as it has come down to us, the movement many have perceived in the 1609 Quarto that makes Shakespeare's *Sonnets* work, and makes them (it?) into a "work" of literature. (I have commented elsewhere on the legacy and limits of the sonnet-sequence assumption.[74]) The first seventeen poems in the Quarto urge the young man to take a wife and reproduce himself in legitimate offspring, it seems, especially, a son. Then, it is the relationship with the poet and his poetry that offers fulfillment and a measure of immortality to the aristocratic patron. By sonnet 129 we have seemingly left even the young man behind, as the poet celebrates and condemns a woman whose moralized racial "darkness" Levinas might well be recalling, from a troubling masculine and European viewpoint, with his evocations of shadow, obscurity, and "disfigurement."[75] The abandonment of the youth is uncertain in sonnet 129 itself, however: the waist of shame may be male or female, for the gender of the hell or the dream is unspecified in a poem whose terrifying scope defies its firm placement in the operational sequence of a narrative or drama. What we can settle on, I believe, is the intense exploration of non-reproductive sexuality in this sonnet and those that follow it in the traditional order. This is one sense, already loaded with negative judgment, of the word "waste." In suggesting, however tentatively, that *Totality and Infinity* gestures toward a reading of the *Sonnets* as a sequence along with *Macbeth*, I am broaching the limitations of the following statement by Levinas, frequently quoted by current commentators: "it sometimes seems to me that the whole of philosophy is only a meditation of Shakespeare."[76] Even without the *Sonnets* in mind, Levinas in effect reverses the succession of ideas in the customary sequencing of Shakespeare's sonnets, bringing the common love-poetry narrative into line with assumptions about gender and sexuality that would have been all too familiar to Shakespeare's readers. He sees the non-possessive hope in the voluptuous relation between man and woman as the accidental means by which self and Other come together to "engender the child." "Already the relation with the child," he writes, "takes form in voluptuosity, to be accomplished in the child himself."[77] The empty future towards which the caress had motioned is suddenly fulfilled in offspring, specifically, the male child of a male father, as a kind of savior: *Totality and Infinity* ends in "Messianic triumph." Levinas has resumed a theme from *Time and the Other*, turning toward what both texts call "fecundity."[78] Moreover, voluptuosity is replaced by "fecundity" as a specifically masculine feeling—as paternity. And yet, "The son coveted in volup-tuosity is not given to action, remains unequal to powers."[79] Like a thing in action at law, the son in Levinas is most powerful as a philosophical idea when it remains a thing in suspense. As pure potentiality reclaimed, fecundity subsumes the tedium of repetition in life, and "continues history without reproducing old age."[80]

Shakespeare may have put it better.

Back in sonnet 3, the poet urges the young man to tell his reflection, "Now is the time that face should form another" (3.2). According to Levinas, the "profanation" of sex does not discover another face beyond the face, beyond the body of the Beloved: "it discovers the child."[81] Levinas ends where Shakespeare began. If it is true, as scholarly legend suggests, that the poet left behind his commission to encourage a young man's marital procreation as his sonnets progressed, then it seems Shakespeare embarked upon an inestimable terrain of need, desire, uncertainty, and unworkability. Another way to describe Shakespeare's journey is to say he left per-sonhood behind: specifically, the masculine aristocratic personhood to which he paid initial tribute, in which property, enjoyment, and their biological and legal continuity through the family line were guaranteed by means of marriage and reproduction. Levinas would one day disclose the no-man's-land beyond this limited sense of the person under the name "infinity." Sonnet 129 is a convoluted indict-ment that ends in an unasked question: how does one shun what the world thinks it knows as an infinite and barren evil when it may also be the very place of bliss, escape, and salvation?

Notes

1. The sonnets are cited from Katherine Duncan-Jones, ed., *Shakespeare's Sonnets*, 2nd edn. (London: Methuen, 2010). Quotations from Shake-speare's works other than the *Sonnets* are from *The Riverside Shake-speare*, 2nd edn. (Boston: Houghton Mifflin, 1997).
2. Walter Benjamin, "Critique of Violence," in *Selected Writings*, vol. 1, ed. Marcus Bullock and Michael W. Jennings (Cambridge, MA: Harvard University Press, 1996), 236.

3. Emmanuel Levinas, *Totality and Infinity: An Essay on Exteriority*, trans. Alphonso Lingis (Pittsburgh: Duquesne University Press, 1969), 86, 89.

4. Levinas, *Totality and Infinity*, 262.

5. Georges Bataille, *The Accursed Share*, vols. 1–2, trans. Robert Hurley (New York: Zone Books, 1991), 197–200; Carl Schmitt, *Political Theology: Four Chapters on the Concept of Sovereignty*, trans. George Schwab (Chicago: University of Chicago Press, 2005), 5–7.

6. Joel Fineman, *Shakespeare's Perjured Eye: The Invention of Poetic Subjectivity in the Sonnets* (Berkeley: University of California Press, 1986), 15.

7. *OED*, "lust, *n.*," 1.c.

8. Bradin Cormack, "On Will: Time and Voluntary Action in *Coriolanus* and the *Sonnets*," *Shakespeare* 5 (2009): 253–70, 257.

9. John Rastell, *Les termes de la ley: or, Certaine difficult and obscure vvords and termes of the common lawes of this realme expounded* (London, 1624), 67v.

10. Stephen Booth, ed., *Shakespeare's Sonnets* (New Haven, CT: Yale University Press, 1977), 441.

11. William Blackstone, *Commentaries on the Laws of England. Book the Second*, ed. with commentary by William G. Hammond (San Francisco: Bancroft-Whitney, 1890), 595–6.

12. Blackstone, *Commentaries*, 600.

13. Blackstone, *Commentaries*, 600.

14. Blackstone, *Commentaries*, 609.

15. Blackstone, *Commentaries*, 610.

16. Blackstone, *Commentaries*, 610.

17. For the term, see Charles Sweet, "Choses in Action," *Law Quarterly Review* 40 (1894): 303–17, 304.

18. Blackstone, *Commentaries*, 609, 676.

19. Sweet, "Choses in Action," 305.

20. A. Wood Renton and Maxwell A. Robertson, eds., *Encyclopedia of the Laws of England*, 2nd edn., vol. 3 (London and Edinburgh: W. M. Green & Sons, 1907), 49.

21. Sweet, "Choses in Action," 306n.2 (quoting Coke).

22. Sweet, "Choses in Action," 309.

23. Stanley J. Bailey, "Assignments of Debts in England from the Twelfth to the Twentieth Century," *The Law Quarterly Review* 190 (1932): 248–71, 256–7.

24. Stanley J. Bailey, "Assignments of Debts in England from the Twelfth to the Twentieth Century," *The Law Quarterly Review* 192 (1932): 547–82, 554 (quoting Bracton).

25. Robert Brooke, *Some new cases of the years and time of King Hen. 8. Edw. 6. and Qu: Mary; written out of the great abridgement, composed by Sir Robert Brook, Knight*, trans. John March (London, 1651), 50–1.

26. Blackstone, *Commentaries*, 597.
27. Levinas, *Totality and Infinity*, 86, 113.
28. Jeremy Tambling, "Levinas and Macbeth's 'Strange Images of Death,'" *Essays in Criticism: A Quarterly Journal of Literary Criticism* 54 (2004): 351–72; Richard A. Cohen, "A Meditation," in *Of Levinas and Shakespeare: "To See Another Thus,"* ed. Moshe Gold and Sandor Goodhart (West Lafayette, IN: Purdue University Press, 2018).
29. Nicholas Doenges, "A Levinasian Meditation on Shakespeare's *Macbeth*," *Levinas Studies* 5 (2010): 167–87, 168; Cohen, "A Meditation," 31–2.
30. Levinas, *Totality and Infinity*, 231.
31. Andrew Cutrofello, *All for Nothing: Hamlet's Negativity* (Cambridge, MA: MIT Press, 2014), 84.
32. Emmanuel Levinas, *Time and the Other and Additional Essays*, trans. Richard A. Cohen (Pittsburgh: Duquesne University Press, 1987), 50, 72–3; Tambling, "Levinas," 362.
33. Levinas, *Totality and Infinity*, 146; Doenges, "A Levinasian Meditation," 179.
34. Jackson G. Barry, "'Had, having, and in quest to have, extreme': Shakespeare's Rhetoric of Time in Sonnet 129," *Language and Style: An International Journal* 14 (1981): 1–12, 11.
35. Booth, *Shakespeare's Sonnets*, 97.
36. See also Booth, *Shakespeare's Sonnets*, 97.
37. Booth, *Shakespeare's Sonnets*, 368; see also Duncan-Jones, *Shakespeare's Sonnets*, 335.
38. Emmanuel Levinas, *Otherwise than Being or Beyond Essence*, trans. Alphonso Lingis (Pittsburgh: Duquesne University Press, 1998), 3.
39. Tambling, "Levinas," 367.
40. Levinas, *Otherwise than Being*, 123, 192n.27.
41. Levinas, *Totality and Infinity*, 90.
42. Levinas, *Totality and Infinity*, 91–2.
43. René Descartes, *Meditations on First Philosophy*, trans. Donald A. Cress (Indianapolis, IN: Hackett Publishing, 1993), 16–17.
44. Levinas, *Totality and Infinity*, 257–8, 259.
45. Levinas, *Totality and Infinity*, 263.
46. Emmanuel Levinas, *Existence and Existents*, trans. Alphonso Lingus (Pittsburgh: Duquesne University Press, 2001), 60–1.
47. Tambling, "Levinas," 361–2; Doenges, "A Levinasian Meditation," 170–4; Cohen, "A Meditation," 30; Sandor Goodhart, "Lear's Darker Purpose," in *Of Levinas and Shakespeare*, ed. Gold and Goodhart, 55.
48. Levinas, *Totality and Infinity*, 262.
49. See Luce Irigaray, "Questions to Emmanuel Levinas: On the Divinity of Love," in *Re-Reading Levinas*, ed. Robert Bernasconi and Simon Critchley (Bloomington: Indiana University Press, 1991), 109–18.
50. Friedrich Nietzsche, *The Gay Science*, trans. Walter Kaufman (New York: Vintage, 1974), 38.

51. Levinas, *Totality and Infinity*, 262.
52. Levinas, *Totality and Infinity*, 259–60, 265.
53. Emmanuel Levinas, *On Escape: De l'évasion*, trans. Bettina Bergo (Stanford: Stanford University Press, 2003), 52–4.
54. Martin Heidegger, *Being and Time*, trans. Joan Stambaugh, rev. and with a Foreword by Dennis J. Schmidt (Albany, NY: State University of New York Press, 2010), 179–81 (German pagination 185–7).
55. Levinas, *On Escape*, 55, 60–8 (brackets in original).
56. Giorgio Agamben, *Remnants of Auschwitz: The Witness and the Archive* (New York: Zone Books, 2002), 104–6.
57. Levinas, *On Escape*, 64.
58. Levinas, *On Escape*, 64–5 (translation modified; brackets in original).
59. Martin Heidegger, *Aristotle's Metaphysics [Theta] 1–3: On the Essence and Actuality of Force*, trans. Walter Brogan and Peter Warnek (Bloomington: Indiana University Press, 1995), 148–56, 188.
60. Aristotle, *The Basic Works of Aristotle*, ed. Richard McKeon (New York: Random House, 1941), 1046b 35–1047a 26.
61. Levinas, *On Escape*, 59.
62. Levinas, *On Escape*, 60.
63. Levinas, *On Escape*, 60.
64. Heidegger, *Aristotle's Metaphysics*, 129.
65. Levinas, *On Escape*, 62; Aristotle, *Basic Works*, 1174b 33.
66. Levinas, *On Escape*, 62–3.
67. Levinas, *On Escape*, 61 (brackets in translation).
68. Levinas, *On Escape*, 61 (brackets in translation).
69. Levinas, *On Escape*, 65.
70. Levinas, *On Escape*, 65.
71. Descartes, *Meditations*, 16–17.
72. Descartes, *Meditations*, 16.
73. Cutrofello, *All for Nothing*, 25–8.
74. John Michael Archer, *Technically Alive: Shakespeare's Sonnets* (New York: Palgrave Macmillan, 2012), 19–24.
75. Levinas, *Totality and Infinity*, 262.
76. Levinas, *Time*, 72; Gold and Goodhart, *Of Levinas and Shakespeare*.
77. Levinas, *Totality and Infinity*, 266.
78. Levinas, *Totality and Infinity*, 284–5; Levinas, *Time*, 90–2.
79. Levinas, *Totality and Infinity*, 267.
80. Levinas, *Totality and Infinity*, 268.
81. Levinas, *Totality and Infinity*, 267.

Chapter 10

Edward Herbert's Cosmopolitan State

Gregory Kneidel

In the opening pages of *The Civilization of the Renaissance in Italy* (1860), Jacob Burckhardt notes that in medieval Italy there was no feudal system that "naturally transformed" over time "into a unified monarchy." Such transformations did occur in England, France, and Spain, but the absence of one in Italy allowed, Burckhardt says, for the incubation of city-states that were to an unprecedented degree "the outcome of reflection and calculation." Each such state was, in Burckhardt's famous phrase, "a work of art" (*Kunstwerk*).[1] This chapter focuses on a 1608 verse satire by Edward Herbert that similarly identifies the "State" as a work of art, specifically as a "proportion'd colour'd table" or perspectival landscape painting.[2] Herbert's perspectival and topographical conceit, I will be arguing, reimagines the English nobility not as feudal lords, nor as loyal subjects to a unified monarchy, but as cosmopolitan persons of a peculiarly modern sort.

Herbert's description of the state as a work of art is less well known and considerably more puzzling than Burckhardt's, and so it merits quoting in full here at the start. It appears as something of a set-piece, two-thirds of the way through his poem, "The State progress of Ill":

> State, a proportion'd colour'd table, is,
> Nobility the master-piece, in this
> Serves to shew distances, while being put
> 'Twixt sight and vastness they seem higher, but
> As they're further off, yet as those blew hills,
>
> Which th'utmost border of a Region fills
> They are great and worse parts, while in the steep
> Of this great Prospective, they seem to keep
> Further absent from those below, though this
> Exalted Spirit that's sure a free Soul, is

A greater privilege, than to be born
At *Venice*, although he seek not rule, doth scorn
Subjection, but as he is flesh, and so
He is to dulness, shame, and many moe
Such properties, knows, but the Painters Art,
All in the frame is equal: that desert
Is a more living thing, and doth obey,
As he gives poor, for God's sake, (though they
And Kings ask it not so) thinks Honours are
Figures compos'd of lines irregular

And happy-high, knows no election
Raiseth man to true Greatness, but his own. (ll. 81–102)

This is an obscure passage, and its obscurity has several causes. A few of those causes cannot be easily remedied (Herbert's notoriously crabbed metaphysical style; his indifference to grammar; the haphazard punctuation of the sole seventeenth-century witness of the poem). But others can be and they are addressed in the three sections that follow: the first discusses how the Renaissance discovery of perspective changed legal conceptions of space, land, and property; the second explains why Herbert invokes the art of perspective to prevent what he calls "The State progress of Ill," which he sees as an assault on his very robust sense of noble personhood; and the third considers how analogous passages—by Herbert himself, by John Donne, and by Francis Quarles—help to mark off, by way of contrast, the curious political and legal status of Herbert's cosmopolitanism.

"vaste and indefinite viewes"

Burckhardt's (admittedly somewhat offhand) assertion that England transformed itself "naturally" from feudalism to monarchy has been challenged, of course, by later historians, and, mostly saliently for my purposes, by historians of what Henry S. Turner has recently called *topographesis*: "the representation of place in any graphic mode—writing, painting, drawing—and particularly in those forms of expression that tend to be more conventionalized rather than less so."[3] The various products of *topographesis*, including city-views, estate surveys, county and country maps, and landscape paintings, were in the early modern period not as readily distinguishable as they are today. All can be seen to "stem from fifteenth-century discoveries which enabled the expression of an awareness of space, of mapping in terms of coordinates and of perspective painting."[4] Cartographic historians have noted the contested political implications of this new perspectival awareness of space. On the one hand, ever since Alberti called the central line of sight of his famed visual pyramid the "prince of rays," early modern practitioners of the perspectival arts seized on the notion that perspective "gives the eye absolute mastery over space."[5] Thus, as Denis Cosgrove explains, landscape painting "achieved visually and ideologically . . . control and domination over space as an absolute, objective entity, [and] its transformation into the property of individual or state."[6] On the other hand, as Cosgrove's phrase "individual or state" suggests, any pretenses to royal absolutism were tempered by the fact that the perspectival arts demanded practical mechanical skills—measuring, estimating, charting—rooted in basic mathematics, so that "the principles which underlay perspective theory were the everyday skills of the urban merchant."[7] For all of its claims of creating a sovereign authority over space, then, "perspective may be regarded as one of a number of techniques which allowed for the visual representation of a bourgeois, rationalist conception of the world."[8]

Cosgrove explains how princely and mercantile interests converge in the *topographesis* of the Italian city-state (Venice in particular), but his kind of analysis changes in interesting ways when transported to England, with its strong, land-based common law tradition. In his influential study of Elizabethan and Jacobean cartography, Richard Helgerson finds, at the level of symbolism at least, an increasing and perhaps even "natural and inevitable" "antagonism between mapping and chorographical description on the one hand and royal absolutism on the other."[9] On this account, as local knowledge of land became more exact, rational, and public, the pretenses of royal absolutism become less tenable. But, as other critics have shown, at a legal level, the Crown benefited enormously from the rapidly advancing skills of land surveyors, and the end of Elizabeth's reign witnessed "the intensified erosion of common rights, and a shift towards a commodified market in land."[10] The interests of the surveyor and estate-owner converge in what Garrett A. Sullivan, Jr. has called the "landscape of absolute property," a form of imagined landscape that emphasizes ownership of known, measured, and legally disposable parcels of land (the bourgeois and sovereign join most notably in the sale of royal property, much of it newly un-concealed, to private individuals or, at a smaller scale, in the sale of private property between individuals under the sovereign's distant but tacitly-approving gaze). Sullivan sets this now-dominant landscape of absolute property against two other, related kinds of landscape: the "landscape of custom," which distributed a bundle of rights and duties between landlord and tenants according to immemorial communal norms, and the "landscape of stewardship," which "presupposes and champions a land-based moral order at the center of which stands the beneficent landlord, moral steward of his estate."[11] The older landscapes of custom and stewardship were gradually displaced by absolute property, in part because of advances in perspectival *topographesis*. As Andrew McRae has shown, the increasing sophistication and professionalization of land-surveyors allowed a landlord to grasp the extent of his property—"to know his own"—with increasing ease and comprehensiveness. Against the customary ideal of the landlord "manuring the land with his feet," John Norden, a leading land-surveyor of the period, encouraged his employer to evaluate and enjoy his property from his study while "sitting in his chayre," all thanks to the maps, estate-surveys, and landscapes that Norden and his ilk provided.[12]

Elements of these conceptual distinctions can be discerned in a notable passage concerning the choice of a location or "scituation" of a family "seat" in *The Elements of Architecture* by Henry Wotton, who was, like Herbert, a member of Donne's literary circle. In this tract, which was published in 1624 but draws on well-established classical and Continental sources, Wotton explains that some of the "precepts" for deciding where to situate a family estate "may bee said to bee Optical":

> Such I meane as concerne the Properties of a well chosen Prospect: which I will call the Royaltie of Sight. For as there is a Lordship (as it were) of the Feete, wherein the Master doth much ioy when he walketh about the Line of his owne Possessions: So there is a Lordship likewise of the Eye which being a raunging, and Imperious, and (I might say) an vsurping Sence, can indure no narrow circumscription; but must be fedde, both with extent and varietie. Yet on the other side, I finde vaste and indefinite viewes which drowne all apprehension of the vttermost Obiects, condemned, by good Authors, as if thereby some part of the pleasure (whereof we speake) did perish. Lastly, I remember a priuate Caution, which I know not well how to sort, vnlesse I should call it Political. By no meanes, to build too neere a great Neighbour; which were in truth to bee as vnfortunately seated on the earth, as Mercurie is in the Heauens, for the most part, euer in combustion, or obscuritie, vnder brighter beames then his owne.[13]

When Wotton describes a "Royaltie of Sight" whereby property is made both the object of and location of vision (the estate is seen and seen from), he condones the visual mastery over space promoted by land-focused perspectival arts. And when he contrasts it with a

"Lordship . . . of the Feete," he evokes a kind of secularized beating of the bounds in imitation of medieval rogation ceremonies, in which spatial boundaries were reaffirmed through the communal performance of (supposedly) ancient rituals. These two perspectives transmute subtly into what Wotton calls a "Lordship . . . of the Eye," which is somehow both fixed and "raunging," both "Imperious" and "vsurping." As Anne M. Myers explains, from this distinctly English fusion of royal and tenurial perspectives, "the patron is to see his estate, and to see his own prerogative reflected in it, as the house becomes a topographical landmark that reveals the expanses and lineaments of his own sprawling possessions."[14] Though dependent upon earlier writers such as Vitruvius and Alberti, who were by and large concerned with situating entire cities or communities, not individual estates, what is most distinctive in Wotton's account is the preoccupation with enhancing the builder's "Political" status relative to other neighboring estates. Although his gaze is "fedde" "with extent and varietie," Wotton derives no pleasure from "vaste and indefinite views which drowne all apprehension"; the best "scituation" has to be known by its relative proximity to other known buildings and boundaries. At the same time, Wotton also cautions against building "too neere a great Neighbour," lest the reflected glory of that neighboring estate outshine (or overshadow?) one's own estate, putting it "in combustion, or obscuritie."

"Nobility the master-piece"

So, when Herbert wrote "The State progress of Ill," *topographesis* in general and the art of perspective in particular had begun to impact legal conceptions of land and property, but both were new enough that Herbert—never one to shy away from an outlandish conceit or to insist on precise terminology—could use its technical vocabulary fairly loosely.[15] What exactly, for example, is a "proportion'd colour'd table" (l. 81)? The implied contrast with the "lines irregular" (l. 100) of purchased honors suggests a kind of mechanical or rule-based perspectival composition, perhaps like an estate map. But the term "table" might suggest a landscape painting (via Fr. *tableau*; compare "Painters Art" [l. 95]), and, as McRae has noted, some estate maps from the period were color-coded to make them both more functional as administrative tools and more attractive as display pieces.[16] And what about the "blew hills" that "fills" "th'utmost border of a Region" (ll. 85–6)? (Herbert evidently cared more about rhyme than subject–verb agreement; or maybe the border fills the hills? It is hard to tell.) The "blew hills" could indicate that Herbert knew the theory that colors blur increasingly as distance increases, and so that, in landscapes at least, blue hues should be added to indicate increased distance. As Henry Peacham explains:

> If you laie your Landtskip in coloures, the farther you goe, the more you must lighten it with a thinne and aiery blew, to make it seeme farre off, beginning it first with a darke greene, so driuing it by degrees into a blew, which the densitie of the air betweene our sighte and that place doth (onely imaginarily) effect.[17]

Peacham's parenthetical "onely imaginarily" concedes the principle point of James Turner's important study of landscape and the perspective/prospective word group in the early modern period: it was possible to praise the art of perspective for "its authoritative handling of space" or to denounce it for "its illusionism"; it could be seen as an art of "cognition" or as an art of "illusion."[18] Perhaps influenced by the possible association of the perspectival arts with *trompe l'oeil* and anamorphism, Eugene D. Hill has asserted that Herbert's point in this passage of "The State progress of Ill" is that by "a kind of optical illusion, men are made to believe that the exalted nobility are superior to other folk."[19] But Herbert does, in fact, believe that the exalted nobility are superior to other folk. The perspective offered by the "proportion'd colour'd table" does not distort reality but clarifies it. The crucial claim for the entire conceit is that the "Nobility" is the landscape's "master-piece" (l. 82). Though it records earlier usages, the *OED* does not record a sense that fits well here. The closest is "a piece of work produced by a craftsman in order to be admitted to a guild as an acknowledged master" (s.v. 1.a.),[20] a sense that, as Walter Cahn has shown, is found in medieval hexameral literature in which humans are the masterpiece of the divine Creator (*Deus artifex*).[21] But Herbert specifies that the "master-piece," like the "blew hills," "[s]erves to shew distances" (l. 86), so that its key function in the "great Prospective" of "State" is as some kind of focal point, something that has been put "'Twixt sight and vastness," in what is otherwise imagined as a colored, bordered, and perspectival landscape.[22] I take the force of "seem" in both lines 84 and 88 to be the exact opposite of what Hill is suggesting: in the perspective that Herbert imagines, the nobility are "farther off" and even "absent," and so they are shown to be "higher" in relation to some imagined horizon. They are "great and worse parts": great because they are in fact great, worse because consigned to "th'utmost border." The distances represented in the image of the state are real, and only through the art of perspective can they be comprehended in one "table." Put differently, Herbert's set-piece on "State" puts nobility or, to use his alternative term, greatness into perspective. Perspective allows greatness to appear small, distant, and fixed on a "proportion'd colour'd table" while still being great, "[e]xalted," and "free."

But how does this topographical set-piece fit within the broader argument of Herbert's verse satire about the "State progress of Ill"? In part, this is a question about what "ill" is. G. C. Moore Smith, whose edition of Herbert's poetry is dated but still standard, provides a long paraphrase of the entire poem ("the satire," he concedes, "is admittedly obscure"). In it, he glosses "Ill" simply as "evil."[23] In doing so, he renders Herbert's verse satire highly conventional and moralistic, when, in fact, it is better described as proto-Miltonic in its scorn for monarchical power and priestly authority and its defense of worldly pride. It is un-Miltonic, however, in its subsequent, cosmopolitan untethering of political status from nationality.

Instead of recycling Christian pieties about ever-proliferating evil, "The State progress of Ill" joins together anti-tyrannical political thought with Aristotelian virtue ethics in a way that highlights Herbert's robust sense of natural right and moral agency, his underappreciated cosmopolitan personhood. As Hill has noted, "The State progress of Ill" owes its political stance to Étienne de la Boétie's *Discours sur la servitude volontaire* (c. 1548; pub. 1576), an anti-tyrannical tract that puzzles over the voluntary and indeed habitual surrender of native liberty to tyrannical power. How is it, Boétie asks, that "so many men, so many villages, so many cities, so many nations, sometimes suffer under a single tyrant who has no other power than the power they give him"?[24] This theme recurs in early modern political beast fables such as "As I my little flock on Ister Bank" by Herbert's kinsman, Sir Philip Sidney, and "Humilitee" by his brother, George.[25] Edward's verse satire occasionally gestures toward this genre. For example, he asks why the same "freeborn man," who by "his own choice" submits his "infinite" "Spirit" and "Wit" to "some eight Monarchs," expresses "wonder" at the fact that humans have achieved their "rule of Horses" (ll. 119–25). (This equine analogy recalls Donne's own theological query, "Why brookst thou ignorant horse subiection?" [*HSWhy*, l. 5].[26]) The same analogy can be traced back to Boétie: "Men are like handsome race horses who first bite the bit and later like it."[27]

But even more important than his anti-tyrannical politics, and unrecognized by Moore Smith or Hill, is Herbert's Aristotelian virtue ethics. Stated positively, Herbert's poem champions greatness of spirit (*megalopsychia*), which is usually translated as pride or, sometimes, proper pride, that is, the ethical stance that one should be recognized as great because one actually is great. Aristotle calls it the "crown" (*kosmos*) of all virtues (*Nicomachean Ethics* 4.3), since it cannot exist without the other virtues and is concerned chiefly with the proper assessment of and renown for those virtues. As Richard Strier has shown, any hoped-for syncretism of classical ethics and Reformation theology foundered over antithetical valuations of the prideful desire "to attain glory and create self-esteem."[28] Such a desire was entirely in keeping with Aristotelian virtue ethics but anathema to Reformation theology. For Luther and Calvin, sinful humility, not proper pride, is the inevitable endpoint of any attempt to pursue pagan virtue ethics. There is a pointedness, then, to Herbert's use of the term "great" in the poem's prologue, as he states that "Ill" has "Great'ned in his long course" (ll. 1–2; "Ill" is mostly, but not exclusively, gendered male in the poem), and Herbert, in the poem's *divisio*, states that he plans to examine "how this Ill / Did come at first, how't keeps his greatness here / When 'tis disguis'd, and when it doth appear" (ll. 14–16). In his typically convoluted way, Herbert explains that "Ill" first progressed in the "infant-world" though his agents, "mischief and sin," who are duly attended by "Fear" in private and "Shame" in public, and now go disguised as "doing of Good" and "Pleasure," respectively (ll. 31–44). Through this elaborate disguising, "doing of Good" and "Pleasure" are both made to seem "Ill." But again, it bears repeating that Herbert is rejecting, not endorsing, the Calvinist view that sees both "doing Good" and "Pleasure" as manifestations of "Ill." Further parodying Roman Catholic hamartiology, he says that "Ill" progresses through sins "com- and o-mitted," sins that work even "after death" and never "come alone, / But sudden fruitful multiply e'r done" (ll. 44–50).

Stated negatively, "The State progress of Ill" identifies "Ill" as humility, and it considers the role of humility in the formation of the early modern state. Early in the poem, Herbert complains that "Ill" has "tamed" "the pride of Goodness" (l. 21), a kind of pride in one's goodness that is in fact good to have. And late in the poem, he asserts that "Ill" works by distracting us from "thinking on / A present greatness" (ll. 112–13). In fact, Herbert explicitly identifies "Religion" as the force that draws "harder minds" (which for Herbert are good) into the "whirlpool" of the judgment of others, specifically of spiteful "officers, and neighbors" (ll. 111–14). Similarly, joining political and religious themes, Herbert blames the clergy for preaching a gospel of humility and servitude. Just as "Priests" "rav'd / And propheci'd" until hereditary monarchies were created (ll. 71–2, with an allusion to 1 Samuel 8), so "sugred Divines" (l. 103) now preach that

> . . . Humility and Patience is
> The way to Heaven, and that we must there
> Look for our Kingdom, that the great'st rule here
> Is for to rule our selves; and that they might
> Say this is better, they to no place have right
> B'inheritance, while whom Ambition swayes,
> Their office is to turn it other ways. (ll. 104–10)

There are a couple of astonishing things about these lines. First, Herbert condemns the conventional, Stoic-sounding ideal of self-mastery—"the great'st rule here / Is for to rule our selves"—as a ploy of the priesthood to frustrate or, at least, steer the "Ambition" of great men away from worldly achievement. Second, Herbert stresses the earthly placelessness of the priesthood. The "Kingdom" they promise is "there," in "Heaven," not "here." They have the "right" "to no place" (which, like "State," I take to connote both status and property), at least by "inheritance." So they preach "Humility and Patience" to constrain those, the great-spirited nobility, who actually do.

Just as Herbert rejects such an ethic of humility, he also rejects a politics of equality. The counter-example of Venice, the only historical location mentioned in Herbert's otherwise nondescript "Prospect," underscores his belief in the "true Greatness" of the "happy-high" man. As Gasparo Contarini explains in his widely read account of the Venetian government, although Venice's constitution favors "nobility of lineage" over "estimation of wealth," it "temper[s]" "men of chiefe and supreme nobility" by granting the right to participate in civic government to "euery other citizen whoseouer not ignobly borne: so that all which were noble by birth, or enobled by virtue, or well deseruing of the commonwealth, did in the beginning obtain this right of gouernment"; to these citizens were added "some forrain men and strangers" "adopted into this number of citizens, eyther in regard to their great nobility, or that they had beene dutifull to the state, or els had done vnto them some notable seruice."[29] By contrast, for Herbert, neither birth alone nor election nor purchased honor ("lines irregular") raises a man to "true Greatness."[30] Venetian-style equality is not a desideratum. Without "the Painters Art," Herbert says, "All in the frame is equal" (ll. 95–6). Herbert opposes equality, and so he appreciates the painter's art. As he figures it, the painter's perspectival art allows space (an empirical measure of distance) to be brought into proper alignment with place (a political measure of greatness). And yet Herbert does not claim for the nobility the central, authoritative vantage of the "prince of rays." Recalling Wotton's condemnation of "vaste and indefinite viewes which drowne all apprehension of the vttermost Obiects," Herbert places nobility *between* "sight and vastness."

But it is also noticeable how unattached Herbert seems to be to the "Region" or landscape that he imagines. There is no local color, no landmarks, nothing native to suggest a direct connection to a specific territory; though both perspectival and topographical, it is hard to see how Herbert's state-as-work-of-art promotes an absolute, customary, or stewardship-based conception of property.[31] In "The State progress of Ill," Herbert argues that the authority of the state— the Crown, the Church, and their officials—has increased due to an "Ill" that he associates with "Humility and Patience." In this context, Herbert's image of "State" as a "proportion'd colour'd table" actually tempers his anti-monarchical and anti-prelatical rhetoric. The view from the "great Prospective" is "steep," but it is unifying; it rejects equality as resolutely as absolutism, but, as the product of reflection and calculation, it is not disordered. It mentions an idealized, urban conception of citizenship, only to reject it in favor of a state oriented toward and by the *kosmos* of Aristotelian virtues, greatness.

"Man is a lumpe"

"The State progress of Ill" might be said to offer Herbert's perspective—undeluded by false humility—on his own political value to the English state. When he wrote the poem, that perspective was not self-evident, nor does his life story until that point add clarity. Herbert was born in 1582, and in 1599, following the death of his father, he married Mary Herbert (an older relative) in order to consolidate their family estates (Edward remained a ward of Sir George Moore, Donne's much-aggrieved father-in-law, from 1599 until 1603, i.e., during the very years of Donne's marriage crisis). In 1608, after a few years of moving between Oxford, London, and Montgomery Castle, and after an evidently tense and failed attempt to negotiate with his wife the legal status of their separate estates should either one die, Herbert took leave of his family and traveled to France. There, after a short stay in Paris, he came under the influence of Henri de Montmorency, the Grand Constable of France, at whose château in the village of Mello "The State progress of Ill" was written.[32] Although Herbert's travels in Europe from 1608 to 1619 (and indeed after) sometimes had elements of public service, they were, as Hill has noted, rarely directed toward a particular or particularly important political objective (e.g. when he returned to England from France in 1609, "the Princess of Conti desired [him] to carry a Scarf into England, and present it to Queen Ann on her part";[33] this errand occasioned a shipwreck and, of course, much heroic conduct by Herbert). In fact, noting Herbert's self-proclaimed intention of making himself "a Citizen of the word as farr as it were possible," Hill likens him not to a diplomat, but to "the Stoic wise man, at home anywhere beneath the sky."[34] The Stoic world-citizen that Hill has in mind here is something like the snail that Donne had described in an early verse letter to Wotton:

> Be then thyne owne home; And in thy selfe dwell;
> Inne anywhere; Continuance maketh Hell.
> And seeing the Snayle, which euery where doth rome
> Carying his own house still, still is at home,
> Follow (for he is easy pac'd) this Snayle,
> Be thyne own Pallace, or the World is thy Gayle. (*HWKiss*, ll. 47–52)

A similar ethic of integrity and impenetrability underpins Herbert's other verse satire, "Of Travellers." Addressed to Ben Jonson and penned just a month after "The State progress of Ill," it excoriates the ready adoption and perverse affectation of French ways by English travelers. But as we have seen, in "The State progress of Ill," Herbert's philosophy was anything but Stoic. As the following three analogs to that poem show, it is not wisdom—with its attendant values of self-understanding and bounded restraint—but greatness that shapes Herbert's cosmopolitan vision.

The first analog comes from Herbert's own writings. In his rollicking autobiography, finished sometime after 1624, Herbert recounts in some detail the months in 1608 that he spent with Montmorency. As Herbert tells it, he spent most of his time with Montmorency proving "how strictly" he held himself to his "Oath of Knighthood."[35] He feuded, for example, with a "Frensh Cavelier" in a dispute involving the theft and retrieval of a young lady's "knot of Reband,"[36] the first of many notionally chivalric challenges that Herbert proudly recounts. In other ways, though, Herbert's version of knighthood was more closely tied to Montmorency's property and the feudal organization of his estates. At his château in Mello, Herbert learned to ride "great horses" under the tutelage of Montmorency's "Escuyer" (i.e. squire), and Herbert hunted wolves and boars with the assistance of a hundred local peasants and dozens of dogs. Despite these pleasures (and although "The State progress of Ill" is subscribed "At Merlow"), it is evident from his autobiography that Herbert was even more impressed by the "extraordinary fairness and scituation" of Montmorency's second château (now the Musée Condé) in nearby Chantilly:

> And Thus I past a wholle Summer partly in the exercises and partly in Uisitts of the Duke of Montmorency at his faire house in Chantilly, which for its extraordinary fairness and scituation I shall here describe: A litle River descending from some higher grounds in a Country which was almost all his owne and falling at Last vpon a Rock in the middle of a Ualley which to keepe its way forwards must on one or other side thereof haue declyned its Course. Some of the Ancestors of the Montmorencyes to ease the River of this Labour mssade diuers Channells through this Rock to giue it free passage, dividing the Rocke by the meanes into little Islands vpon which he built a greate and strong Castle, ioyned together with Bridges and sumptuously founded with hangings of silke and gould, rare Pictures and Statutes, All which Buildings vnited as I formerly tould were incompassed about with water, which was paved with Stone (those which were vsed in the building of the House being drawne from thence). One might see the huge Carps Pikes and Trouts which were kept in seurall Divisions gliding along the waters very easily, yet in my opinion nothing added soe much to the Glory of this Castle as a Forest adioyning close to it, and vpon a level with the house, for being of a very large extent and sett thick both with tall trees and vnderwoods the wholle Forrest which was replenished with wilde Bore Stagg and Rowe was cut out into Long walks euery way, soe that although the doggs might follow their Chace through the Thicketts, the Huntsmen might ride along the said walks and meete theire Game in some one of them, as being Cutt with that Art that they led to all the parts in the said Forrest and here also I have hunted the wilde Bore diuers tymes: Both then and afterwards when his sonne the Duke of Montmorency succeeded him in that incomparable place.[37]

This lovely passage of prose is as fluid and graceful as Herbert's poetry is dense and obscure. Stylistically and topographically, Herbert's key themes are symmetry and continuity, as the distant hydraulic engineering of Montmorency's "Ancestors" results, by the end of the passage, in the present terrestrial pleasure of his son. Herbert is careful to find equivalences between the artificial and the natural, between the castle (with its "hangings of silke and gould, rare Pictures and Statutes") and the forest (with its "Carps Pikes and Trouts" and "Bore Stagg and Rowe"), and between the man-made archipelago (with its "diuers Channells" and connecting "Bridges" encompassing round the château itself) and the natural forest (with its "walks" and cut-throughs calculated to allow hunters to "meet" their prey).

The castle is "greate and strong," and the forest, though "level" with the house in absolute terms, is "the Glory of this Castle."

The critical legal theorist Alain Pottage, in an article on "The Measure of Land," has argued that early modern land law underwent a difficult "translation of memory into geometry," when traditionally understood conceptions of communal space were replaced by mathematically measured parcels of private property.[38] Herbert's topographical description of Montmorency's château in Chantilly might be said to arrest that translation mid-process. It memorializes Montmorency's ancestors, but the past is distant both temporally and spatially. Ancestral memory gives way to a fascination with symmetry and the "Art" of topographical division, but that geometry does not impose the commercial or legal ideals of absolute property. Save for the initial descent of the river Nonette "from some higher grounds in a Country which was almost all [Montmorency's] own," this is essentially a non-perspectival and non-proprietary topographical description. We follow the course of the river, the division of the channels, even the chase through the forest without any elevated, privileged view of the estate. What reflection and calculation there is in the construction of the estate—altering the course of the river, funneling game through the forest—is oriented toward the unlabored achievement of traditional aristocratic pleasure, not the relaxed, all-encompassing, sovereign posture of dominion. Put differently, though artfully laced with intersecting paths, the forest feels unmapped, without coordinates: in a passage that follows, Herbert remembers Montmorency, who was famous for his military valor though reputedly scarcely literate, advising Herbert that, should he find himself lost in "this Admirable Laborinth," he should look for the trees' "roughest and hardest" side, which always points northward, and so orient his direction of travel that way.[39] Correspondingly, Herbert insists that this unmapped estate is invaluable: Spain's Carlos V had offered "one of his Provinces in the Lowe Countreys for such a place"; years later, France's Henri IV "offered to Exchange any of his houses with much more land then [sic] [Montmorency's] Estate thereabouts was worth."[40] The lordship imagined in this passage may be more of the saddle than the feet, but it is certainly not exerted from the comfort of a chair or aided by the products of *topographesis*. This description of Chantilly might be said to constitute Herbert's idealized landscape, and, if nothing else, underscores his detachment from the "Region" of "State" in "The State progress of Ill," which feels even more like a satire written by an Englishman abroad after looking at his loving description of Chantilly.

A second analog is from Donne. Although the two poems are keyed to events two years apart, critics have long assumed that Donne's verse epistle "To Sir Edward Herbert at Iulyers" (*EdHerb*) is a reply to Herbert's verse satire. The conclusion of Herbert's poem— "The World, as in the Ark of Noah, rests, / Compos'd as then, few Men, and many Beasts" (ll. 125–6)—does seem to provide Donne's jumping-off point: "Man is a lumpe, where all Beasts kneaded bee; / Wisedome makes hym an Arke where all agree" (ll. 1–2). In addition to the Ark analogy, Donne's Pauline "lumpe" (cf. Rom. 9:21) contrasts sharply with Herbert's noble "master-piece" and indicates that his poem will, in the end, advance a much more conventionally moralistic argument. So, for example, Donne touts fallen human nature ("Poysonous tincture of Originall Sin" [l. 20]) and the corresponding necessity of self-knowledge ("you knowe man" [l. 46]). By comparison with Herbert's, Donne's poem is quite preachy; he rebukes Herbert's apology for the unelected "happy-high" man as comprehensively as any "sugred Divine" could have hoped. Donne pointedly targets Herbert's self-diagnosed tendency toward anger (cf. "Anger" [l. 8], "rage" [l. 17], and "wrath" [l. 28]), which suggests that the occasion for the verse letter was not, as it is sometimes supposed, Herbert's actions at the military siege of Jülich, but rather his incessant issuing of challenges, even to allies, prompted by his amplified sense of noble codes of honor.[41] According to Donne, "Wisdom," not greatness, is what Herbert needs, and Donne's characteristic play on man as both micro- and macrocosm denies the perspectival vantage point that allowed Herbert to distinguish greatness from mere "vastness":

> Since then our busines ys to rectifye
> Nature, to what she was, we are led awry,
> By them, who Man to vs, in litle showe;
> Greater then due, noe forme we can bestowe
> On him: for man into himselfe can drawe
> All: All his Faith can swallowe, or Reason chawe.
> All that is fill'd, and all that which doth fill,
> All the round world, to man is but a pill. (ll. 33–40)

Although his conceit is primarily medicinal, there is an element of *trompe l'oeil* ("All the round world, to man is but a pill") that seems intended to counter Herbert's "steep" perspectivalism.

Donne's poetic response to "The State progress of Ill" reasserts both Calvinist and absolutist perspectives on the poetic landscapes that Herbert had imagined. While Herbert talks extensively about landscape and perspective but concludes with animal imagery, Donne talks extensively about animals (as metaphors for emotional loss of control) but includes a couple of allusions to land-policy:

> Howe happye is hee which hath due Place assign'd
> To his Beasts, and disaforested his Mynde?
>
> Empayld hymselfe, to keepe them out, not in,
> Can sowe, and dares trust corne, where they haue beene,
> Can vse his horse, Goate, wolfe, and everye beast,
> And ys not asse hymselfe to all the rest? (ll. 9–14)

Citing these lines, Erica Fudge has explained that "the animal exists as the other against which the human is constructed," which means that the animal is what human persons can return to should they "stop acting according to their education" and "revert back to their natural sensuality."[42] Although the bestial analogy dominates the poem, Donne here refers to two legal categories used to classify territory in direct opposition to customary rights. Because these categories originate in the assertion of sovereign authority, they make clear that decisions to "stop acting" and "revert back" are vested not in native inhabitants but in the sovereign. The first category is the forest, which "was a jurisdiction over a territorial area rather than a wooded game preserve."[43] Though considered Crown lands, forests were notoriously difficult to administer, and informal or tradition-based local economies thrived in the absence of strong administration from a distant, centralized authority. Disafforestation destroyed those informal local economies by removing the Crown's special jurisdiction so that the territory could be listed on sales commissions. In theory, then, disafforestation boosted the royal coffers at the expense of local inhabitants, another manifestation of the same tension between private property and communal rights that shaped the period's discourse of estate mapping. As David Underdown explains,:

> Disafforestation . . . upset the delicate balance between national and local institutions, between "Court" and "Country". . . . Disafforestation left the areas affected with a worse problem of poverty than ever, with a population less inclined to see the King as their benevolent protector or the court as anything but an oppressive, alien force, and with well-developed habits of collective action.[44]

The second legal category that Donne refers to is the Pale. To "Empayl[e]" oneself meant not only to create a fenced-in boundary, but, as with the English Pale in Ireland or in Calais, to establish sovereign jurisdiction over part of an otherwise foreign, native-ruled territory. Although, as with Sidney's "Ister Bank" poem, the proliferation of animal imagery in *EdHerb* at times makes humans seem more consummately animalistic, Donne ties his beast imagery to land policy that assumes a landscape of absolute property, controlled by the sovereign and indifferent to the customary rights and duties of the native populations. For Donne, that is what a wise, ordered mind is like.

A final analog is a slightly later moralizing emblem by Francis Quarles, which provides an apt point of contrast to Herbert's use of both perspectival imagery and his use of the term "master-piece." The emblem is keyed to Job 15.31: "Let not him that is deceived trust in vanity: for vanity shall be his recompence."[45] The corresponding image shows two angels standing in a bare landscape next to the stump of a tree, whose only apparent function (aside from perhaps symbolizing earthly fallenness) is to establish a proper perspective that connects the viewer with the rising hills, lightly sketched forest, and hazy city-scape in the distant horizon. The larger angel is standing behind and holding up a shiny, circular, mirror-like shield. In front of the shield is a smaller, childish angel who postures puckishly, and whose image appears slightly larger when reflected in the shield, that is, as one would expect from an image projected onto the convex surface of an orb. A Latin motto explains *Sic decipit orbis*: "Thus the globe deceives."[46] The accompanying poem rehearses numerous examples of visual misperception and concludes with an admonition directed at the preening smaller angel: "The least is greatest; And who shall / Appeare the greatest, are the least of all."[47] The concluding epigram for the emblem reads:

> Be not deceiv'd, great Foole; There is no losse
> In being small: Great bulks but swell with drosse:
> Man is heav'ns Master-peece; If it appeare
> More great, the valu's lesse; If lesse, more deare.[48]

For Quarles, the fun-house perspective contained in the mirrored orb is a deception, one that distorts Christianity's "less-is-more," pro-humility morality. It is perhaps an unintended irony that this deception is quite literally supported by the emblem's chief divine agent, the larger and well-haloed angel. That is, the earthly, linear perspective turns out to be true (as least regarding the actual stature of the smaller angel), while the divine orb's perspective deceives by exaggerating his stature. Still, according to the text, at least, man remains "heav'ns

Sic decipit orbis.

Figure 10.1 Francis Quarles, *Emblems, divine and moral* (London, 1634), Bk 2, emblem 6. Image courtesy of the Pennsylvania State University Libraries.

Master-peece"; God's artistry is that of a miniaturist. According to the text, heaven has transvalued earthly values, so that small is great and worthlessness is value.

Quarles's slightly-ambiguous global perspective returns us to Herbert's "The State progress of Ill," which fashions for the great, "happy-high" man what I earlier called a cosmopolitan personhood of a peculiarly modern sort. Against the ill of humility, Herbert champions the political value of *megalopsychia*, which Aristotle had called the *kosmos* or crown of virtues. So Herbert's championing of Aristotelian ethics speaks to a certain kind of cosmopolitanism. But only with considerable difficulty could one learn from his verse satire the four lessons—cultural modesty; international cooperation; basic human dignity; the moral arbitrariness of national boundaries—that Martha Nussbaum, in an essay that sparked a widespread critical re-evaluation of the term, has identified as cosmopolitanism's core values.[49] And yet, in a poem that at times parodies fables of political constitutionalism, Herbert defies the authority of hereditary monarchs ("some eight Monarchs") and their ecclesiastical apologists ("sugred Divines"); he scorns petty "officers, and neighbors," as well as equality-minded, locally-centered Venetian citizens. Though somehow bordered by distant "blew hills," Herbert's "happy-high" man is not confined by local, national, and imperial boundaries. Thanks to the art of perspective, he is situated in, but not rooted to, the land; he is neither a traditional tenant, exemplary steward, nor private owner. He claims no special privilege by birth or even by election. As against the Stoic cosmopolitan traveler, who learns from but resists the influence of strangers in strange lands, Herbert's cosmopolitan is fixed between "sight and vastness." Herbert's noble "master-piece" resembles nothing so much as the modern globalist elite who, it is sometimes observed, use the hammer of cosmopolitanism to flatten out local variation, diminish burdensome group affiliations, and reduce barriers to individual self-fulfillment, which may itself include aspects of altruism (recall that, uncompeled, Herbert's "happy-high" man cares about the poor).[50] As a work of art, Herbert's strangely global "State" is there chiefly to recognize his greatness.

Notes

1. Jakob Burckhardt, *The Civilization of the Renaissance in Italy* [1860] (Mineola, NY: Dover, 2010), 2.
2. "The State progress of Ill," ll. 81–2; qtd. from Edward Herbert, *The Poems in Latin and English*, ed. G. C. Moore Smith (Oxford: Oxford University Press, 1923). Further citations to this edition will be given parenthetically in the text.
3. See Henry S. Turner, "Literature and Mapping in Early Modern England, 1520–1688," in *The History of Cartography*, ed. David Woodward, 3 vols. (Chicago: University of Chicago Press, 2007), 3:412–26, 424–5. I owe this reference to Kader Hegedüs. Turner's excellent survey does not mention Herbert's poem, even though it uses (at least) two of the five techniques Turner associates with *topographesis*: 1) "techniques of framing or bordering a representational field or setting it apart from the object or world to which it is presumed to refer"; his 4) "an analytic posture that explicitly relies on artificial projections and models to present information that could not be gained by the naked eye alone" (424).
4. A. Sarah Bendall, *Maps, Land and Society* (Cambridge: Cambridge University Press, 1992), 5–6. The scholarly literature on the Renaissance discovery of perspective is enormous. In addition to the scholarship on perspectival representations of land cited below, this chapter draws on the scholarship of Svetlana Alpers, *The Art of Describing* (Chicago:

University of Chicago Press, 1983), 72–168 and Lucia Nuti, "The Perspective Plan in the Sixteenth Century: The Invention of a Representational Language," *The Art Bulletin* 76:1 (March 1994): 105–28. For perspectival representation and metaphysical poetry in particular, see Lucy Gent, *Picture and Poetry, 1560–1620* (Leamington Spa: James Hall, 1981); Ernest B. Gilman, *The Curious Perspective* (New Haven, CT: Yale University Press, 1978). Angela Benza has alerted me to Baldassare Castiglione's use of perspective to describe courtly performance. See Wayne A. Rebhorn, *Courtly Performances* (Detroit: Wayne State University Press, 1978), 30–1.

5. Denis Cosgrove, "Prospect, Perspective and the Evolution of the Landscape Idea," *Transactions of the Institute of British Geographers* 10:1 (1985): 45–62, 48. "The central ray is that single one which alone strikes the quantity directly, and about which every angle is equal. This ray, the most active and strongest of all the rays, acts so that no quantity every appears greater than when struck by it. We could say many things about this ray, but this will be enough—tightly encircled by the other rays, it is the last to abandon the thing seen, from which it merits the name, prince of rays." Leon Battista Alberti, *On Painting*, trans. John R. Spenser (New Haven, CT: Yale University Press, 1956), 48.
6. Cosgrove, "Prospect," 46.
7. Cosgrove, "Prospect," 50.
8. Cosgrove, "Prospect," 49.
9. Richard Helgerson, *Forms of Nationhood* (Chicago: University of Chicago Press, 1992), 146.
10. Nicholas Blomley, "Law, Property, and the Geography of Violence: The Frontier, the Survey, the Grid," *Annals of the Association of American Geographers* 93:1 (March 2003): 121–41, 126.
11. Garrett A. Sullivan, Jr., *The Drama of Landscape* (Stanford: Stanford University Press, 1998), 12.
12. Andrew McRae, *God Speed the Plough* (Cambridge: Cambridge University Press, 1996), 169–97, 192.
13. Henry Wotton, *The Elements of Architecture* (London, 1624), 5–6.
14. See Anne M. Myers, *Literature and Architecture in Early Modern England* (Baltimore: Johns Hopkins University Press, 2012), 60–3, on this passage and the seventeenth-century English country house poem tradition.
15. The first technical treatises on landscape painting, in Italian, date to the 1580s; the first English tract to consider it in detail is usually said to be Henry Peacham's *Art of Drawing with the Pen* (London, 1606). See esp. E. H. Gombrich, "The Renaissance Theory of Art and the Rise of Landscape," in *Norm and Form* (London: Phaidon Press, 1966), 107–21.
16. For the decorative color-coding of estate maps, see McRae, *God Speed the Plough*, 189–97.

17. Peacham, *Art of Drawing*, 30; compare Alberti, *On Painting*, 48.
18. James Turner, "Landscape and the 'Art Prospective' in England, 1584–1660," *Journal of the Warburg and Courtauld Institutes* 42 (1979): 290–3, 290–1. Turner quotes the miniaturist Edward Norgate (d. 1650): "Landscape is nothing but Deceptive visions" (qtd. 290). In a similar way, Peacham relays this comical account of a perspectival landscape gone awry: "I haue seen a man painted comming downe a hill some mile and a halfe from mee, as I iudged by the Landskip, yet might you haue told all the buttons of his dublet: whether the painter had a suttle inuention, or the fellows buttons were as big as those in fashion whe[n] Mounseir came into England, I wil leaue it (friendly reader) to thy iudgement. Your eie may easily bee deceiued in remote thinges, that is when the bodies appeare to your sighte farre bigger then indeede they are, by the corruption (as wee saie) of the Medium." Peacham, *Art of Drawing*, 41–2.
19. Eugene D. Hill, *Edward, Lord Herbert of Cherbury* (Boston: Twayne Publishers, 1987), 69.
20. "masterpiece, *n.*," I.a. *OED Online* (Oxford: Oxford University Press, July 2018), <http://www.oed.com/view/Entry/114781> (last accessed May 31, 2019).
21. See Walter Cahn, *Masterpieces* (Princeton, NJ: Princeton University Press, 1979), esp. 23–42. In a poem roughly contemporary with Herbert's, Donne uses the term in something like this sense ("you are then Gods Masterpeece" [*BedfReas*, l. 33]) in praise of the Countess of Bedford. For Donne's idiosyncratic use of the term "master-piece" in his later religious prose, see Kirsten Stirling, "Dr. Donne's Art Gallery and the *imago dei*," *John Donne Journal* 27 (2008): 67–80, 75–6. Compare Milton's use of "Master work" with "Magnanimous" in *Paradise Lost* (1667): "There wanted yet the Master work, the end / Of all yet don; a Creature who not prone / And Brute as other Creatures, but endu'd / With Sanctitie of Reason, might erect / His Stature, and upright with Front serene / Govern the rest, self-knowing, and from thence / Magnanimous to correspond with Heavn'n" (7.505–11).
22. In a way, as both compositionally "best and worst," Herbert's "masterpiece" resembles the royal insignia on early modern maps: as Helgerson has argued, at the beginning of the cartographic revolution, the Elizabethan royal insignia were prominently placed on state-sponsored maps, only then to be increasingly marginalized, so that the "dimunition of the place accorded the insignia of royal power" corresponded to "a corresponding increase in the attention paid to the land itself." Helgerson, *Forms of Nationhood*, 114.
23. Herbert, *Poems*, 142–3.
24. Étienne de la Boétie, *Anti-dictator, the Discours sur la servitude volontaire*, trans. Harry Kurz (New York: Columbia University Press, 1942), 4.
25. See Laurie Shannon, *The Accommodated Animal: Cosmopolity in Shakespearean Locales* (Chicago: University of Chicago Press, 2013), 66–75.

26. For Donne's poetry, I have used the *Variorum* short-form titles (which can be found on *DigitalDonne*) and quote from the relevant volume of that edition throughout.
27. Boétie, *Anti-dictator*, 26; see also 16.
28. Richard Strier, "Milton against Humility," in *Religion and Culture in Renaissance England*, ed. Claire McEachern and Debora Shuger (Cambridge: Cambridge University Press, 1997), 258–86, 260; see, more generally, Daniel C. Russell, "Aristotle's Virtues of Greatness," in *Virtue and Happiness* (Oxford: Oxford University Press, 2013), 115–47.
29. Gasparo Contarini, *The Commonwealth and Gouernment of Venice* [1543], trans. Lewes Lewkenor (London, 1599), 18.
30. On the unpopular practice of selling titles by the English Crown, see Lawrence Stone, "The Inflation of Honours, 1558–1641," *Past and Present* 14 (1958): 45–70.
31. So Herbert's poem does not use another of the techniques of *topographesis* identified by Henry S. Turner: 2) "a referential semiotic mode that posits as conventional a one-to-one relationship of correspondence between the signifier inside the frame of the text and the object or world outside of it." Turner, "Literature and Mapping," 424.
32. In its sole seventeenth-century printing, the poem is subscribed "Aug. 1608. / At Merlow in France" (correcting the date per the volume's errata slip). Herbert's other verse satire, the worldlier "Of Travellers: (from Paris.)," is dated "Sept. 1608."
33. Edward Herbert, *The Life of Edward, First Lord Herbert of Cherbury, Written by Himself*, ed. J. M. Shuttleworth (Oxford: Oxford University Press, 1976), 50
34. Herbert, *Life of Edward*, 17; Hill, *Edward, Lord Herbert*, 17.
35. Herbert, *Life of Edward*, 44.
36. Herbert, *Life of Edward*, 42.
37. Herbert, *Life of Edward*, 47.
38. Alain Pottage, "The Measure of Land," *The Modern Law Review* 57:3 (May 1994): 361–84, 366.
39. Herbert, *Life of Edward*, 48.
40. Herbert, *Life of Edward*, 48.
41. In the early print tradition (i.e. from its appearance in the 1633 *Poems*), *EdHerb* was said to be occasioned by "the siege of Iulyers," which began on July 17, 1610 and ended a month later on August 22. But in the manuscript tradition, only the Group I manuscripts (from which the print tradition was derived) mention Jülich, and none of them mention the siege proper, and Herbert spent an eventful period in the region after the siege as well. For Herbert's quarrelling off and on the battlefield, see Herbert, *Life of Edward*, 54–8.
42. Erica Fudge, *Brutal Reasoning: Animals, Rationality, and Humanity in Early Modern England* (Ithaca, NY: Cornell University Press, 2006), 60.

43. Richard Hoyle, "Disafforestation and Drainage: The Crown as Entrepreneur?," in R. W. Hoyle, ed., *The Estates of the English Crown, 1558–1640* (Cambridge: Cambridge University Press, 1992), 353–88, 355.

44. David Underdown, *Revel, Riot and Rebellion: Popular Politics and Culture in England 1603–1660* (Oxford: Oxford University Press, 1985), 112.

45. Francis Quarles, *Emblems, divine and moral* (London, 1634), 84–7. I owe this reference to Kirsten Stirling. The emblem is modeled on one that originally appeared (with Latin, French, and Dutch verse) as the sixteenth emblem in *Typus mundi* (1627), which was published anonymously in Antwerp by the Jesuits.

46. For the presence of globes and cartography in sixteenth-century emblems and the "landscape of emblems" more broadly, see Thomas Conley, *An Errant Eye* (Minneapolis: University of Minnesota Press, 2011), 81–116.

47. Quarles, *Emblems*, 86.

48. Quarles, *Emblems*, 87.

49. Martha Nussbaum, "Patriotism and Cosmopolitanism," *Boston Review* 19:5 (October/November 1994): 3–16. See also the numerous responses printed alongside Nussbaum's article, as well as the essays collected in *Shakespeare Studies* 35 (2007).

50. See David Harvey, *Cosmopolitanism and the Geographies of Freedom* (New York: Columbia University Press, 2009).

Index

EU representative:
Easy Access System Europe
Mustamäe tee 50, 10621 Tallinn, Estonia
Gpsr.requests@easproject.com

www.ingramcontent.com/pod-product-compliance
Lightning Source LLC
Chambersburg PA
CBHW070843300326

41935CB00039B/1404